GIVEN UP FOR DEAD

Also by the Author:

*The Fighting First: The Untold Story
of the Big Red One on D-Day*

*The Rock of Anzio:
From Sicily to Dachau
A History of the 45th Infantry Division*

*Soldiers on Skis: A Pictorial Memoir of
the 10th Mountain Division (with Bob Bishop)*

GIVEN UP FOR DEAD

American GI's in the Nazi
Concentration Camp
at Berga

FLINT WHITLOCK

Author of *The Fighting First*

BASIC
BOOKS

A Member of the Perseus Books Group
New York

All maps courtesy of Flint Whitlock.

Hardcover first published in 2005 by Westview Press, A Member of the Perseus Books Group
Paperback first published in 2006 by Basic Books, A Member of the Perseus Books Group

Books published by Basic Books are available at special discounts for bulk purchases in the United States by corporations, institutions, and other organizations. For more information, please contact the Special Markets Department at the Perseus Books Group, 11 Cambridge Center, Cambridge MA 02142; or call (617) 252-5298 or (800) 255-1514; or e-mail special.markets@perseusbooks.com.

Set in 10.5 Minion by the Perseus Books Group

Cataloging-in-Publication data is available from the Library of Congress.
HC: ISBN-13 978-0-8133-4288-7; ISBN 0-8133-4288-0
PBK: ISBN-13 978-0-465-09115-7; 0-456-09115-6

Dedicated to the memory of the millions
who never made it home.

CONTENTS

ACKNOWLEDGMENTS

MANY PEOPLE DESERVE credit for helping me tell this story, which had gone virtually untold for half a century. First and foremost, the late filmmaker Charles Guggenheim must be acknowledged, for it was his documentary, broadcast over PBS stations on Memorial Day weekend, 2003, that first made me (and millions of others, I'm sure) aware of this incredible tale.

The next person needing to be thanked is Mel Rappaport, of Douglaston, New York—a World War II veteran, a liberator of Buchenwald, and a person with very good connections. It was he who first put me in contact with some of the survivors, who then introduced me to others.

I am deeply grateful to the surviving veterans of Berga and Stalag IX-B who allowed me to interview them and told me their often painful stories. Without their willingness to share, the unspeakable things that went on in these terrible places may have passed into obscurity, dismissed as fantasy simply because the reality is so horrific and unbelievable.

Once I had decided to visit the locales written about in these pages, one person provided immeasurable assistance: Frau Sabine Richter, Berga-an-der-Elster's finance director. It would have been virtually impossible to find the relevant sites in Berga without her generous assistance. She devoted many hours to escorting me to the sites of the camps and the sealed-up tunnels, and to answering my endless stream of questions. I am also indebted to the current mayor of Berga, Stephan Büttner, for his kindnesses.

Then, in no particular order of importance (for they are *all* important) are Will Mahoney of the Modern Military Records Branch of the National Archives II in College Park, MD; Dr. Mitchell Bard, author of *Forgotten Victims*; Helen Fowler, who lent me her late husband's memoirs; the operators of the website www.LoneSentry.com; Dr. Patricia Wadley, national historian of the American Ex-POW organization; Peter House, Jr., for his father's memoirs; Barbara Geisler; and my good friend Dr. Richard Sommers and the staff of the U.S. Army Military History Institute in Carlisle, PA. I thank my agent, Jody Rein, and my editor at Westview Press, Steve Catalano, for their keen insights and unflagging desires to see this project through.

Last but certainly not least, my wife, Dr. Mary Ann Watson, and the members of her Denver book club, also deserve recognition for their careful reading of the rough manuscript and their thoughtful comments. To them and everyone else involved in this endeavor, I humbly offer my deepest appreciation.

Flint Whitlock

PROLOGUE

A LONG FILE of olive-drab American tanks, the vanguard of the 11th Armored Division's "Task Force Wingard," rumbled southward across eastern Bavaria along the Czechoslovak border. The April air was alive with a wild mixture of fragrances: engine exhaust, burning villages, torn-up earth, new spring growth, decomposing corpses, and victory.

Riding high in the turret of a well-worn, thirty-three-ton M–4 Sherman tank was a sergeant whose name has been lost to history. Like the battle-scarred tank, the sergeant had seen plenty of combat since the 11th Armored Division first ran into the enemy in Belgium at the end of December 1944. Then came pitched battles at Herzfeld, Leidenborn, Sengerich, Roscheid, Eschfeld, Reiff, Ormont, Lissigen, Kelberg, Andernach on the Rhine, Worms, Hanau, Fulda, Gelnhausen, and so many other towns that they all began to blur into an indistinct, amorphous mass. Then Bayreuth fell on 14 April, the big German armored training camp at Grafenwöhr on 19 April, and the city of Weiden on 21 April.

The last couple of days, the going had gotten a little easier. Instead of bullets and tank-busting *panzerfaust* rounds flying in deadly profusion from the windows of every town and village they approached, the "Thunderbolts" of the 11th

Sherman tanks of the 11th Armored Division roll down an *autobahn* in
eastern Germany, April 1945. (Courtesy National Archives)

Armored were now greeted by silent white bedsheets fluttering from every window, a sign that the Germans—at least the civilian townsfolk—had had enough
of war and were finally admitting defeat. The German army, if one could even
call it an army, was retreating faster than the Americans were advancing.

Heading toward the multi-spired Bavarian city of Cham, Task Force Wingard
suddenly sped up and struck out for the village of Rötz. The sergeant in the lead
tank looked across a fresh-green expanse of farm fields and saw a most unusual
sight. Up ahead, the tank commander could make out what appeared to be a
couple hundred stick figures, some of whom began waving their scarecrow-like
arms at him. He ordered the driver to halt and raised his binoculars for a closer
look. Strange, he must have thought; the stick figures appeared to be wearing
the same mustard-colored wool uniform that he wore, except that their uniforms were torn and stained and covered with patches of mud. Many of the
stick figures were also long-haired and some were bearded. If they were soldiers,
he thought, they certainly looked like no soldiers he had ever seen.

One of the stick figures staggered toward him, waving its arms, a ghoulish grin spreading across its emaciated, unshaven face, tears streaming into hollows that were once its cheeks. Who was this sepulchral figure? The sergeant wanted to know.

The tanker put his hand on the grip of his holstered forty-five-caliber pistol, unsure of what was happening, of what to do. As the figure drew closer, the sergeant could hear words—unbelievable words—rasping from the gaping hole that was its mouth: "Don't shoot! We're Americans!"

And then another aroma filled the spring air, one that blocked out the fragrance of the verdant April countryside: the terrible stench emanating from the living skeleton.

What Task Force Wingard had stumbled upon were the remnants of a group of American GIs who had been taken prisoner some four months earlier and who had been on a death march to nowhere since being removed from their slave-labor camp at Berga, 300 kilometers to the north three weeks earlier.

—*w*—

In the autumn of 1944, Nazi Germany was being crushed from three sides. From the east, Joseph Stalin's huge Soviet army, burning with hatred to avenge the atrocities Hitler's forces had been committing within the Motherland since June 1941, was slowly pushing back the Wehrmacht and SS divisions like a glacier pushing back a mountain range.

From the west and south, American, British, and Free French forces, too, were on the march, inexorably forcing the German army into a massive retrograde action. From overhead, daily raids by thousands of Allied aircraft were pounding the Third Reich into shattered, smoldering, unrecognizable rubble. The whirlwind that Hitler had unleashed against Poland and the world on 1 September 1939, when he began history's most devastating war, was being reaped tenfold.

The war in Europe, however, was far from over. Millions of soldiers and civilians had already perished; within the next six months, hundreds of thousands more would join those already dead. The most cataclysmic conflict of all time was racing toward its bloody dénouement. In *Götterdämmerung* (The Twilight of the Gods), the final work of German composer Richard Wagner's monumental series of operas known as the Ring Cycle, the spirits ruling the world meet a fiery end; if Germany could not be victorious, Hitler, a great devotée of Wagner's music and anti-Semitic philosophy, was determined to bring his nation, and perhaps even civilization itself, down with him.

Although many of his generals and most of his soldiers had long ago abandoned the idea of a German victory and were merely trying to save their own skins, Adolf Hitler continued to live in a dreamworld, or, as one of his minions put it, in a "cloud-cuckoo-land." In his delusional state, he ordered divisions and armies that no longer existed to rush to the front on trains that no longer ran and throw themselves in an orgy of self-immolation against the advancing enemy hordes. His fifty-five-year-old body, still wracked by injuries sustained in the 20 July 1944 assassination attempt at Rastenburg, East Prussia, was old and feeble now, his reasoning by turns shrewd and delusional. His raspy voice railed against those traitors who had plotted to kill him and who had been agonizingly hung from meathooks as punishment for their perfidy. Even his favorite general, Erwin Rommel, had given tacit approval of the plot and would soon be forced to commit suicide; Hitler could trust no one but the shrinking coterie of loyal members of his Fascist family—Heinrich Himmler, Josef Goebbels, Martin Bormann, Eva Braun.

No matter where on the maps he looked, the German chancellor saw that his Reich—the empire he had created with nothing but his own indomitable will—was crumbling, but he refused to believe the evidence. Now, in September 1944, arrows drawn on the maps showed that the Russians—those subhuman Bolsheviks Hitler had boasted he would conquer and enslave before the winter of 1941 came on—were driving westward along a thousand-mile front that stretched from the Baltic to the Caspian Seas. Slowly, like being sucked into a continent-wide threshing machine, his best troops were being pulverized by the advancing Soviets.

Only in the west, Hitler thought, was there any hope of redemption. The Americans and British and French, while militarily powerful, were squabbling allies. Perhaps they could be divided, both physically and emotionally. Their peoples, like the German civilians, were war weary. But, unlike the Germans, they were products of soft democracies; Hitler could order his people to fight to the last bullet and the last man if need be, but Roosevelt and Churchill and de Gaulle could not. Viewing the mounting casualty lists, the American, British, and French home fronts would rise up and demand an end to the awful bloodletting. Perhaps, Hitler reasoned, if he could deliver a massive blow in the West, he could reach a negotiated peace, then turn what was left of his armies against the Soviets. Hitler knew that the Western Allies had no love of Stalin and Communism, and had come to Russia's aid only to forestall an inevitable German victory. Perhaps he might even persuade them to join forces with him and go to war against the Bolsheviks; surely America and Britain did not want to see much of Europe dominated by Russia![1]

By the summer of 1944, the Allies were on a roll. To pile on the metaphors, on 6 June, British, American, Canadian, and Free French units had landed along a sixty-mile swath of Normandy coastline and delivered a mighty blow to the German jaw. A Soviet operation known as Bagration, mounted on 22 June, was a proverbial kick in the German ass. On 15 August, another Allied landing, this one on the French Riviera, was a knife-thrust into the gut, while the continual fighting in Italy was like a pit bull with its jaws locked onto the Fascist leg. Showing no mercy, the aerial assault on Germany was also stepped up, raining millions of tons of bombs onto the Third Reich's head.

Reeling from the massive blows, German troops on all fronts began retreating, despite Hitler's numerous "stand and fight" orders. While the Führer's soldiers were putting their collective shoulders against the back door that was being battered by the Russians, the Americans and British were on the front porch, kicking in the front door. Germany's heavily fortified frontier, the Westwall, along its border with France, Belgium, Luxembourg, and the Netherlands, proved to be no match for the invaders.

But fierce fighting along the wall, especially at Aachen, Metz, the Hürtgen Forest, and in Alsace-Lorraine—along with ferocious winter weather and an over-extended supply line—had brought the Allied advance to a crawl.

Giving him the breathing space the combination of factors had provided, Hitler made plans for one final effort to reverse the tide swelling against his beloved Deutschland. Whereas the Allies would later call the operation the "Battle of the Bulge," the German leader code-named it Wacht-am-Rhein (The Watch on the Rhine), after a well-known German song. It was not the Rhine River, however, that Hitler planned to secure; it was the port at Antwerp, some seventy-five miles west of the front at Aachen, that he hoped to reach. Antwerp had become the Allies' nearest port, through which millions of tons of ammunition, fuel, rations, weapons, clothing, and other vital supplies were pouring.

Antwerp also was the terminus of the dividing line between the Allies' two great western armies: Field Marshall Sir Bernard Law Montgomery's Twenty-first

British Army Group to the north and Lieutenant General Omar Nelson Bradley's Twelfth Army Group to the south. If his troops could split the two forces, inflict massive casualties, and capture the port of Antwerp, Hitler believed it would be possible to convince the American and British people that continuing the war was futile and that a negotiated settlement was the only logical way to end the dying.

Hitler's eyes darted across the maps for a suitable place from which he would launch his counter-assault. Then he saw it. The Wehrmacht would plunge like a flaming spear through the dense Ardennes Forest—the same improbable place through which his divisions had begun their surprise invasion of France and Belgium in 1940. At this point, he envisioned hundreds of panzers, self-propelled artillery, and infantry divisions plunging in a violent thrust through the "impenetrable" forest and straight into the soft spot of the American front lines.[2]

That soft spot happened to be, for the most part, occupied by thousands of scared, fresh-faced Americans, many of them Jewish, newly arrived in Europe and strangers to combat. What happened to them during the battle—and afterward, as prisoners of war—is an incredible, virtually unknown story of fear, courage, desperation, brutality, survival, triumph, and betrayal.

1

RAW RECRUITS

"TODAY I AM a man."

So declared thirteen-year-old Morton Brimberg,* wearing a prayer shawl and yarmulke, on a cold January day in 1939 in the Emanuel synagogue in the bustling, vibrant borough of Brooklyn. His traditional Bar Mitzvah ceremony marked the end of his childhood, the culmination of weeks of religious schooling, and the beginning of his obligations as an adult to observe the commandments of his faith.

His father, Hyman Brimberg, recited the Hebrew blessing, thanking God for removing the burden of being responsible for his son's sins. Observing the ceremony were his proud mother, Betty, his younger, fraternal twin siblings, Max and Francine, and various relatives and family friends.

Despite the elaborate trappings of ceremony, the family was not especially religious. "My parents were somewhat observant," Brooks recalled. "We knew what our religion was because we were born into it, but that was about it. We, as a Jewish family, did recognize the high holy days, but not very much more than that."

---

*After the war, he changed his last name to Brooks. The name Brooks will be used throughout the rest of the book.

The family was, however, observing the worrisome events taking place in Europe. In 1933, Adolf Hitler and his Nazi Party had come to power in Germany and seemed to transform the face of that cultured nation almost overnight. Laws were passed that stripped German Jews of much of their identity, possessions, and ability to make a living. Harassment and discrimination of the Jews became accepted, even encouraged, by the Nazi authorities.

"We knew that the Jews in Europe were being persecuted and having a difficult time," Brooks noted. "I didn't have any relatives living in Europe; my great-grandparents came to America with my grandparents in the late 1800s or early 1900s."

With the effects of the decade-long Great Depression still lingering, the family of the first-year student at Brooklyn College struggled to make ends meet. Brooks's father and uncle ran a small automobile business—repairing cars, selling gas, and dealing auto parts to other mechanics. "We didn't have a lot, but we got by," Brooks remarked.

The family repeatedly moved from one rented place to another. "When I was about twelve, there was a house available for taxes. My uncle loaned my parents the money to pay the taxes and get the house. My father's friends came by and, just for the cost of the plumbing parts and other stuff that was necessary, they fixed it up for us without any charge for the labor. We were finally able to settle down."

As a teenager, Brooks pondered what to do with his life. He had been encouraged to become a dentist at some time in the future, but hadn't fixed his plans. "Because of my family's financial situation, I knew that I would have to work my way through school to pay for expenses, so I worked full time during the summers." By scrimping and saving, he was able to afford to attend Brooklyn College.

By the summer of 1943, war was raging across Sicily and the Pacific Islands. Germany had already annexed Austria; had conquered France, Belgium, Poland, Denmark, Norway, Czechoslovakia, and the Netherlands; had invaded the Soviet Union; battled the British across North Africa; and had subjected the cities of Great Britain to months of aerial bombardment.

In the Pacific, the Japanese attacks on the American military bases at Pearl Harbor, Midway Island, Wake Island, the Philippines, Adak, and elsewhere had severely damaged the United States's ability to defend itself. But America had swiftly mobilized for war and was now taking the fight to the enemy on two fronts. The factories that had been idled by a decade of economic depression were rebuilding America's arsenal. Millions of young men, too, were being drafted to fill the many divisions being formed and trained for combat. Slowly, Pacific island after Pacific island was being reclaimed from the Japanese, the U.S. had asserted itself in North Africa and, in July 1943, had evicted the Italian and German defenders from Sicily. But victory was a long way off and, in the autumn of 1943, was by no means assured.

To Morton Brooks, his carefree college lifestyle seemed like an extravagant luxury he could no longer afford. Two options were open to him: He could do nothing and wait to take his chances with the draft; or he could enlist and join a new program known as the Army Specialized Training Program, or ASTP, in hopes of becoming an officer.*

"Knowing that I faced being drafted shortly," Brooks said, "and that I also learned that I was successful on the exam for the ASTP program, I enlisted in the Army." In the fall of 1943, while Allied troops were storming ashore at Salerno, Italy, the Army sent him to Syracuse University. "In 1943, I had just started the first semester at Syracuse. I was not interested in joining the Navy, having a fear of being stuck someplace out in the middle of the ocean. So I thought I would stay in college, get a degree, and then get a military commission."

Like most parents in wartime, Brooks's were not thrilled with the prospect of him joining the service—even if he was headed for the ASTP. But Brooks and a friend had discussed "the war and the Germans and how they were advancing and what was going on in Europe and how, as Americans, we would have to do something."[1]

The Army Specialized Training Program did not last long. Expecting heavy casualties once the Allies invaded the continent of Europe in the summer of 1944, the Army brass knew it would need a vast pool of replacement soldiers to restock the depleted divisions. And so, ASTP was dropped in early 1944, and its members were ordered to report for active duty.[2]

Private Morton Brooks wound up as a rifleman in the infantry and was assigned to the 42nd Infantry Division, which was in training at Camp Gruber, near Braggs, some fifty miles southeast of Tulsa, Oklahoma—an experience totally alien to his life in New York, but one which he hoped would prepare him for the rigors of combat.[3]

—◆◆◆—

---

*The ASTP was set up in December 1942 to identify, train, and educate academically gifted enlisted men, with the eventual goal of turning them into officers. ASTP students were to receive a four-year education, combined with military training, at major colleges and universities across the country.

Morton Brooks,
photographed
in October
1944.
(Courtesy
Morton Brooks)

For Gerald Daub, the son of an architect, New York City was the greatest city in
the world. Growing up across the East River from Manhattan, he could watch
the city's skyline change on an almost daily basis. Even though the country's
spirits were mired in the Great Depression, a building boom was sending New
York skyscrapers—and their architects' reputations—soaring. William Van
Alen's seventy-seven-story, 1,046-foot-tall Chrysler Building, at Lexington and

42nd Street, had risen with the stock market in 1928 and survived the crash the following year, opening its doors in 1930.

This Art Deco gem was eclipsed a few months later by William Lamb's mighty Empire State Building, which climbed 102 floors (1,250 feet high; with a TV antenna added in 1953, it now stands 1,454 feet) into the sky. Opened in 1931, the Empire State Building cost $41 million to construct, and quickly became one of the architectural wonders of the world and a symbol of American strength, ingenuity, and optimism.

Of all the buildings in Manhattan, though, Gerry Daub's favorite was famed architect and industrial designer Donald Desky's masterpiece—the Radio City Music Hall. Opened on 27 December 1932, the Art Deco edifice enclosed what was then the world's largest indoor theater. With its marble walls and floor to its twenty-four-karat gold-leaf ceiling in the Grand Foyer, it was a glittering jewel set in the heart of Manhattan—and one of the inspirations for young Daub to follow in his father's footsteps. "I would go to my father's office and play with the colored pencils and look at the drawings of the various projects his company was working on," he recalled.

Born in Brooklyn in 1925, Daub lived in an upper middleclass neighborhood that was, generally speaking, predominately Jewish. "At the time, I was too young to realize that Brooklyn was just a microcosm of the United States. I attended a grammar school called PS-99. In fact, the neighborhood was so Jewish, we had one girl in our school who was not Jewish. Her name was Lillian Torricelli and I felt sorry for her because she had to go to school on Jewish holidays."

On his first day in kindergarten, Daub met a shy little boy named Robert Rudnick. The two remained classmates and acquaintances through eighth grade, but were not the closest of friends. The two then lost contact, with Daub going to a special school known as Brooklyn Technical High School while Rudnick attended the local James Madison High School; World War II would see them reunited—in a most unusual way.

After graduating from Brooklyn Tech, Daub was admitted to the prestigious Pratt Institute, also in Brooklyn, to study architecture. But the war soon sidetracked his dreams of an architectural career, just as it sidetracked the dreams of so many others. In 1943, Daub was in his first year of architecture when he turned eighteen and was notified that he was to report for active duty. "Most people who were in college at that time were offered the choice of going either into the Army and the Army Specialized Training Program, or into the Navy in

Gerald Daub in the ASTP program at The Citadel, winter 1943/44. (Courtesy Gerald Daub)

what was called the V-12 Program; I chose the ASTP. When I went to my draft board to report, I was told that I would be deferred until the spring to finish my first year of college, and I was. Then I went into the Army; Fort Dix, New Jersey, was the reception center." Daub was then sent to Fort McClelland, Alabama, for three months of basic infantry training.

In the fall of 1943, he was assigned to the ASTP program at The Citadel in Charleston, South Carolina. "I spent two semesters at The Citadel, and then when the invasion of Europe was contemplated, the Army was searching for young men to flesh out the remaining infantry divisions and to be available as replacements for the divisions that were already in or going to Europe. So the ASTP programs were closed down and all of us eighteen-year-olds were sent to a lot of infantry divisions. I wound up in Fort Bragg, North Carolina, with the 100th Infantry Division. The very first morning there, when they called the roll, about the second or third name that I heard was 'Robert Rudnick.'"

At the first break, Daub approached the fellow who had answered to the name Rudnick. "I asked him if he was from Brooklyn and he said 'yeah.' I asked him if he went to Grammar School PS-99 and, of course, it turned out to be the same guy. In fact, he and I were assigned to the same infantry company; we even started out in the same platoon."[4]

Before long, Daub's outfit received orders for overseas movement. Major General Withers A. Burress's "Century Division" left Fort Bragg in September 1944 and staged at Camp Kilmer, New Jersey. On 6 October 1944, the division departed from New York, landing at Marseilles fourteen days later. No one, least of all Daub, had any idea of what lay ahead.[5]

—◦◦◦—

In Durango, Mexico, on the other side of the continent from Morton Brooks and Gerald Daub, an eighteen-year-old lad by the name of Anthony Acevedo expected to receive his draft notice at any moment. He had been born in San Bernadino, California, but because of the economic difficulties brought on by the Depression, his father, Francisco, a professional engineer, had moved the family to Durango to find work. Still, as an American citizen, Tony Acevedo was subject to the draft.

"My father was an official for the Mexican government," Acevedo said. "He was a construction engineer and a consultant to the hydraulic industry in Mexico City. Later he became an engineer on the Pan-American Highway and Director of Public Works."

In 1942, Mexico entered the war on the side of the Allies and contributed an air force unit to fight in the Pacific Theater. The war also came close to Mexican shores. "One of my friends was the nephew of a railroad conductor who knew Morse code," Acevedo recalled. "He said he knew there was spying going on in Baja California, with communications with a German submarine. I reported it to my father. Sure enough, there were U-boats spying on the West Coast."

Anthony
Acevedo,
1943.
(Courtesy
Anthony
Acevedo)

When he turned eighteen in 1942, Acevedo finally received his "greetings" from Uncle Sam, along with orders to report to an induction center in the States. Since his stepmother's sister Carmen was living in Pasadena, California, he reported there, only to be told that he needed to finish one more semester of school. This puzzled Acevedo because his schooling in Durango had been very rigorous. "I had graduated from the Institute of Technology in Durango. We went to school from six in the morning to seven in the evening. I felt the induction center was discriminating against Mexican-Americans, but I finished my semester and was inducted and went to Fort MacArthur in San Pedro. I wound up in Camp Adair, Oregon. We called it 'Swamp Adair,' because it rained nine months a year there."

Ever since he was a youngster, Tony Acevedo had had his heart set on becoming a physician. "I even had papers from the governor of the state of Durango, stating that I wanted to be a doctor. I was later transferred to the Medical Corps. I went into training as a medic and was sent to O'Reilly General Hospital in Springfield, Missouri. I graduated as a surgical and medical technician. My goal was to become an officer."

He was assigned to the 91st Infantry Division, training at Camp Adair but came down with the measles shortly before the division shipped out for Italy in early 1944 and was quarantined. Upon recovering, he was assigned as a medic to Company B, 275th Regiment, 70th Infantry Division, also at Camp Adair.[6]

For a while, it looked as if the war might be over before the "Trailblazers" would see action. In June 1944, the Allies landed on the Normandy coast of France and began to slowly push back the German army. In Italy, too, Rome had fallen, and the Germans there were on the run. It seemed to many of the new recruits that the war might be over any day.

But, in July 1944, the 70th Division, under the command of Major General Allison J. Barnett, received orders alerting it for overseas movement. The 14,253 men of the division entrained and moved from Oregon to Camp Myles Standish, near Boston. In mid-December 1944, the three infantry regiments of the division deployed overseas, destination Marseilles.[7]

Acevedo remembered without fondness the two-week ocean voyage aboard the U.S.S. *West Point,* a converted luxury liner: "The sea was really rough. We were like a toy on the ocean. I was lying on my back for thirteen days because I was so seasick. We went through Gibraltar and docked in Marseilles [on 18 January], and then moved up to where the fighting was."[8]

The three infantry regiments of the 70th arrived ahead of the rest of the division and were formed into Task Force Herren, a temporary unit under the command of Assistant Division Commander Brigadier General Thomas W. Herren, and assigned to Lieutenant General Alexander Patch's Seventh Army, which was engaged in heavy fighting in the Vosges Mountains, along the French-German border near Strasbourg.[9]

———

Norman Fellman was a fellow medic assigned to the same company in the 70th Division as Tony Acevedo. He grew up close to the U.S. Naval Base at Norfolk, Virginia. "I was eighteen," he said, "and had just finished high school at Augusta Military Academy in Fort Defiance, Virginia. At that time, any graduate of that school was automatically accepted into VMI—the Virginia Military Institute. I was actually sent to military school as a prescription for my mother, Edith, who had had a nervous breakdown. The war was on and they wanted to get me out of the house and yet in friendly territory for a while. I don't know if her breakdown was related to the war. All I know is that she had a problem and they thought it best to get me out of the house."

Fellman's father, Al, had been in the footwear business for most of his adult life. Al Fellman was not only a merchandise manager for a rather substantial business in Norfolk but also a footwear consultant for the Navy and an inventor who created a number of innovations for protective footwear, including the first safety-toe shoe in America.

Norfolk was—and is—a great naval base and one of America's major seaports. Norman Fellman recalled that "Some of dad's friends were naval officers. One of his customers was a commandant of an armory nearby where they stored shells for the big naval guns, and they had a problem with shells rolling off of gurneys and crushing men's toes. So my dad came up with a shoe rated, I think, to seven hundred pounds that was credited with saving quite a few toes. They are common shoes these days; you can find them everywhere. But Dad, being so naïve, hadn't bothered to patent any of his stuff. One of the employees of the firm that built the test models stole the idea, and it became the vanguard of safety-toe shoes. My dad never saw a nickel from his invention."

Fellman said his father also developed a safety sole used by Navy deck crews on aircraft carriers. "Sailors couldn't go on the deck without a pair of these safety sole shoes on. The 'Fellman Tri-Back Sole' had triple vacuum-like, concentric circles on the sole to get a better grip." Fellman's father also invented a submarine sandal and a type of slipper-sock that naval aviators could wear; if shot down and forced to seek shelter on a coral reef or atoll, the lightweight slipper-sock enabled the pilots to swim, while the leather sole gave them sufficient protection to walk on the jagged, poisonous coral without cutting their feet.

With the war now on, Fellman knew that he probably would be drafted. Despite being brought up in a Navy town—or perhaps because of it—he decided to go into the Army Air Corps. "I hated sailors," he related. "We used to get the fleet in once a year, and it was mayhem in town. I had a desire to fly. At the time, to get your wings in the Navy took a little over a year; in the Army you could get your wings in, I think, four or five months. I wanted to fly in the worst way; so, for several reasons, I decided to go for the Army."

Fellman entered the service in April 1943 and was inducted at Fort Lee, Virginia; from there he went to Camp Grant, Illinois, for medic basic training.

Norman
Fellman,
photographed
at Fort Lee,
Virginia,
June 1943.
(Courtesy
Norman
Fellman)

"When I went into the service, I had my three letters of recommendation and all the requirements needed to go into the Air Corps—letters from school, school records—everything." Fellman went to speak to his company commander about a transfer to the Air Corps. The unsympathetic officer told Fellman, "Listen to me. I'm from the Infantry. I don't like being in the medics any more than you do. Unless *I* get out of here, *nobody* is getting out of here."

But fortune began to shine on Fellman. He said, "During the last week of basic, they came through with an announcement that they needed people in the Air Corps and asked those who were interested to apply. I did, and I passed all the tests and was transferred into the Air Corps. I did basic in Miami and from there they sent me to a college training detachment in Stevens Point, Wisconsin.

Then we were sent to Santa Anna, California. At that time, it was just around D-Day [6 June 1944], and I wound up in the pilot training pool at Santa Anna. They had a thousand of us there and no training officers. *Nobody* was getting into any kind of school. Then they came down with the edict that all of us who had come into the Air Corps from the ground forces had to go back."

Fellman and the others were washed up as pilot cadets. "At that time, there was a program going on called ASTP. They were training people for occupation duty in Europe in anticipation that we'd win the war. That was shut down about the same time, and everyone who had gone into that program or the Air Corps cadet program had to go back to ground forces. I was sent for reassignment to Monterey, California, and across the table from me was a kid that I had gone to high school with.

"He was doing the reassigning, so I told him, 'Get me into the coast artillery with you.' I think he laughed so hard that he almost fell off the chair. 'That's been closed for a long time,' he said. I said, 'So get me into something that says I don't have to walk—and I don't want to go back to the medics; if I have to go into combat, I want to be able to defend myself.' So he gave me an MOS [Military Occupation Specialty] number that said I was a half-track driver. I never saw a half-track in my life and had no idea what one looked like, but I figured I'm a quick study.

"They put us on the train and sent us up to Camp Adair, Oregon, right outside Corvallis, where they were forming this new division—the 70th Division. At battalion headquarters, this light colonel said, 'Now I know all of you guys have orders. You can forget about them. We are building the artillery portion of our division and we're building the infantry. If you come onto this base on an even-numbered day, you are in the artillery; if you come here on an odd-numbered day, you are in the infantry.' Well, it was the seventeenth of the month—so I was now in the infantry."

Fellman went through infantry basic training at Camp Adair, and then was designated a scout and given extra training. "From there we went to Fort Leonard Wood, Missouri. Things were getting bad over in Europe, so they sent the infantry regiments on ahead of our artillery. We were sent on to Camp Miles Standish, outside of Boston, and we went across the ocean on the *West Point*; it had been the S.S. *America*, the largest ship ever built in the United States. It was built in Newport News, across the bay from Norfolk.

"We went over, no convoy, and landed in Marseilles. From there we were sent up to Alsace; we got there in the middle of December. We were designated a 'task force,' and were named 'Task Force Herren,' and were attached to the 45th Infantry Division. The 45th had landed in Italy and fought at Salerno and Anzio, and now they were in Alsace at that point. They had been on the line a long time."[10]

—⁓—

An only child, Joseph C. Mark,* was born in 1920 and grew up in the Hunt's Point section of the South Bronx, New York. His immigrant parents divorced when he was in sixth grade, and he lived with his mother. "My mother was a very competent person," he recalled. "She worked at making linings for fur coats in the Garment District. I lived with her on the fourth floor of an apartment house. It was very pleasant at the time. I went to P.S. 48 and had lots of friends. We were always playing various games."

His parents had come from a section of Europe called Transylvania. "It's now in Romania, but then it was part of Hungary," he explained. "Before the war, we still had relatives there. My folks were Hungarian Jews and I learned to speak Hungarian as a child. We visited Hungary when I was eleven years old. My two uncles, Ferencz Herrmann and his brother Ignatz, owned a whiskey distillery there. You had to be able to speak German, Hungarian, and Romanian in order to get along."

After grade school, Mark attended Townsend-Harris High School, a special, three-year school that allowed students to enroll in New York City College without any testing. He attended City College and graduated in 1940, then received a fellowship in the college's department of psychology and was on the staff for a year.

"Five hundred dollars per annum didn't buy much," he recalled, so he picked up some extra money by offering his services as a ghostwriter. "I wanted to get into government service. In order to do that, I needed civil service status, so I took a job in the Brooklyn Navy Yard as a messenger; later, I was promoted to storekeeper. I bought a car for twenty dollars—a 1928 Chevy. I remember that, if you let the clutch out too fast, the axle would break. For fifty cents, we could go to the junkyard and buy another axle."

---

*Previously Markowitz. He changed it to Mark after the war.

Joseph and Stella Mark on their wedding day, 6 June 1943. (Courtesy Joseph Mark)

Mark met his future wife, Stella Kaltman, who was working in the supply department at the Navy Yard. "We got married in 1943. My mother got remarried a week before I got married."

The war that had been consuming Europe ever since Hitler invaded Poland in September 1939 became a very personal matter for Mark, as he and his mother feared for the safety of their relatives still in Hungary. "My mother corresponded with my relatives before the war, but there was no correspondence during the war. None of the mail got through. We didn't know what happened to them until afterward."*

While he probably could have obtained an exemption due to his job in a war industry, Mark felt duty calling. "Even though I was married, I volunteered to go into the Army rather than wait to be drafted; it wouldn't have been patriotic." He went on active duty three weeks after his wedding, and was assigned to the 106th Infantry Division, a new unit that had been activated in March 1943 and was training at Camp Atterbury, Indiana.[11]

———⟊⟊⟊⟊———

William Shapiro was born 29 July 1925 in the East Bronx section of New York City, the youngest of five sons. His parents, Jacob and Dora, emigrated from Russia in 1903 to escape the Tzar's anti-Jewish pogroms. They arrived separately, met in the Lower East Side, and were married shortly thereafter. Jacob had his own business in the Garment District but lost it in the Great Depression; he then found work making children's coats.

In January 1943, William graduated from Christopher Columbus High School in the Bronx. "During my high school years," he said, "I worked after school in a drugstore as a stockboy and delivery boy. My minimal salary went to my mother and I kept the tips. I was rather self-sufficient since age twelve. I had great support and friendship of my next older brother, who was five years older. My other brothers were much older and had little influence upon me.

"My father used to speak of the Nazi invasions and his concern for England. Roosevelt was his hero and became mine. I had no significant knowledge of the SS and their horrors, but I knew that I wanted to fight when the U.S. entered the war." Before Shapiro was able to enlist, however, he was drafted three months after his eighteenth birthday and sent to the Medical Corps' basic training course at Camp Grant, Illinois, then on to Walter Reed Hospital for surgical training. "After D-Day, I was shipped overseas to a replacement depot. I joined the 28th Division in England and landed in Normandy via Omaha Beach in July."[12]

---

*Their fears were well-founded; after the war, they learned that two uncles, two cousins, and an aunt survived, but the rest of the family had been wiped out by the Nazis.

Private
William
Shapiro,
1943.
(Courtesy
William
Shapiro)

After the division landed in France, it was thrust into combat against German units still holding out in the hedgerow country near St.-Lô. The 28th
marched through liberated Paris on 29 August 1944 then, as a part of VIII
Corps, fought its way eastward and entered Germany through Luxembourg
in September. Under Major General Norman D. Cota, the 28th was in the
thick of fierce fighting in the month-long battle for the Hürtgen Forest. By
the time the battle was over, the division had lost nearly a third of its men.

In November, the 8th Infantry Division relieved the battered 28th, which
was then sent to rest and refit along a twenty-five-mile front in the "quiet"

Ardennes region, near Wiltz, Luxembourg. By that time, Medic Bill Shapiro had seen plenty of combat and had helped save scores of wounded buddies.[13]

———✥———

In 1941, shortly before America became embroiled in the war, Peter Iosso felt that his life was not headed in a positive direction. "Although I was always one of the best students," he said, "when I turned sixteen, I didn't think my life had much promise. Whether or not I got a high school education didn't seem to matter. It seemed that maybe I was to become a foreman in a factory. So I quit high school in the tenth grade and got a job in a factory as a mechanical adjuster working on radio condensers and things like that."

Born in Newark, New Jersey, on 25 October 1925, the son of an Italian immigrant father and an American mother of Italian heritage, Peter Iosso grew up in a large, loving household, with three brothers and three sisters. His father had come to America from Italy in 1916 and had lived in the States for about a year when, the following year, the U.S. entered the First World War and he was conscripted. As a member of the 90th Division, the elder Iosso was gassed in combat in France, returned to the States, and was given a medical discharge.

Peter Iosso said, "My father spent some time in the VA hospital in the Bronx for his lung condition. He was a diabetic and died at sixty-five. His military experience and the gassing that he incurred may have shortened his life a bit. After the war, my father was a watchman at a candy factory between Newark and Bloomfield. He had to be there at five o'clock in the morning and he didn't get home until about seven or eight at night."

Iosso had two older brothers, Frank and Philip, and both had been drafted when they turned eighteen. He assumed the same would happen to him—and it did.

A small person—five-foot-five and a half—Private Iosso passed the physical and completed basic training in Georgia, then was assigned to Company E, 422nd Regiment, 106th Infantry Division, at Camp Atterbury, Indiana. "I was in the fourth platoon, which was the weapons platoon," he noted. "We had thirty-caliber 'light' machine-guns and sixty-millimeter 'light' mortars; I became a light machine-gunner. The summer was hot and the training rigorous. Enough of the 'dry runs'; we were eager for the 'real thing.'"

Peter Iosso, photographed in Newark, New Jersey, May 1943. (Courtesy Peter Iosso)

Major General Alan Jones's "Golden Lion" Division would soon get its wish. In October 1944, while heavy fighting was going on along the "Siegfried Line" on Germany's western border, the 106th left for Britain. "In November," Iosso said, "heavy rains pelted us as we crossed the English Channel and got closer to the front. December finally found us on line, spread thin in a quiet sector in Belgium, having left the rainy autumn of the flat land of northern France to be suddenly thrust into the snowy winter of the hilly Ardennes Forest region." The sector would not remain quiet for long.[14]

———

Before long, Tony Acevedo, Mort Brooks, Gerry Daub, Norm Fellman, Peter Iosso, Joe Mark, Bill Shapiro, and several hundred thousand other American young men who had either signed up to do their patriotic duty or were drafted, and who may have been dreaming about the war being over by Christmas, would be fighting for their very lives in struggles of great magnitude. And their fates would be intertwined in ways they never could have imagined.

2

TRIAL BY FIRE

It took the H.M.S. *Queen Elizabeth,* the largest passenger liner afloat, only five days to transport 15,000 men of the 106th Division from New Jersey to Glasgow, Scotland, making port on 17 November 1944. The troops were then taken by trains to Portsmouth, England, and transported across a storm-tossed English Channel to France and up the Seine River. The young soldiers of the "Golden Lion" Division who had hoped to spend a few days in Paris were disappointed. The division was loaded like cargo into hundreds of unheated trucks and hauled eastward, crossing into Belgium on 10 December. The troops did not see Paris.

What they saw instead from the backs of their "deuce-and-a-halfs" (cargo trucks) was a burnt and broken landscape that bore grim testimony to the ferocity of the no-holds-barred type of fighting that had taken place for the past six months. Hardly a town, village, or bridge was left intact; the ruins of homes, shops, churches, and factories—the enormous reality of which exceeded a thousand-fold what the young soldiers of the 106th had seen in newsreels or read about in newspapers—spoke mutely of the desperate battles that had been waged across the continent.

A member of the 106th Infantry Division stands guard in the snowy Ardennes region of eastern Belgium. (Courtesy U.S. Army Military History Institute)

Scattered along the roadsides and in the fields were the twisted and blackened carcasses of tanks, trucks, halftracks, ambulances, artillery pieces, jeeps, aircraft, and military hardware of all kinds. And not all of it was German; plenty of wrecked and blood-stained American vehicles littered the fields, farms, roads, and towns. The men of the 106th collectively gulped and hoped that things were considerably quieter wherever they were going.

On 11 December, the Golden Lions, half-frozen from their long, wintry ride across France and Belgium, found themselves detrucking in St. Vith, a quaint, east Belgian town that had existed for over 600 years. It didn't look too bad here. In the center of town stood the impressive Pfarrkirche, while the Büchelturm, a stone tower that had been part of the landscape since 1689, provided a picturesque glimpse into the town's medieval past.

The town was almost as old as Europe; named in honor of the martyr St. Vitus, the first settlers had put down roots in the area in 863 A.D., although there is evidence of much earlier settlement. In the twelfth century, St. Vith began building its reputation as an important market town for produce and manufactured

The intersection of Belgium, Luxembourg, Holland, and Germany—
site of the "Battle of the Bulge."

goods. Over the centuries, the town was ruled by many nations—Spain, Austria, and France, to name but three—and has found itself in the center of numerous wars, during which it was destroyed and rebuilt many times.

After the Congress of Vienna remapped the Continent following Napoleon's defeat in 1815, the town became part of Prussia (even today, St. Vith's official language is German). In August 1914, St. Vith found itself in the path of Kaiser Wilhelm's armies as they swept through on their way to the Somme and beyond. When Germany was stripped of her conquered territories at the end of World War I, St. Vith was restored to Belgian control. This status remained in place until July 1940, when German troops plunged across the border in Hitler's surprise invasion of France through the Ardennes Forest. Banners bearing the swastika hung from the town's buildings, and St. Vithians, perhaps hoping that

Concrete "dragon's teeth" anti-tank obstacles along the German-Belgium border near Aachen. (Author photo 2004)

a friendly welcome would spare the town from destruction, stood on the street corners and greeted the first panzers with the stiff-armed Fascist salute.

And now, at the end of 1944, with Hitler's armies having been forced out of France and Belgium by the advancing allies, St. Vith again became a vital and attractive prize for both sides.[1]

This eastern part of Belgium is the country's least populous. The broad farmlands and thick groves of trees are spread over a series of rolling hills and deep river valleys, intercut by narrow, winding roads. At St. Vith, just north of Luxembourg, the Ardennes Forest of Belgium melds with the Schnee Eifel region of Germany; the two areas are indistinguishable from one another. To call the region "mountainous" would be to use a misnomer; while steep in places and heavily forested in others, the region's undulating terrain is perhaps more akin to the gently rolling Appalachians of central Pennsylvania than the Alps.

A high, tree-covered ridge that runs basically from the northeast to the southwest, the Schnee Eifel was, in 1944, heavily fortified with reinforced-concrete bunkers, pillboxes, and anti-tank "dragon's teeth" obstacles—part of the Germans' Westwall defensive line. As the official Army history of the campaign says, "The Eifel is thickly covered with forests and provides good cover from air observation even in the fall and winter. The area has no large towns but rather is marked by numerous small villages, requiring extensive dispersion for any forces billeted here. The road net is adequate for a large military concentration. The rail net is extensive, having been engineered and expanded before 1914 for the quick deployment of troops west of the Rhine."[2]

On 7 December 1944, General Dwight D. Eisenhower, head of the Supreme Headquarters Allied Expeditionary Force, met with his highest American and British commanders in Maastricht, Holland, to map out plans for future operations. Autumn's broad Allied push had come to a dead stop along the German-Belgian border at Aachen and the Hürtgen Forest, as well as elsewhere along the front, due to a variety of factors: bad weather, heavy casualties, a serious shortage of fuel and ammunition, increased German resistance, and plain exhaustion. It was decided that a fresh offensive, set for early 1945, must be mounted in order to keep the German defenders on their heels and prevent any further loss of offensive momentum.

By the middle of December 1944, the Allies held a 400-mile front—from Nijmegen, Holland, in the north, to the French–Swiss border at Basel, in the south. Occupying the northern front, or left flank of the Allied line, were British Field Marshal Sir Bernard Law Montgomery's Twenty-first Army Group, composed of the First Canadian and Second British Armies; General Omar Bradley's Twelfth Army Group occupied the area to the south. Lieutenant General William H. Simpson's U.S. Ninth Army was squeezed into a small sector from west of Jülich and south to Aachen, while Lieutenant General Courtney Hodges's First Army had the broadest sector to cover—from Aachen to the southern border of Luxembourg, a distance of 120 miles. Below Luxembourg

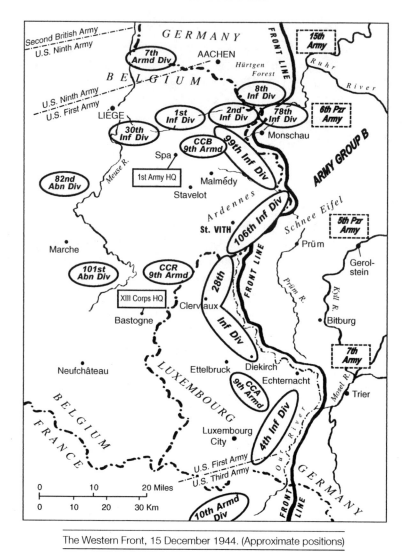

The Western Front, 15 December 1944. (Approximate positions)

stood Patton's Third Army; at Saarbrücken, the front turned east and was the responsibility of Patch's Seventh Army, which had landed on the French Riviera in
August. From just below Strasbourg to Basel, the French First Army held the line.

Along the Belgian border with Germany was Hodges's First Army—the veteran 1st, 2nd, 29th, and 30th Infantry Divisions, plus the 2nd Armored Division—all of which had seen months of heavy fighting in and around Aachen

Lieutenant General Alexander Patch, commander of the U.S.
Seventh Army. (Courtesy National Archives)

and the Hürgten Forest. On their right flank, from Monschau south, were spread the 99th, the 106th, and the badly stretched-out 28th Infantry Divisions.* To the rear of the 28th were the 101st Airborne Division and Combat Command R from the 9th Armored Division.

---

*Brigadier General James Wharton's 28th Infantry Division (Pennsylvania National Guard) had arrived in Normandy on 22 July 1944 and got its first taste of combat in the hedgerows around St.-Lô. Wharton was killed on 12 August; Norman D. Cota replaced him. The division paraded through liberated Paris on 29 August, and then saw considerable fighting during its drive across France, Belgium, Luxembourg, and the Hürtgen Forest. It suffered 5,000 casualties in four months. (Stanton, pp. 104–106)

Below the 28th was the 4th Infantry Division, which had landed at Utah Beach on 6 June 1944 and battled its way across France and Belgium. It had been in the area since September.

It was decided that Montgomery would send his forces in an all-out thrust toward the Rhine north of the Ruhr; Simpson's U.S. Ninth Army would be attached to the British force. Farther south, as part of a one-two punch, Eisenhower would send Lieutenant General George S. Patton's Third Army, in line south of Luxembourg, racing toward Frankfurt-am-Main. Supporting these attacks would be strong offensive action along the Saar front by Lieutenant General Jacob Devers's Sixth Army Group, with Patch's Seventh Army hitting the enemy in Alsace-Lorraine and the Saverne Gap.

Lieutenant General Courtney Hodges's First Army, consisting of the V, VII, and VIII Corps, would also play a major role in the coming fight; the VII Corps, commanded by Major General J. Lawton Collins, would spearhead the First Army's offensive and head for Cologne. Major General Leonard T. Gerow's V Corps, comprised of the 8th, 78th, 99th Infantry Divisions,* along with two armored combat commands and a cavalry group, would follow up and exploit any VII Corps successes. To take part in the V Corps offensive, the 2nd Infantry Division was pulled out of its positions east of St. Vith and trucked northward to the vicinity of Dom Butgenbach. The date of 13 December was set as D-day for the start of the offensive.

Major General Troy H. Middleton's VIII Corps, on the First Army's right, or southern, flank, had no immediate role in the offensive operations, but would be ready to follow up Allied gains. The VIII Corps would remain in place in the St. Vith sector, between Losheim and Eppeldorf. In reality, the units were in no shape to fight. Two of the infantry divisions—the 4th and 28th—were worn out and, added to Middleton's corps, were two new, untested divisions: the 99th (which had arrived on the front lines on 9 November) and the 106th.[3]

Although a veteran of World War I, the 106th's commanding general, fifty-two-year-old Major General Alan Jones, a stocky man with a Clark Gable mustache, had never led a unit of any size in combat, let alone a 14,253-man infantry division. Most of his officers, non-coms, and enlisted men were equally green.

---

*The 78th had arrived in theater in late November and reached the front lines on 1 December; the 99th landed in France on 3 November and was at the front by the ninth. (Stanton, pp. 145–146; and 175)

Generals Eisenhower and Bradley had earlier decided that the thickly wooded hills in the vicinity of St. Vith would be the perfect place for the new divisions—which had still been training back in the States during the heavy fighting of the summer and fall—to get a taste for living near the front, hearing the occasional distant rumble of artillery fire, and acting as reserves. As the seasoned divisions that had been slugging their way across the Continent since June 1944 became depleted on the difficult march toward Berlin, these fresh units, it was felt, could be quickly brought to the front.

Through no fault of its own, the 106th was about as ill-prepared for combat as any division America ever put into the field. From September to December 1943, 2,756 enlisted men were pulled out of the 106th at Camp Atterbury and either sent overseas as replacements or transferred to divisions that had been alerted for overseas movement. That was just the beginning; from activation to departure for its port of embarkation, the 106th lost a total of 12,442 men— more than eighty percent of its total. The official history of the Army Ground Forces notes, "The withdrawals were often made in driblets, aggravating the disruption of training. For example, there were fourteen separate withdrawals, involving from 25 to 2,125 men at a time."[4]

Bringing the division back up to its full Table of Authorization complement was a flood of ASTP students, fresh from their college classes—as well as the rookies from the infantry replacement centers at places such as Camp Wheeler, Georgia—whose military training was minimal at best.

There were other problems, too. One historian noted, "Unlike Regular Army and National Guard divisions, [the 106th] had no distinctive history or achievements, unit pride, or connection with any particular state or region."[5]

Once it arrived at the front, the 106th had not had time to acclimate itself to its new positions. While the 2nd Infantry Division, which the 106th replaced, had earlier plotted out preregistered artillery concentrations to its front, and established liaison with the 14th Mechanized Cavalry Group to its north, the 106th had yet to adequately carry out either of these two essential tasks. The officers of the 106th may have thought that, as new arrivals at the front, they would be given time to get their feet wet before anyone expected them to engage in any "real" soldiering. And they may also not have realized that the division, in its positions in the Schnee Eifel, represented a deep penetration into German territory.[6]

Besides unknowingly taking up positions in a salient, being deployed thinly across an extended front, having inadequate artillery cover, having little liaison with adjoining units, having not even a day of combat experience, and not having "distinctive history or achievements, unit pride, or connection with any particular state or region," the 106th was also extremely young. One member of the division noted that the 106th "was the youngest division, with an average age of twenty-two."[7]

The situation was ripe for disaster.

The American high command saw no reason to expect a German counter-thrust of any great magnitude in the Ardennes. Intelligence reports indicated no major enemy buildup or unusual "chatter" in communications that might suggest that the Germans were planning anything big. Even ULTRA, the system that had broken the German ENIGMA codes and was reading the high command's messages almost as quickly as they could be sent, deciphered nothing conclusive. Just as the Allies had hoodwinked the Germans about the Normandy invasion, the Germans had devised a deception plan to convince the Allies that Germany was going to stay strictly on the defensive; they made sure that the Allies received this carefully planted information.[8]*

––––––

The middle of December saw Americans back home getting ready for their fourth Christmas of the war. Shoppers stormed New York's brightly decorated avenues hoping to find just the right last-minute gift at Macy's or Gimbel's or Wanamaker's or Lord and Taylor; gifts for their servicemen overseas had been mailed many weeks earlier.

To help Americans take their minds off the war, Hollywood offered Elizabeth Taylor in *National Velvet* and Judy Garland in *Meet Me in St. Louis*. But films with a military theme also abounded: Moss Hart's *Winged Victory*; *Thirty Seconds Over Tokyo* with heartthrob Van Johnson; as well as *Since You Went Away*, *Hollywood Canteen*, and *Doughgirls*. Some theaters specialized in nothing but newsreels.

In New York, Broadway staged such hits as *One Touch of Venus*, *I Remember Mama*, *Life with Father*, *A Bell for Adano*, and *Soldier's Wife*; and *Miracle of the Warsaw Ghetto* played at the New Jewish Folk Theater.

---

*To avoid tipping their hand, all communications regarding the upcoming German offensive was conducted either in person or via couriers. (Parker, pp. 39–40; and MacDonald, *A Time for Trumpets*, p. 40)

Inside Radio City Music Hall, which budding architect Gerald Daub admired so much, the Rockettes were going through their annual high-kicking holiday show. Gallagher's Steak House on 52nd Street was giving away a free dinner with the purchase of a hundred-dollar war bond. Even the stockbrokers could smile; on 14 December, the Dow Jones 30 Industrials closed at 151 points.

Somehow, though, with the war dragging on, there was a hollowness to the holiday season. Each day, the *New York Times* published long listings of New York, New Jersey, and Connecticut war dead, divided under the headings of "Army," "Navy," "Marines," "Air Corps," "Coast Guard," and "Merchant Marines." Sometimes the listings ran to a full page. Frequently, photographs of prominent area servicemen killed or missing in action also appeared. Wedged in as it was between the cheery Christmas ads and the sports pages, the death toll was a grim and graphic reminder of the cost of liberty.

On Friday, 15 December, however, the *New York Times* was full of favorable war reports. The big news was the bombing by the B-29s of Curtis LeMay's Twentieth Bomber Command, based in India, against Japanese targets in Bangkok, Thailand, and Rangoon, Burma, with "excellent results." Other air assaults against the Japanese home islands and targets in China were also noted as being "successful."

In southeastern France, Alexander Patch's Seventh Army was reported to have gained four miles along a thirty-five-mile front. A war correspondent, writing from Supreme Headquarters Allied Expeditionary Force (SHAEF) in Paris, noted that Patch's army had "smashed northward through the snowy Vosges Mountains within seven miles of the Wissembourg Gap today [December 14] and Marauders [B-26 medium bombers] of the First Tactical Air Force hammered the Siegfried Line defenses . . . in Gen. Dwight D. Eisenhower's bid to break the German defenses at a comparatively weak point and reopen the war of movement in the west." A map helped readers visualize the situation.

Farther north, Courtney Hodges's First Army had, after a month of vicious fighting in the gloomy Hürtgen Forest following the battle for Aachen, finally resumed its push toward Bonn and the Rhine. Things were looking up; perhaps the war would, as some had predicted, be over, if not by Christmas, then surely early in the new year.[9]

While it appeared that the war was being prosecuted to a successful conclusion, the nation as a whole could turn its worries to another pressing concern: the state of the president's health. Having just waged another knockdown, drag-out presidential campaign and defeated New York governor Thomas Dewey, Franklin Delano Roosevelt, the old campaigner and consummate politician, was weary. In photos and newsreels he looked worn and haggard, with darkened circles beneath his eyes; and, indeed, his health was flagging. But FDR could still grin that famous grin and whip off a quip that would have everyone except Republicans laughing. For most Americans, Roosevelt had been like a father figure; in fact, for many, the man now in his eleventh year in the White House was the only president they could remember. Many were privately concerned that Roosevelt might not live to celebrate the victory and enjoy a world of peace that he had done so much to bring about.[10]

—⁊⁊⁊—

On the night of 11 December 1944, a number of high-ranking German generals were summoned to Feldmarschal Gerd von Rundstedt's headquarters in a castle at Langenhain-Ziegenberg, a small town about twenty miles north of Frankfurt-am-Main. At the headquarters, they were told to leave their briefcases and pistols behind, and were directed to board a gray-painted Wehrmacht bus.

Puzzled, the generals nevertheless complied. For half an hour, the officers were driven through the dark, snow-covered landscape, through the narrow, winding streets of nearby Ober Mörlen, then through open countryside, making one turn after another until they had lost all sense of direction. Only then did the bus deposit them at their secret destination: the Führer's underground forward headquarters, known as the Adlerhorst, in the resort city of Bad Nauheim.

"Most of the visitors," noted the historian Hugh Cole, "seem to have been more impressed by the Führer's obvious physical deterioration and the grim mien of the SS guards than by Hitler's rambling recital of his deeds for Germany which constituted this last 'briefing.'"[11]

The Führer began his long-winded historical discourse:

> Gentlemen! A fight like the struggle in which we find ourselves right now, which is being fought with such unlimited bitterness, obviously has different aims than the quarrels of the 17th or 18th Centuries, which might have concerned minor inheritances or royal dynastic conflicts. People and nations don't start a long war of life and death

without deeper reasons. One can't deny that the German nation, in terms of size and value, has (earned the claim) in central Europe to become the leader of the European continent. . . . [12]

Eventually, Hitler got around to the reason why he had summoned them to the Adlerhorst: In four days, the Germany army would launch the biggest offensive since the invasion of the Soviet Union.

Stunned, the generals could not believe their ears. Many privately believed that the Führer had, long ago, lost all touch with reality, and this news certainly confirmed their beliefs. They did their best to change Hitler's mind, pointing out that their formations were much too weak, the Allies were much too strong, and the chances for victory were nonexistent.

But Hitler had heard this type of defeatist talk from his generals before; he would not be moved. The operation would go ahead as planned—whether they liked it or not. After listening to the details of the scheme, the reluctant generals clicked their heels, gave their leader the Nazi salute, shouted *"Heil Hitler,"* climbed back into the bus, and began trying to figure out how they could pull off such a massive operation in just four days. [13]

As early as September 1944, when the American and British drive began to lose steam along the Westwall, Hitler had begun to concoct a plan to throw everything he had at the Americans in an attack so violent it would rival Operation Barbarossa, Germany's invasion of the Soviet Union, in everything except scale.

Launched at the height of Germany's military might in July 1941, Barbarossa had involved seven armies, four panzer groups, 150 infantry, panzer, and motorized divisions, three million men, 3,580 armored fighting vehicles, over 7,000 guns, 1,830 aircraft, and 750,000 horses. [14] The resources now available for Operation Wacht-am-Rhein were a mere fraction of the Barbarossa force: three armies with thirteen infantry and seven panzer divisions (plus an additional five infantry divisions in OKW [Oberkommando der Wehrmacht—German Army High Command] reserve on alert or en route to the front), 290,000 men, 2,617 artillery pieces and rocket launchers, 1,038 tanks and self-propelled guns, a handful of aircraft. But perhaps it would be enough; only eighty thousand Americans held the seventy-five-mile line between Monschau and Luxembourg City. And the 99th and the 106th Divisions, occupying the *schwerpunkt*—the point of attack—in front of St. Vith, Belgium, were too inexperienced to put up much of a fight.

The five infantry and four SS panzer divisions of the Sixth Panzer Army, under SS-Obergruppenführer Sepp Dietrich, would strike Major General Leonard
T. Gerow's V Corps lines between Aachen and Monschau. Dietrich's army consisted of over 140,000 men, 642 tanks and self-propelled assault guns, and 1,025
pieces of artillery. Spearheading the attack was SS-Obersturmbannführer
Joachim Peiper's Kampfgruppe Peiper, a unit that would soon earn eternal in-
famy for its actions near the Belgian village of Malmédy.

To the south, General der Panzertruppen Erich Brandenberger's Seventh
Army, the weakest of Hitler's attacking force, would hit Major General Troy H.
Middleton's extended VIII Corps's line along the German-Luxembourg border.
Still, the unmotorized Seventh Army had some 60,000 men and 629 artillery
pieces and rocket launchers, a formidable force by any calculation. Fortunately
for Brandenberger, the Americans facing him—one regiment each from the 4th
and 28th Infantry Divisions and a combat command from the 9th Armored
Division—were also regarded as weak.

The center thrust would send General der Panzertruppen Hasso-Eccard von
Manteuffel's Fifth Panzer Army crashing toward Bastogne and into the unsuspecting ranks of the U.S. 28th, 99th, and 106th Divisions. Von Manteuffel's force
consisted of four infantry and three panzer divisions (90,000 men), 396 tanks
and assault guns, and 963 artillery pieces and rocket launchers.

In addition, a thousand parachutists of a provisional Fallschirmjäger battalion would be dropped behind American lines in the early morning hours of 17
December near the Mont Rigi crossroads on the highway from Eupen to
Malmédy in Operation Stösser, Germany's last airborne operation. The commander of the parachute operation, Baron Oberst Frederich-August von der
Heydte, inquired about the composition of the American reserve forces his
paratroopers might encounter and was angrily told by his superior, Sepp Dietrich, "I am not a prophet! You will learn earlier than I what forces the Americans
will use against you. Besides, behind their lines there are only Jewish hoodlums
and bank managers!"

As an extra surprise, a thousand English-speaking Germans, dressed in American uniforms, driving captured American vehicles, and commanded by the bril-
liant commando SS-Obersturmbannführer Otto Skorzeny, would be employed in
Operation Greif to sow confusion and disinformation behind the lines. Additionally, Skorzeny's men were to dash ahead of the panzer columns and seize at least
two Meuse bridges. It seemed that Hitler had thought of everything.[15]

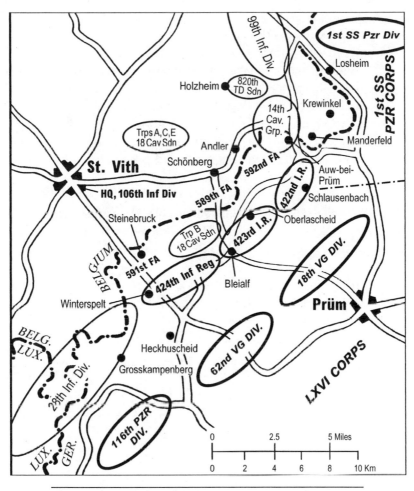

Approximate positions of units of the 106th Infantry Division, adjoining, and enemy units, 15 December 1944.

Although it appeared formidable on paper, the German force was something of a paper tiger. According to Hugh Cole,

> In December 1944, Germany was fighting a "poor man's war" on the ground as in the air. This must be remembered when assessing the actual military potential of the divisions arrayed for the western of-

fensive. Motor transport was in sorry shape; the best-equipped divisions had about 80 percent of their vehicular tables of equipment, but many had only half the amount specified in the tables. . . . Spare parts, a necessity in rough terrain and poor weather, hardly existed. There was only a handful of prime movers and heavy tank retrievers. Signal equipment was antiquated, worn-out, and sparse. . . . Anti-tank guns were scarce, the heavy losses in this weapon sustained in the summer and autumn disasters having never been made good. The German infantryman would have to defend himself against the enemy tank with bravery and the bazooka. . . .

Adding to the attackers' woes, ammunition stocks were dangerously low and there was insufficient fuel to allow the Germans to reach their main objective, Antwerp. Many of the supply wagons and artillery pieces were pulled by horses.[16]

But strange things happen in war; victory does not always go to the best trained or the best equipped. Hitler gambled that German desperation, surprise, and audacity would be enough.

3

THE SURPRISE

THE THREE REGIMENTS OF THE 106th Infantry Division were thinly spread across nearly ten miles of a gently sloping ridge in the Schnee Eifel, just inside Germany's border with Belgium.

The left flank of Colonel George L. Descheneaux, Jr.'s 422nd Infantry Regiment touched the village of Schlausenbach; the right flank met Colonel Charles C. Cavender's 423rd Regiment near Oberlascheid. The 423rd's lines then extended southwest to the town of Bleialf. The third regiment, Colonel Alexander Reid's 424th, was located four miles southwest of Bleialf, around Winterspelt. Covering a road between the 423rd and 424th were Company B of the 106th's 81st Engineer Battalion and Troop B, 18th Cavalry Squadron. Division headquarters was six miles behind the front line in a schoolhouse in St. Vith.[1]

To the 422nd's and 423rd's front lay wide farm fields. Beyond the fields stood groves of tall fir trees. No one expected much action in this sector. Except for the distant and sporadic thud of artillery, and occasional patrols by both sides, the situation along the front was about as quiet as war could get. And that suited many of the nervous new arrivals just fine. Scanning the far side of the valley with binoculars, officers saw no reason to think that a major attack was imminent. But the binoculars were not X-ray glasses; they could not penetrate the

37

thick woods before them to see the stores of ammunition and fuel being built up; the hundreds of panzers, half-tracks, and self-propelled artillery pieces lined up track-to-track; the thousands of heavily armed men assembled for the great operation.

Still, some front-line soldiers, inexperienced though they were, did suspect something was up. Nineteen-year-old Private First Class William Shapiro, a medic assigned to the 110th Regiment, 28th Division, said, "For many days in early December, we heard activity on the other side of the Our River. These were German troop movements. . . . We sent our reports back to company headquarters and were reassured to ignore the movements across the river."[2]

According to historian Hugh Cole, shortly before the offensive began, the 28th and 106th Divisions sent in reports of increased vehicular activity on the nights before the attack. The 28th discounted its own report by noting that this was the normal accompaniment of an enemy front-line relief and that the same thing had happened when a German unit had pulled out three weeks before. The 106th was a green division and unlikely to know what weight could be attached legitimately to such activity. In fact, one regimental commander rebuked his S-2 [Intelligence officer] for reporting this noise as "enemy movement."[3]

These and other indicators, such as aerial reconnaissance that showed heavy concentrations of men and equipment (which was misinterpreted as enemy units merely passing through the Eifel area on their way to bolster German lines to the north or south) should have alerted the American high command that something big—or at least unusual—was in the works. Even General Omar Bradley, head of the American Twelfth Army Group, failed to attach adequate importance to the ominous signs, admitting later, "I had greatly underestimated the enemy's offensive capabilities. . . . We could not believe he possessed sufficient resources for a strategic offensive."[4]

For most of the men trying to keep warm in bunkers and foxholes along the Eifel ridge, everything was as peaceful as a Hallmark Christmas card. According to Peter Iosso, a machine-gunner in E Company, 422nd Infantry Regiment, 106th Division, dug in eight miles east of St. Vith, the loudest thing in his sector was "the snow that fell off the branches of the evergreens."

Iosso added, "We had been on line for a few days. We had just arrived there and replaced the Second Division. The guys in the Second Division told us there wasn't much going on. We had a machine-gun nest in a pillbox with logs over it—kind of a primitive shelter. We thought we would probably serve a couple of

View toward German lines from the 422nd Regiment's positions
near Schlausenbach. (Author photo 2004)

weeks there and then get R and R [rest and recuperation] and have a good time somewhere else, then return to this kind of phony war."[5]

Robert Kline, a communications sergeant from Iowa with Company M, 423rd Regiment, 106th Division, noted, "We had taken over the sector from the 2nd Division—they had been up there for two or three months. We were on the end of the line. We were on a hill and there wasn't anybody between us and the bottom of the hill. About five miles away was the highway—our anti-tank company was there."

Kline was in a large, concrete, former-German bunker with his company commander. "I couldn't stand sleeping in that bunker. James Hardy was our company commander, and he smoked and smoked. So I went outside and slept with the other guys. By that time, they had a little dugout with logs over the top. The Germans ran patrols up through us about every night. You weren't supposed to shoot at them, because you'd give away your position. One guy had a dog jump in on him—scared him to death. I had to put telephone lines in from

Two soldiers from the 106th Division roll up their sleeping bags
after a night in the open. (Courtesy National Archives)

our headquarters up to our front line, and it snowed, and I could see dog tracks;
the Germans even stuck swastikas on the trees to scare us."[6]

Clifford Savage, a twenty-three-year-old from Oxford, Mississippi, and a
heavy machine-gunner with Company M, 393rd Regiment, 99th Division, was
several miles farther north, near Krinkelt. He recalled, "We relieved the 29th Division which had pushed right up to the Siegfried Line and had dug in there. I
guess they thought they were going to be there all winter. We were in a bunker
with logs over us and our machine-gun in there. There was about eighteen to
twenty-four inches of snow on the ground. We didn't have any other shelter, but
we did have an emplacement in back of the gun a little ways, so we could maybe
sleep once in a while. Of course, every day or two the Germans would test us out
to see what we were up to."[7]

All along the American lines, the night of 15–16 December 1944 was pretty
much like the previous few nights: a little distant gunfire; a lot of hand-rubbing

and foot-stomping by sentries trying to keep warm; hours of monitoring the radio net to hear if anything important, or even interesting, was happening; trying to sleep while one's wet, cold clothing caused the body to shiver and shake; thinking about what tomorrow—and the day after—would bring. For those who had been "gung-ho" and had enlisted enthusiastically for the cause, their military ardor had waned; war was a cold, dirty business. Uncomfortable, too. And, at times like this, exceedingly boring.

For many married soldiers, like Joe Mark and Bob Kline, that night's thoughts drifted homeward, picturing what their wives might be doing at that exact moment in New York and Iowa, respectively—making breakfast, getting ready for work, listening to the latest songs on the radio, writing a letter, or, more likely, still asleep in a nice, warm bed.

Peter Iosso probably mulled over his future—whether he should return to work at the radio factory or seek a different direction with his life.

Philadelphian Jack Crawford, in the 106th's 590th Field Artillery Battalion, trying to catch some sleep near the guns, perhaps dreamed that he might return to the grocery business in Philadelphia; after all, it wasn't every eighteen-year-old who had been promoted to manager.

Richard Lockhart, in the 423rd Regiment's Anti-Tank Company, likely figured he would return to his studies at Purdue University—if he survived the war.

Twenty-one-year-old James V. Smith of Columbus, Georgia, an ammunition carrier for the mortar platoon in Company H—the heavy weapons company—2nd Battalion, 423rd Infantry Regiment, 106th Division, no doubt glanced at the snapshot he carried of his girlfriend, Mary Virginia Fuller, and wondered when he would see her again. They had been pretty serious before he left; if he got out of this alive, he'd ask her to marry him.

As a child of the Depression, Cliff Savage might have been thinking about money—the thirty dollars a month he had earned with the Civilian Conservation Corps back in Oxford, Mississippi, or the eighteen dollars a week he was making at a mop factory in Memphis right before he got drafted in November of 1942, or the fifty dollars a month he was making now—and wondering where his postwar life would lead him.

For William Shapiro with the 110th Regiment, 28th Division, life was good. Instead of freezing in a foxhole, he was relaxing in the warm kitchen of a farmhouse in the Luxembourg hamlet of Nachtmanderscheid, not far from Clervaux, and thinking of his sweetheart, Betty Ostrowsky, back home in the Bronx.

Thousands of men on the night of 15–16 December in the woods and hills to the east of St. Vith thought about home and pondered their future. For many, however, there would be no future.

—·∿∿·—

In the dark chill of 15–16 December 1944, a few miles to the east of the American lines, beneath the towering, frosted pines of the Ardennes, the German unit commanders drew their troops around them and read to them the reason why they had been secretly assembled along the Belgian frontier—von Rundstedt's stirring order of the day:

> Soldiers of the West Front:
> Your great hour has struck. Strong attacking armies are advancing today against the Anglo-Americans. I do not need to say more to you. You all feel it. Everything is at stake. You bear in yourselves the holy duty to give everything and to achieve the superhuman for our Fatherland and our Führer.[8]

Then the massive German war machine stirred to life. Soldiers shouldered their K-98 Mauser rifles and MP-40 Schmeisser machine-pistols and tank-busting Panzerfausts, and climbed aboard their trucks and half-tracks. Panzer commanders gave their men the signal to move out, and the cold, night air was suddenly filled with the roar of engines and clouds of choking diesel exhaust. All along the eighty-mile front, the snow crunched beneath the tires and tracks of the vehicles as over a quarter million men and their thousands of pieces of motorized transport headed west, grimly determined to do their holy duty to save the Fatherland—or die trying.

—·∿∿·—

In military matters, the greatest sin is to be taken by surprise. Poland was surprised when Germany invaded on 1 September 1939; France was surprised when German divisions attacked her in the summer of 1940; Stalin was surprised when Germany invaded the Soviet Union a year later; and the United States received a shocking surprise on 7 December 1941 when Japan bombed American military installations in Hawaii. So, too, were the Allies caught napping once again in the small hours of 16 December 1944.

As the sleepy, unsuspecting American sentries scanned the terrain in front of them, the predawn blackness of the eastern horizon suddenly lit up like an artificial dawn, as though the end of the world were at hand. Thousands of German artillery pieces, mortar tubes, rocket launchers, and panzer barrels flared as they sent their rounds screaming toward the American lines. Seconds later, the projectiles began splattering on the ground, bursting in the air, and tearing into the trees, spraying hot, jagged fragments on their unsuspecting victims.

Men who had been dozing just moments before were now jerked out of their slumber by noise and concussions that none had ever experienced before. Shaking the sleep from their brains, and suddenly fueled with adrenaline, soldiers screamed "Incoming!" as they grabbed for their rifles and rushed to their assigned defensive positions. Others, terrified at the bright white-orange flashes and the splintering of tall pines that accompanied the eruptions of thousands of shells, took off running to escape the steel storm.

A confident group of German paratroopers, 17 December 1944. (Courtesy U.S. Army Military History Institute)

After a barrage that seemed to last several eternities, the fires lifted. Those soldiers who had survived the saturation saw ghostly shapes moving toward them through the trees—white-washed panzers, accompanied by infantry in snow camouflage. While elements of the 18th Volksgrenadier Division kept the men of the 106th occupied to their front, the rest of the enemy division was already slipping around the flanks, between the seam of the 422nd Regiment and the 14th Cavalry Group to the north, and between the 423rd and the 424th to the south, at Bleialf. The immediate objective of the German units was Schönberg, between the rear of the 106th and St. Vith.[9]

Before the assault began, Private First Class Peter Iosso, Company E, 422nd Regiment, 106th Division, was shivering. "I had been out in the snow from about six o'clock at night [15 December] until about six o'clock the next morning. My equipment and clothing were still wet, freezing at night and thawing during the sunless days. We had a half dozen pairs of socks but no change of shoes; my boots were soaked through. Winter gear, we were told, was on the way. We changed our damp socks a couple of times a day, drying the ones removed with body heat under our shirts."

In the dark, early morning hours of 16 December, Iosso suddenly had more important things to worry about than wet socks. He was heading back out to his machine-gun post when German shells began dropping. A round exploded nearby and knocked him unconscious; when he awoke, it was daylight and he was lying in the snow with a bloody chin and throbbing feet. "Though my stiff legs and frostbitten feet resisted," he said, "I managed to get to company HQ for sick call. At another time I would probably have been taken to the 'rear,' but this was December 16, and the Germans had broken through our lines. Somebody bandaged my chin. But the battle began and the aid station was no help to me because they were getting ready to retreat. I was cut off from my company and had to retreat with the company headquarters people."[10]

Joe Mark was at his switchboard in a German pillbox in the Siegfried Line that served as headquarters for the 3rd Battalion, 106th Division, when the Battle of the Bulge suddenly erupted. "I was putting through switchboard calls from our artillery observer in the front to our artillery in the back. Our position held initially. We stopped them cold in front of us, but they got around us on both sides.

"After that artillery barrage, I said to this young fellow—eighteen—from Iowa, 'I think things are bad.' We put on all the clothes we had, because I once asked an old sergeant, 'What's your best friend?' When you train, your best friend is your rifle. This old sergeant said, 'Your best friend is your overcoat.' Especially when it's

German assault troops dash across a road littered with burning vehicles and equipment
belonging to the 14th Armored Cavalry Group near
St. Vith, Belgium, during the Battle of the Bulge. (Courtesy National Archives)

the dead of winter. So we put on all our clothes—the ODs [olive-drab wool uni-
forms] and all the other stuff we had—and we fell back."[11]

James V. Smith, Company H, 423rd Infantry Regiment, 106th Division, was
with his mortar platoon in a rest area a few miles behind the lines. On the
morning of 16 December, he learned that the Germans had infiltrated the artillery positions of the 28th Division. "We were supposed to go up to the front
lines and chase the Germans out of [the 28th's] artillery positions," he said. "We
started having these three-quarter-ton trucks passing us, heading for the rear.
We could see all these dead soldiers stacked up in the trucks. That didn't cheer
us up very much.

"We went on up, but instead of going to the artillery position, we came to a
mountain. We were on one side of the mountain and the Germans were on the

A dead American soldier lies in the foreground as his buddies hastily dig foxholes in a roadside ditch during the German breakthrough in the Ardennes, December 1944. (Courtesy National Archives)

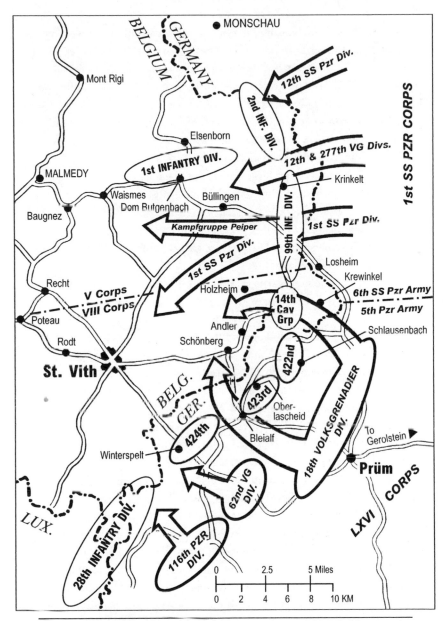

MONSCHAU

BELGIUM
GERMANY

Mont Rigi

12th SS Pzr Div.

2nd INF. DIV.

1st SS PZR CORPS

Elsenborn

1st INFANTRY DIV.

12th & 277th VG Divs.

MALMEDY

Krinkelt

Waismes
Dom Butgenbach
Büllingen

99th INF. DIV.

1st SS Pzr Div.

Baugnez

Kampfgruppe Peiper

1st SS Pzr Div.

Recht

Losheim

Krewinkel

6th SS Pzr Army

Holzheim

V Corps
VIII Corps

14th
Cav
Grp

5th Pzr Army

Poteau

Andler

Schlausenbach

Rodt

Schönberg

422nd

St. Vith

BELG.
GER.

423rd

Ober-
lascheid

424th

Bleialf

18th VOLKSGRENADIER DIV.

To
Gerolstein

Winterspelt

Prüm

LXVI CORPS

LUX.

62nd VG DIV.

28th INFANTRY DIV.

116th PZR DIV.

0   2.5   5 Miles

0   2   4   6   8   10 KM

The German Ardennes counteroffensive (Wacht-am-Rhein) against the 106th Division
and other American positions near St. Vith, 15–16 December 1944.
(Approximate positions)

other, firing V-1s, or what we called the 'buzz-bombs.' When the flame went out on the back of that thing, everybody started heading for some kind of cover. We destroyed several of those things with just fifty-caliber machine-guns. We had fifty-caliber machine-guns mounted on some of our jeeps and trucks, and they were shooting at those buzz-bombs as they came over the mountain. We were using tracer ammunition, so we could tell whether the bombs were being hit or not."[12]

Historian Hugh Cole noted, "The V-weapon turned out to have no tactical significance, although the German high command stepped up the attack on the Allied depots at Antwerp and Liège during the Ardennes offensive, averaging at least 135 firings a week against Liège and 235 against Antwerp. These mostly were the pilotless aircraft, or V-1 type, bearing 2,240 pounds of explosive. The military casualties inflicted by this V-weapons attack were slight, except for one strike on 16 December which destroyed an Antwerp cinema, killing 296 British soldiers and wounding 194." [13]

Farther north, the same carnage and confusion that reigned in the 106th's area was being repeated in the 99th Infantry Division's sector. The 12th SS Panzer, 12th Volksgrenadier, and 277th Volksgrenadier Divisions were all hitting the 99th's positions in and around the twin towns of Rocherath-Krinkelt. Clifford Savage, a machine-gunner with Company M, 393rd Infantry Regiment, dug in there, said, "Early on the 16th, about four o'clock in the morning, the Germans started shelling us. We figured something big was happening, but we didn't see any soldiers until just about daylight. They made a big push and we all opened fire; we had four machine-guns set up there, and also the riflemen. We was cross-firing all out through there, and we drove them back maybe two times, then they sent another group.

"We were right at the edge of the wooded area in what's called the Hürtgen Forest. We could see the German bunkers in the Siegfried Line and they would come out of there all dressed in white to go with this snow, so it was hard to distinguish people. Further down on either side of us they broke through. We held our position there until they came in from our rear and cut off our ammunition supply. Everything we had back there in reserve, they took that. Later on in the afternoon, they made a push into our rear and we couldn't get our machine-guns out to fire in that direction, so just the riflemen was all that was capable of putting out any fire."

Savage's position was soon overrun. "Our platoon leader already had gotten shot through the opening in the front of our bunker. He got shot right between

Private James V. Smith. Photo taken 21 February 1944.
(Courtesy Mary E. Smith)

the eyes pretty early in the morning. I don't know why he was in that particular position, but he was. We had an opening in the back of our pillbox and several Germans were right over us with their guns pointed at us and our section leader was in there, also. He put his handkerchief on the end of his rifle and held it up and they told us to come out and we did.

"The Germans were all around us there and we couldn't fire our machine-guns. I don't think we had any ammunition left, anyway. We had been firing all morning out front trying to hold them off that way, but they broke through somewhere else and came around to our rear. It was one of the SS divisions. They searched us and we had to throw everything we had down on the ground—watches, money, everything. Then they made us take all the dead and wounded Germans back to their bunkers. We did that for, I don't exactly re-member how long—maybe a couple or three hours, and we got them all out of there."

While Savage and his buddies were carrying the enemy's casualties, artillery shells began plastering the area, and he was hit in the side and leg. "None of the shrapnel was imbedded; it just glanced. I got a pretty good gash on my side and two places in my leg about as big as a half dollar. Both sides were firing, so I don't know whose hit me. I never got to see a medical doctor at all." He was hus-tled off to a prisoner collection point.[14]

In the 106th's sector, James V. Smith and his mortar section were set up not far from Bleialf. "We set up our mortar on some logs. The mortar was designed to have the base plate dig into dirt, but when we fired, it skidded all the way back to the end of the log. The first round we fired out of the mortar, it hit a church steeple in the town and blew the church steeple apart. The next round—we had used a magnesium round—it hit very near a tank that was coming around a corner in the town. Our observers said a lot of Germans came out of the tank and several things were on fire there."

Later that day, as the ammunition supply was running low, Smith was sent back to pick up more. "I had to go about a half mile to a truck that had our am-munition. While going over there, I walked across a small creek. It was frozen over, so I had no problem. I got to the truck and they gave me this apron; it had pockets front and back, and they loaded it with 81mm rounds. I started back and came to that little creek. With all that extra weight, I broke through the ice and went up to my knees in ice water. Of course, I had no way to dry myself, and no heat or anything like that. My feet were basically almost frozen. Anyway, I got

A squad leader of the 1st SS Panzer Division signals for his men to move forward near St. Vith. (Courtesy National Archives)

the rounds back to the mortar, and then they decided we should move out, which we did.

"We got about a half mile or so away from that position and all of a sudden the sun came out and these [American] P-47 fighters came over. We had one master sergeant who had been with the anti-aircraft artillery in Washington, D.C. The first thing he did, he opened up with his M-1 rifle at the P-47s, and got attacked by about forty enlisted men there, right quick—he of all people should've known better. They had a dogfight and the P-47s were grossly out-numbered; one of them was shot down and the pilot parachuted in about a mile from where we were. We tried to figure a way to get to him, but he was well be-hind the lines, so it wouldn't have been practical."

Smith and his unit were then ordered to move to another area; they spent the frigid night in an open field. "We dug a large pit for our mortar and then we took some logs and our raincoats and covered it with dirt so we had a place where we could crawl in to sleep. Early the next morning, out of nowhere came this German reconnaissance plane that flew over us, about 100–150 feet. Then we knew that they knew where we were. So then we started moving out and moved to another little town. The Germans were firing a lot of mortars into the area that were landing about 150–200 yards from where we had set up our mor-tar—in a cow lot by a very nice two-story farmhouse."[15]

By late morning on the 16th, the 14th Cavalry Group was being pushed back to the Holzheim-Andler line, uncovering the 422nd's left flank in the process. On the 423rd's right flank, in the village of Bleialf, a street battle resembling a Wild West shootout—only this time using automatic weapons, armored vehi-cles, and artillery—took place; the seam between American units was torn. The German breakthrough above and below the 106th's 422nd and 423rd Regiments was about to snare the division in a classic double envelopment.[16]

St. Vith was in a panic, with civilians attempting to flee while German shells, fired from batteries at Prüm, fifteen miles away, bombarded the town; German armored columns were spotted closing in. No one, least of all General Jones, seemed to know what was happening to the 106th's forward regiments.[17]

4

CAPTIVE

AT HIS PARIS headquarters, General Eisenhower was not panicked, or even terribly concerned. To him, the Ardennes counteroffensive signaled that the war was nearly over. He wrote, "We had always been convinced that before the Germans acknowledged final defeat in the West they would attempt one desperate counteroffensive. It seemed likely to Bradley and me that they were now starting this kind of attack."[1]

The SHAEF brass huddled about the situation. It was decided that the 7th Armored Division, a part of Courtney Hodges's First Army to the north of the penetration, and the 10th Armored Division, in Patton's Third Army operating to the south, should be immediately rushed to the area of the breakthrough to pinch off the threat. Such moves would necessitate the postponement of other offensive operations that were scheduled to begin in the next few days, but it could not be helped.

The situation for the Americans on the front lines was fast becoming untenable. On 17 December, the Germans had driven the 14th Cavalry Group, to the north of the 106th, back to St. Vith. South of St. Vith, the Germans had pushed the 424th Regiment back and taken the town of Winterspelt.

SS Grenadiers of the 1st SS Panzer Division move past destroyed American
vehicles during the Battle of the Bulge. (Courtesy National Archives)

A plan was formulated to gather whatever troops could be found in and around St. Vith and head for Schönberg, thereby opening an escape corridor for what was left of the 106th's 422nd and 423rd Regiments. Meanwhile, the 7th Armored Division was ordered to rush to St. Vith.[2]

If Eisenhower was calm and confident, General Jones was despondent. Wrongly informed that the 7th Armored Division, just starting out from Maastricht, Holland, sixty miles to the north, would arrive early on the 17th, Jones was losing hope that his besieged regiments could hold out that long.[3]

Speeding south from Maastricht several miles in advance of his Combat Command B tanks was Brigadier General Bruce C. Clarke. He first reported to General Middleton at VIII Headquarters in Bastogne, who informed him of the deteriorating situation in the 106th's sector. The next morning, the forward elements of the 7th Armored reached Poteau, five miles west of St. Vith. Already there were problems; the SS spearhead had cut the 7th's route of march and killed Colonel Church M. Matthews, the division's chief of staff.*

Meanwhile, in Luxembourg, south of St. Vith, the Germans were hitting the 28th Division. Medic and combat veteran William Shapiro recalled that his company was ordered to vacate the farmhouses it had been occupying, proceed along a high ridge, and dig in in preparation for repelling the enemy assault. He said, "No matter how often you are in a foxhole and are subject to a bombardment by artillery, mortars, or from the air, your physical actions and silent prayers are the same. Additionally, on the front lines, after a bombardment by the enemy stops, you know that the tanks and infantry are heading toward your position. . . .

"We were on the Luxembourg side of the Skyline Drive near Marnach. After digging in with several infantrymen about me, we just laid there, awaiting orders. Waiting stimulates tenseness. The more waiting, the more tenseness. . . . You say to yourself that the job has to be done, you cannot go anywhere and you cannot do anything differently. You wait.

"The high ridge road blocked our view in front of us. We could not see the Our River which the Germans had to cross to enter Luxembourg. It was all quiet

---

*Following behind the 7th Armored column was B Battery of the 285th Field Artillery Observation Battalion. The small convoy had passed through Malmédy and was a few hundred yards south of Baugnez when it came under fire from Peiper's panzers. The lightly armed Americans who survived the initial assault surrendered, but they were lined up in a field and gunned down; eighty-six GIs were murdered in cold blood by Peiper's SS *kampfgruppe*. (Cole, pp. 261–265; and Ramsey, "The Battle of the Bulge," *After the Battle* magazine, No. 4)

and it was dawn. Suddenly, there was a tremendous barrage of German artillery from across the river. Despite the knowledge that I was expecting it to occur, the sudden loudness, [and] massive amounts of flashes lightening up the sky on the other side of the river shocks you into reality. . . . You hear many repeating explosions as the shells land one after another. . . . The machine-gun firings, mortar shell bursts, and 'Screaming Meemies* are all about you as you dig deeper and deeper into your foxhole. You are helpless and alone. Suddenly, I saw a very bright flash of light in front and to the right of me. There was a deafening loud explosion."

Shapiro was knocked unconscious by the concussion of the exploding shell and woke up several hours later in the battalion aid station, which was set up in the Clervaux railroad depot. Shapiro had no memory of anything that happened after the shell went off near his foxhole. He checked himself out: no broken bones, no bandages, just "a tremendous headache, my ears felt stuffed, my vision was blurred, and there was a constant ringing in my ears."

Evening came and with it the sounds of German firing coming nearer to the depot. "I heard someone say that we are going to surrender. Someone—perhaps Major Clyde Collins—said that Jewish soldiers should throw their dogtags into the potbelly stove [in the center of the room] because we were surrounded by SS troops." Shapiro complied with the order. "I do not recall any thoughts about what this action meant, or even related the facts that I was Jewish and these were SS troops. I had not known of any incident in which Jewish soldiers had been shot."

Shapiro walked out of the railroad station with his hands up. "My head felt stuffed, my ears were pulsating as if blood was rushing about my head. . . . Outside, you could hear the repeating bursts of the burp guns and pistols being shot into the air. It was the first time that I heard the loud, staccato, guttural shouting of 'Raus! Raus! Raus!' [Out!] I would come to hear this command repeatedly in the next four months as a prisoner and in my nightmares for the rest of my life.

"As we were pushed into groups, I heard the most unexpected and incredulous shouting of, 'Hands up, Chicago gangsters!' They were repeating something some saw and remembered from an old, grade B American movie about cops and robbers. It was repeated again and again. The SS troopers . . . were part of the 116th Panzer Division that swept over Skyline Drive and entered Clervaux. . . ."

---

*The GIs' nickname for the Germans' six-barrel *Nebelwerfer* rocket launcher.

The Americans were searched and the Germans relieved Shapiro of his watch, a gold ring that his brother David had given him for his Bar Mitzvah, his medical supply packs, all his cigarettes except for a small four-cigarette package that the Red Cross distributed, his helmet with the Red Cross insignia, and his combination eating tool. Shapiro was then directed to fall in with a column of prisoners that was being marched into town with their hands up.

Shapiro was unsteady. "I was stumbling, had a tremendous headache, was confused and simply followed others walking in line with their hands held high above their heads." He and the rest of the prisoners were taken to a hotel and packed into a meeting room or restaurant; they were there the entire night without food or drink.

The next morning, the group was marched eastward into Germany. The column of POWs frequently had to scatter from the road as German tanks, trucks, tracked artillery pieces, motorcycles, wood-burning vehicles, bicycles, and horse-drawn wagons dashed by, heading for the battle front. Shapiro noted that "the German equipment was poor, makeshift, and assembled by commandeered vehicles of every variety that could move supplies and troops to the front. . . . Troops were sitting and riding atop this varied transportation, as well as walking alongside. . . . All of us remarked at the shabbiness of the equipment when compared to the American troops on a march."[4]

The situation around St. Vith quickly came to a head on the 17th. At noon, General Jones passed along a message to the 422nd Regiment that the Air Corps would attempt to air-drop supplies in the vicinity of Schlausenbach that night. The announcement only raised the men's hopes unnecessarily; higher headquarters postponed the drop, then canceled it altogether.[5]

Then, at about 1430 hours that afternoon, with two of his three infantry regiments—9,000 men—surrounded and the third fighting for its life, two-star general Jones made the remarkable decision to turn over the defense of the St. Vith sector to one-star general Clarke. Clarke, however, could do little to change the situation for the better; he was still waiting for his Shermans to arrive.

At last, on the evening of the 17th, the first tanks of the 7th Armored clattered down the cobblestone streets of St. Vith. The next day, Combat Command B (roughly the equivalent of an infantry regiment) linked up with the 9th Armored Division, moving up from south of town. The two armored units, along with an ad hoc assemblage of infantry, engineer, artillery, and support units, formed a defensive line east of St. Vith and prepared to hold back the attack or die trying.[6]

Sgt. Robert Kline,
photographed
May 1944.
(Courtesy
Robert Kline)

Robert Kline, the commo sergeant with Company M, 423rd Regiment, 106th Division, felt that the situation was going from bad to worse. "The second or third night of the Bulge," he said, "we heard that the Anti-Tank company had changed hands three times. They sent twelve tank destroyers up but they all got knocked out. In the afternoon, Captain Hardy told us to go get into the foxholes that were all around there. The corporal and I crawled into these slit trenches and a German patrol came through there—boy, they're good; you don't hardly see 'em. The corporal was about six or eight feet off to my right in the one o'clock position and one of those 'potato-masher' grenades landed about a foot from his head and went off. It made a hole in the ground but it never touched him.

"A little bit later, I heard somebody say, 'You gotta turn in your gas mask.' I said the hell with that; I'm not turning in my gas mask. I didn't know who they were—just a bunch of guys in American uniforms. I found out later that they were *Germans* in American uniforms." Worried that perhaps the enemy might use gas on his unit, Smith had one comforting thought: "If they'd have gassed us, they'd have gassed themselves, too. They kept telling me to turn in my gas mask, so I finally turned it in."

The sun made a brief appearance that afternoon, and so did Allied and enemy aircraft. Kline saw an aerial dogfight take place about five miles to the north of where he was being held. "It looked like there was a hundred planes going in every direction. The next morning, we were in kind of the same spot. There was a Focke-Wolfe 120 that came over us at treetop level with two P-47s right on his butt. They let him have it and the smoke came out and he hit a hill about five miles away and blew up."

On the second night of the battle, Kline was the only one in the whole battalion who had been able to string a telephone line from the observation post down to battalion headquarters. "Normally, you just roll your telephone lines out on the ground, but I told the corporal helping me, 'We're not putting our telephone lines on the ground; we're putting them up in the trees.' So we had to climb the trees."

Kline's smart thinking paid off, for it prevented the Germans from snipping or tapping into Company M's phone lines to battalion headquarters. "Captain Hardy kept on sending messages to Lieutenant Colonel Earl Klinck, the battalion commander, while I stood guard all night long outside the bunker with a little carbine and two clips—sixteen bullets to fight a major battle! I hadn't had any sleep for about two or three days. Captain Hardy told me that Colonel Klinck said, 'We're going to pull out and he wants you to go with him'—which is the dumbest thing we've ever done in our life. When you're dug in, you don't pull out. Where're you gonna go? If you're dug in, make 'em come get you.

"I went back to battalion headquarters and the colonel told me, 'You're gonna get the Bronze Star for having the telephone lines up off the ground.'" Kline was then ordered to pack up the battalion's big radio and be prepared to move out. "I thought—good deal; now I can carry that seventy-pound radio on top of all my other stuff. So we pulled out and walked all day."[7]

The Germans began shelling the 423rd Regiment heavily. Colonel Cavender's executive officer was seriously wounded, then Lieutenant Colonel William Craig, commanding the 423rd's 1st Battalion, was killed by machine-gun fire.[8]

Kline noted, "About ten o'clock at night, we stopped in the woods, and Colonel Klinck pulled a 'klinker.' He took out his flashlight to look at a map without covering up and all hell broke loose. We started getting bombarded with all these shells. My PFC hit the ground and I was right after him. I had the radio. A bomb went off to the right of me and it must have been concussion— or else I was so damned tired because I hadn't slept for three or four days—I didn't wake up until daylight the next day. There wasn't one person in sight; everybody went off and left me. Maybe they thought I was dead. There I was by myself, in the daylight.

"I was also supposed to be the reconnaissance sergeant, but I didn't have a compass or a map—not a damned thing. I had an idea which way everything was going, so I walked and walked, and pretty soon I met a first lieutenant from our company, Lieutenant Wigger, the executive officer. He was five-foot-two, a Missouri hillbilly boy, and had been a private and worked his way up. He was really a soldier's officer. He had his head all bandaged up and his eyes were staring. I should have told him to stay with me, 'cuz he was in shock and was going the wrong direction. He told me that Captain Hardy had been killed."

Kline was then wounded in the calf with a wooden bullet and taken prisoner.[9]

At dawn on the 18th, General Jones ordered the 106th's 422nd and 423rd Regiments to disengage with enemy units to their front and fall back to St. Vith. To accomplish this mission, the already confused regiments—their communications in tatters, many of their leaders dead, and the weather worsening—would need to make their way through the dense forest, descend a steep hillside, cross the Ihrenbach stream, and climb another slope; the wounded would be left behind with medics who volunteered to be taken prisoner.

A few hours later, the regiments received another, even more startling, order from Jones: Instead of merely withdrawing, they were to go onto the offensive and attack elements of the 18th Volksgrenadier Division that had captured

Schönberg! Even for seasoned troops, this would have been a tough assignment; for cold, frightened, inexperienced, and disorganized troops who had lost hundreds of comrades already, and who had never before been in combat, it was an impossibility. The attack never stood a chance. The men who chose to stand and fight were killed; the others were taken prisoner.[10]

The Germans had managed to encircle the 106th Division's regiments and were attacking them from the rear. Further, the tankers who had come to save the two cut-off regiments were themselves now fighting for their lives between St. Vith and the Schnee Eifel. They had to pull back; they were in no condition to rescue Cavender's and Descheneaux's men.

Having failed utterly in his first action as a combat commander, the disgraced General Jones departed his CP in St. Vith and joined the long procession of men and vehicles heading west, toward safety.*[11]

According to a history of the battle,

> All kinds of rumors were being spread; men who had fled from the front, apparently seeking to justify their action, gave an exaggerated and inaccurate picture of what was taking place. The situation most certainly was bad, and the impression that the officers of CCB [of the 7th Armored Division] got was that the 106th no longer existed as an effective division.
>
> As staff sections of CCB began to arrive [at the St. Josef's *Klosterschule* in the southeast part of St. Vith that served as the 106th's command post], carrying their equipment into the building, they met men from the 106th Division Headquarters leaving with their equipment.[12]

James V. Smith's unit—Company H, 423rd Regiment, 106th Division—was still lobbing shells from their cow lot when German mortar rounds began crashing all around the position. "There were two large oxen there that they used for plowing the fields," Smith said, "and with all the mortars landing all around us, the oxen began to run everywhere, their bellowing making a terrible noise."

A panicky mortar gunner in Smith's squad "dropped a shell in upside down [into the tube] and, of course, that's very dangerous. Two of our more

---

*On the night of 22 December, Jones, who had been charitably made assistant corps commander, suffered a heart attack and was evacuated. (Whiting, pp. 141–143)

The school at St. Josef Kloster in St. Vith, taken over by General Jones for the headquarters of the 106th Infantry Division. (Courtesy Heimatmuseum St. Vith)

experienced infantrymen took the tube away from the baseplate and another young man, Charlie Dopp—he had been an ex-paratrooper and was a very good soldier—he had to take off his gloves and catch the round when it came out of the end of the tube and put the firing pin back. It was so cold that if you touched metal, your hand would stick to it. We successfully got that round out and we started firing back at the Germans. We had a pretty good morning of it."

With the situation worsening, Smith's unit was soon ordered to redeploy once more. "They told us to move forward, so we moved to this field that was just covered with camouflage netting that the Germans had put up. All of a sudden, we got pinned down by German mortars again, and we were held in that field for quite a long time. I had taken cover in a deep tank track in the mud."

Smith was very hungry, having had nothing to eat since the morning of the 16th. He saw a burning American kitchen truck, the dead driver still behind the steering wheel. Smith still wore the multi-pocket ammunition apron, so he filled it with K-rations. "I didn't get to eat any of them," he said, "but I did get a large tin of tomato juice. I laid there in that tank track and drank that entire number ten can of tomato juice all by myself; it was delicious.

"After about two or three hours in that position, the enemy fire let up and we were told to move forward. We moved up to the edge of the woods and found our company commander; he had been run over by his jeep driver—his right arm and shoulder. He had his forty-five out and he was very nervous. He was waving it around with his left hand—we were glad to get away from him. He told us to take a certain road and go into the next town. He had already sent Sergeant Webb, who was the platoon sergeant of one of the machine-gun platoons." What the captain didn't know was that Sergeant Webb was already dead, killed in an ambush. "We went down that same road and ran into the same ambush that Sergeant Webb had run into. They opened up on our line of jeeps with machine-guns —I think there were three of us at that time, three jeeps and trailers—just raking the jeeps and trailers. A lot of people got hit. All of a sudden they started firing rifle grenades."

The lieutenant of Smith's section was eighteen-year-old Herman Phillipson from Dallas, Texas—an officer Smith called a "real hero." Smith said, "As Phillipson started to get out of the jeep on the passenger side, a rifle grenade landed under the dashboard and went off; he was hit several times in his back and he fell forward into the snow. We had a section leader, Staff Sergeant Oakley, and he had a lot of people around him who'd been hit, so he started trying to surrender. In fact, he did."

Smith attempted to work up the hill to where the machine-gun was firing, but Sergeant Oakley ordered everyone to cease firing and surrender. "I went back down to the road and Lieutenant Phillipson was laying in the snow with a huge puddle of blood around him. I thought: This man is dead. But he was still alive. The Germans told my good friend Johnny Beaver to pick him up. Johnny was a pretty good-size person, so he picked him up and carried him down the road about a half mile to an aid station. The next morning, Beaver took him to a railhead and put him on a box car. The Germans wouldn't let Beaver on the car with him; they said the car was full. Later that day, fighter planes came over and raked the train with machine-gun fire and Lieutenant Phillipson got hit by three fifty-caliber machine-gun bullets. They got him to a hospital and he stayed there a few days, and then he escaped and got back to the American lines. It was almost unbelievable."

A German escorts a group of American POWs away from the battle zone, 17 December 1944. (Courtesy U.S. Army Military History Institute)

When Smith was captured, a teenage German soldier befriended him. "He gave me two blankets and some mess gear. I took the blankets and cut them into strips and cut a place to put my head through and put it under my field jacket; it saved my life later. Some of it I passed on to my friends. Our field jackets at that time were not lined; they were a poor substitute for a good jacket."

Smith reported that the Germans then marched him and the survivors of his unit eastward, where they were loaded into boxcars and shipped out of the battle zone.[13]

On 19 December, Joe Mark's unit had managed to avoid capture for three days and was heading west. He was in a jeep in a long line of American vehicles trying to flee to St. Vith. It was pandemonium. "The Germans were laying in some fire on the road," Mark recalled, "so I jumped out and ran into the woods. The firing was up front so I decided to go the other way. I went the other way and saw hundreds of Americans giving up in a field. I ran back into the woods and I thought, 'Gee, that's the wrong thing to do.' So I broke up my rifle as ordered and finally left the woods because I felt they're going to get us for being yellow. I thought that the war was over for me and that the worst was over—but I was wrong. The worst was coming."[14]

On the same day that Mark surrendered, Jack Crawford, with the 106th's 590th Field Artillery Battalion, was also taken prisoner. "It was early in the morning and I had managed to get my breakfast. All of a sudden, we started getting shelled again, and everybody started taking cover in the wooded area there; we were down in a valley. Finally, the shelling stopped and the fellows started saying, 'Throw down your weapons; they've got us surrounded,' and the Germans started coming out of the woods. We didn't even see them coming; they just started coming out of the woods. Some of the guys didn't even have a chance to get dressed; they got captured without even their boots on. It really killed their feet. I managed to go back and get my coat. I grabbed another guy's coat at the same time, and we were led away."[15]

Peter House, another member of the 590th Field Artillery Battalion, was also hightailing it to the rear, towing a 105mm howitzer with a three-quarter-ton weapons carrier. He reported that, after daylight on the 19th, "We pulled off the road and up a hill to the left and went into firing position. Only had three rounds in the battery. Took tremendous fire from the Germans. . . . After the shelling lifted, Joe Krause came by and told me we were going to surrender. [But] we decided not to become prisoners [and] started running through the woods. We came to a clearing where a number of officers were standing around, including our battalion commander, Lt. Col. Vaden Lackie. With his permission, about twenty of us attempted to get back to our lines. We ran in a westerly direction for what seemed about an hour until we came over the crest of a hill where we came under direct fire from German anti-aircraft 20mm guns in position along a north-south road. Those of us that survived surrendered. I believe this was the road between Bleialf and Schönberg.

"After capture, we were assembled by the side of the road and Krause shared a K-ration with me. While waiting, the Germans prepared their AA weapons for transport. A German officer told one of the Americans to help. The American said it was against the Geneva Convention to help. The German said, '*Ja*, Geneva Convention,' and shot him.

"After they had several hundred Americans, we started walking to Germany. We had to carry our wounded the best we could until we arrived in a town

American prisoners are marched to the rear as German armor rolls toward St. Vith and beyond. (Courtesy U.S. Army Military History Institute)

where we were told to leave them. I believe this was Bleialf. The road east through the mountains was crowded with German men and equipment moving into battle. What surprised me were the number of horses used to move men and equipment. Their armored infantry were riding bicycles.

"The roads that day were packed with tanks, artillery, and other gear. . . . We were under the command of a German warrant officer who was riding in what looked like a Volkswagen. As soon as he could get by the equipment on the road, he would come speeding through our column blowing his horn. Then he would be stopped by more tanks and trucks.

"I was a very tired twenty-year-old who finally was too stubborn to move out of his way. This upset him, so he got out of his vehicle, pulled out his pistol, and aimed it at my head. I heard a click. The German in the turret of a tank alongside the road had cocked his machine-gun, aimed it at the warrant officer, and yelled something in German. The warrant officer put his pistol back in the holster and got back in his vehicle. This German tank commander who saved my life wore the silver skull [insignia] of the SS." House and his group were marched first to Prüm and then to Gerolstein.

On the march to Gerolstein, it became evident to House and his fellow Yanks that the Germans' transportation system was in bad shape. "Almost every truck was towing another truck due to fuel shortages." He also noticed numerous wood-burning vehicles operating on charcoal.

While waiting to be loaded into boxcars at Gerolstein, House was approached by a German colonel. "He asked me in American dialect how the 106th Infantry Division was doing. What a surprise, as there was no insignia on my uniform. I said it was doing OK."[16]

The official U.S. Army historian of the battle wrote,

> The number of officers and men taken prisoner on the capitulation of the two regiments and their attached troops cannot be accurately ascertained. At least seven thousand were lost here and the figure is probably closer to eight or nine thousand. The amount lost in arms and equipment, of course, was very substantial. The Schnee Eifel battle, therefore, represents the most serious reverse suffered by American arms during the operations of 1944–45 in the European theater.[17]

—♦—

At a 19 December meeting in Verdun with Bradley, head of Twelfth Army Group; Lieutenant General Jacob L. Devers, Sixth Army Group commander; Third Army chief Lieutenant General George S. Patton, Jr.; and Air Chief Marshal Sir Arthur W. Tedder, Ike decreed, "The present situation is to be regarded as one of opportunity for us and not of disaster. There will be only cheerful faces at this conference table."

Patton, as befitted his brash, aggressive nature, dared the Allies to "have the guts to let the sons of bitches go all the way to Paris. Then we'll really cut 'em off and chew 'em up."

Ike smiled and replied that the enemy would never be allowed to cross the Meuse.[18]

Ike's old friend and public relations aide Navy Captain Harry Butcher, noted in his diary, "Third Army officers welcomed this venture of the Germans from

Generals Omar N. Bradley, Dwight D. Eisenhower, and George S. Patton, Jr.
(Courtesy U.S. Army Military History Institute)

St. Vith in ruins after the battle.
(Courtesy U.S. Army Military History Institute)

the Siegfried Line, and relished the idea of Patton and his Third Army in the role of saviors of the situation."[19]

Butcher also said that it was decided "the whole front south of the Moselle would go strictly on the defensive and would give up all penetrations across the Saar River. Devers was to take over most of the present Third Army front, freeing Patton to move north with six divisions and temporarily to take over the VIII Corps. Patton was to organize a major counterattack with target date of December 23 or 24."[20]

For many of the GIs caught in the blast furnace of the violent German assault, Ike's grand strategy for stopping the German advance was already too late. Hundreds of Americans lay dead, their corpses frozen in the snow, their blood turned to ice. For thousands of others, they were on their way to months of incarceration in Nazi prisoner-of-war camps, far behind enemy lines.

5

BAD TIMES
AT BAD ORB

AMERICAN NEWSPAPER READERS on Monday, December 18, were tumbled out of their smug, complacent beds. NAZI OFFENSIVE PIERCES FIRST ARMY LINES; CHUTISTS AND LUFTWAFFE SUPPORT PUSH, screamed the *New York Times*'s front-page headline. The story began,

> A German offensive against the southern flank of the American First Army bit several miles into Belgium today [December 17] and crashed across the Luxembourg frontier in two areas.
>
> Several German armored infantry divisions are being employed in Field Marshal Karl [*sic*] von Rundstedt's counter-blow, which is described here as a major effort. Parachute troops dropped in small groups behind the First Army front and today the Luftwaffe flew 450 sorties, its largest effort since D-day, in support of the veteran divisions attacking on a seventy-mile front. . . .
>
> The size of the air effort and use of paratroops indicated Marshal von Rundstedt was throwing every reserve he had into the assault. It is

> not an offensive that should be underestimated, but as yet there is no cause for alarm, although it should be realized that the German attack has not yet reached its climax.

The article continued: "The Germans intensified their ground effort all along the First and Ninth Army fronts from Monschau to north of Trier today. They progressed several miles in the area of Honsfeld and Hepscheid, the former eight miles east of the important road junction of Malmédy in Belgium and seven miles west of the German frontier. Other thrusts were made into Luxembourg. . . ."

Another correspondent in the same edition wrote, "The German counter-offensive . . . looks like the real thing. It is too early yet to gauge its possible extent and scope and whether this is to be Germany's final all-out effort to stave off defeat. But the rate at which the Germans are throwing in divisions, including some crack ones, shows that it is a serious, major counteroffensive and serious exertions will be needed to meet it."[1]

If the United States was not exactly thrown into a state of hysteria by the news, Americans were at least very concerned. After all, the Allies had been on Germany's western doorstep for months, with victory seemingly within their grasp. And for months, the American public had been told repeatedly by cautiously upbeat war correspondents and official communiqués about crumbling German resistance; about the mass surrenders of German units; about the hundreds of liberated towns and cities; about the German war industries being bombed into rubble; about the low state of enemy morale. And yet, in spite of the relentless pounding the Germans had been receiving, Hitler's men proved they were still capable of mounting a serious challenge to the Allied drive from the west.

In response, many American civilians who had allowed themselves to feel a glimmer of optimism about the war's progress and had begun to enjoy life's little pleasures again, responded almost penitently to the news. Although the Green Bay Packers had just beaten the New York Giants, 14-7, to win the American professional football title, other leisure activities suddenly became taboo. In *Time*'s 1 January 1945 issue, the editors noted:

> Nazi tanks, crunching west through the mud and sleet of Luxembourg and Belgium last week, gave the U.S. two separate setbacks:

one on the Western Front, one on the home front. The size of the military defeat would be measured some day in American soldiers killed, wounded, captured. The shape of the home front defeat was already obvious. U.S. civilians would begin a not-so-happy New Year by paying penance for incorrigible optimism.

Suddenly, with the news of the breakthrough, many U.S. preoccupations—even Christmas—seemed like luxuries. It was no time to scramble into a peace-time job, or talk about manufacturing refrigerators. Last week's communiqués were a resounding vindication of those who had been denouncing over-optimism for three long years. . . .

Official Washington set about, through a series of small but significant actions, taking the bloom off the "victory-is-just-around-the-corner" rose that some had been nurturing. For example, James Byrnes, head of the Office of War Mobilization, fearful that too much frivolity was taking the nation's collective focus off the serious business of winning the war, ordered that all dog- and horse-racing tracks be shut down "until war conditions permit." He also excoriated the Selective Service for allowing supposedly 4-F (unfit for military service) professional athletes to avoid serving their country in its time of need. "They proved to thousands by their great physical feats upon the football or baseball field that they are as physically fit . . . as the 11,000,000 men in uniform," he said.

There was more. The OPA (Office of Price Administration and Civilian Supply) announced that certain foods that had recently become "point free" would be rationed again, as would shoe leather. The WPB (War Production Board) slashed the number of automobile tires that would be available for civilian purchase, and froze all consumer-goods production at current levels. And the January and February draft quotas were increased from 60,000 per month to 80,000. It did not look as if the war would be over anytime soon.[2]

———⁓⁓⁓———

Across Germany and the conquered territories lay scattered scores of bulging POW camps. Each was different, yet depressingly alike. All had barbed-wire enclosures, guard towers, floodlights, and living conditions that were usually less than ideal.

In Germany during World War II, there were at least fifty-six prisoner-of-war camps.* By the end of the war, it was estimated that nearly 100,000 American airmen and ground troops had been held in German custody.[3]

The German term for a prisoner-of-war camp is *Kriegsgefangenenlager* (*Krieg*=war, *gefangenen*=prisoners, *lager*=camp), while those interned were known as *Kriegsgefangener*. The average American POWs, finding the German word a tongue-twister, simply shortened it and called themselves "Kriegies." On the backs of their uniforms they had painted a large white letter "K" or "KG" to clearly identify them to the populace in the event of escape. (Unlike the "political prisoners" in concentration camps who were dressed in blue-and-white striped uniforms, POWs wore the military uniforms in which they were captured.)

Officers and enlisted men were normally placed in different camps, the camps for officers being referred to as *Offizierslager*, or *Oflag*, while the enlisted men's camps were called *Stammlager*, or, more commonly, by the abbreviation *Stalag*. Air force personnel were confined to camps that had the German word for "air" attached (e.g., Stalag Luft III).

Camps varied widely as to their accommodations. Some even resembled well-appointed country clubs. Believing that prisoners who were kept occupied by a variety of activities would be less likely to cause trouble and less likely to attempt escape, some camp administrators were happy to keep their inmates busy. For example, a large number of camps had sports facilities and equipment to permit the kriegies to expend their energy playing softball, football, basketball, soccer, volleyball, ice hockey, and other sports. Card games were immensely popular, with cigarettes and the contents of Red Cross parcels being used as the stakes. Camps also permitted prisoners to engage in boxing, weight lifting, working out on gymnastic equipment, ice skating, and swimming. Stalag Luft III, near Sagan, even had a six-hole golf course!

Many camps had their own "underground" prisoner-published newspapers, which often contained surprisingly accurate news from the home front and reports on the war's progress. The news came from a variety of sources: illegal, clandestine radio sets tuned to the British Broadcasting Corporation; newly arrived prisoners; even announcements made over the camps' loudspeakers.

---

*There were forty-two general camps for lower-ranking army personnel; seven camps for officers; six camps exclusively for enlisted airmen; and one camp for naval personnel and merchant mariners. (Foy, pp. 62–63)

Libraries offered popular diversions; the library at Stalag II-B, near Hammerstein, for example, had 5,000 volumes, while the one at III-B, near Fürstenburg-an-der-Oder, had 6,000 books as early as September 1943. Some enterprising inmates started "kriegie colleges," in which interned teachers and professors could impart their wisdom through the offering of a variety of courses.

The opportunity to pursue hobbies was also available at many camps. Some prisoners carved model airplanes out of scraps of wood while others engaged in soap sculpture; Stalag III-B had a complete woodworking shop, while Oflag 64, in Poland, had its own cobbler shop and watch-repair facility. Some inmates planted vegetable gardens to supplement their camp rations, and flower gardens added a touch of color to the drab surroundings.

Some of the camps boasted professional-quality bands and symphonic orchestras, glee clubs, and full-blown musicals and theatrical productions (complete with props and costumes). Some camps had film projectors and regularly treated the inmates to German and American movies, or occasionally took prisoners to civilian cinemas in nearby towns. There were often well-stocked camp stores and houses of worship, complete with Bibles and hymnals provided by the Red Cross.

Sanitation facilities were generally adequate, with most camps providing drinking water, hot showers, and delousing equipment. Medical and dental facilities, with sufficient amounts of medicines and wound dressings, were available at many camps.

For many Allied prisoners (the French and Russian prisoners were never well treated by the Germans, and the Japanese were notoriously brutal to those in their custody), there were worse things in life than to wait out the war in the safety and relative comfort of a POW camp.[4]

For many of the Americans taken prisoner during the Battle of the Bulge, however, no such niceties awaited them.

Although Germany had signed the Geneva Convention on 27 July 1929, four years before Hitler's Nazi regime came to power, it was still legally bound to abide by the provisions. But like so many other treaties, conventions, and other agreements he broke, Hitler felt free to observe or ignore the Geneva Convention as it suited him.

The Convention outlined clearly the manner in which the camps were to be maintained and the prisoners treated. For example, prisoners were supposed to receive the same type and quantity of food as their captors received. Prisoners were also supposed to be provided with adequate clothing, footwear, underwear, and bedding. Prisoners were to have access to medical and dental care, and were to be allowed to send and receive mail and receive packages containing items such as food, clothing, books, tobacco, and other personal items.

The camps themselves were to be maintained in a clean and orderly manner, with proper dining, exercise, washing, and sanitary facilities. Prisoners who performed work outside the camps (such as farm labor) were supposed to be paid. While prisoners could be disciplined for committing infractions of camp rules, they were not to be beaten, tortured, starved, or forced to work in unusually harsh or dangerous conditions.

The loophole, of course, was that if Hitler and his Nazi minions wanted to make life miserable for the enemy prisoners—and they most assuredly did—there was no agency on earth that could enforce the regulations. As a result, as will be seen shortly, the administrators at Bad Orb/Stalag IX-B and at Berga-an-der-Elster, and at many other camps, totally disregarded these provisions of the Geneva Convention.

The conditions from one camp to another varied widely, depending on the mood of the *kommandant* and the proclivities of the guards, the availability of medical care, and the abundance or shortage of decent food and fresh drinking water. Some—probably the minority—of the camp administrators did their best to adhere to the provisions of the international law concerning the treatment of POWs and resisted attempts by the sinister Gestapo (Geheimstaatspolizei, the Secret State Police) or SS (Schutzstaffel, or Elite Guard) to kill, torture, or otherwise mistreat their captives. They perhaps sensed that if the word leaked out that the POWs were being mistreated, a similar fate might befall the Germans who were being held in Allied POW camps.[5]

Many of the POW camps were inspected on a periodic basis by members of the International Red Cross. In actuality, with Hitler the final judge as to how the prisoners would be treated, many of the camps fell far short of the intended mark. It was not uncommon during these inspections for the Germans to engage in "eye-wash" (temporarily issuing blankets, warm clothing, sports equipment, extra rations, etc.) to fool the inspectors. (The 1953 Hollywood film *Stalag 17*, although fictional, nevertheless gives a fairly realistic portrayal of camp life and the efforts that were made to disguise the harshness of the conditions during visits by the Red Cross inspectors. Given the Nazis' track record of human-rights abuses, it is surprising that conditions weren't worse than they were.)

The railroad station at Prüm. (Author photo 2004)

In the end, while they may have been spared the dangers and rigors of combat, many Allied prisoners of war found themselves subjected to physical and mental cruelties at the hands of their captors that none of them could have possibly imagined.

———✕✕✕———

When soldiers are captured in battle, it is vital that their captors remove them quickly from the battlefield, as much to protect them from a counterattack as to make any escape back to friendly lines as difficult as possible. Prisoners also can be a potential gold mine of intelligence to their captors, and removing them to a secure area where skilled interrogators can go to work on them is imperative.

The unexpectedly large number of prisoners taken during the Battle of the Bulge must have presented the Germans with a dilemma: On one hand, the eight thousand or so captives represented a huge gash in the American lines through which Hitler's troops were now pouring; on the other hand, a way to house and feed the prisoners—while Germany itself was facing major shortages—would need to be found.

Joe Mark and his group were marched east, away from the Schnee Eifel. "They marched us back to a town called Prüm," he reported, "where a German took my galoshes, and then they searched me. I had a little tin of aspirins, Bayer aspirin, and this German who was searching me thought I had taken them off of a German because Bayer is a German product and he was going to shoot me, but a sergeant told him that Bayer was commonly distributed, so I wasn't shot."[6]

According to William Shapiro, his group of 28th Infantry Division soldiers marched for three or four days until they came to the railroad station at Gerolstein. "There were many, many American prisoners and we were congregated in large groups. This was the first time that we were guarded by soldiers holding German Shepherd dogs on leashes."[7]

Clifford Savage, of the 28th Division, recalled, "They marched us to a railroad station. As far as mistreating us, they didn't. The only thing is, we didn't have no food or water or heat or anything. We were just out there in the elements."[8]

P. Robert Fowler, another member of the 28th, captured on 18 December, recalled that his captors "marched us for several hours without water and food to a town called Gerolstein, where we were crowded into German trains."[9]

The GIs were divided into groups of ten, given small scraps of food, and packed into the boxcars that were standing in the marshaling yard. The doors to the boxcars were rolled shut, latched, and the shrill whistle of the steam locomotive pierced the icy air. The locomotive chugged slowly away from the station, towing behind it hundreds of scared and nervous Americans who had no idea where they were going or what lay ahead. Fowler noted that the train "traveled very slowly eastward and stopped in every big town or factory district where they thought our planes might hit."

On 23 December, the train pulled into the town of Dreis; within a half hour, the unnerving air-raid sirens began to wail and soon the bombing began. "Those bombs sounded like they were three times larger than they were," wrote Fowler. "For about two hours, the Allies steadily bombed the railroad yard. The flashes had the place lit up brighter than daylight." He reported that his train remained there for three or four days before the prisoners were finally given water; four men shared one Red Cross package that contained food.*

---

*The standard Red Cross package contained a can each of corned beef, pork luncheon meat, powdered milk, margarine, salmon, orange concentrate, coffee, and liver paste, a package of cheese, two chocolate bars, a box of sugar cubes, a box of raisins, a package of biscuits, several bars of soap, and four packs of cigarettes.

Gerolstein railroad station. (Author photo 2004)

Not all of the prisoners were taken to the same place. Savage was sent far from the battlefield to the camp at Moosburg (Stalag VII-A, north of Munich);[10] others, however, soon found themselves herded into boxcars like hogs headed for the slaughterhouse and rolling eastward toward Stalag IX-B at Bad Orb, some thirty miles east of Frankfurt.

After being taken prisoner late on the afternoon of 19 December in Bleialf, Private First Class Charles D. McMullen, Anti-Tank Company, 422nd Regiment, 106th Division, recalled, "I, along with several thousand others, were captured near St. Vith. . . . We slept in a churchyard that night, and the next day we were walked to Gerolstein in zero weather and eight or ten inches of snow, during which time I had my feet initially frozen." From Gerolstein, McMullen would be taken to Stalag VII-A, the first of four POW camps in which he would be interned.[11]

Boxcar typical of the "40 and 8" type that transported POWs to Bad Orb.
Photographed in Bad Nauheim. (Author photo 2004)

Richard Lockhart, from Fort Wayne, Indiana, and a member of the 423rd Regiment's Anti-Tank Company, 106th Division, remembered, "They marched us out for about two days until we got to the town of Gerolstein, Germany. We were held there for a day or two, waiting for the trains to come in. I don't remember the precise day we were loaded into boxcars—about sixty-five or seventy men to a boxcar. Everybody could not sit down at the same time."[12]

To Joe Mark, the boxcars "were made with square wheels that were imported from Italy. It wasn't a comfortable ride. When we first got captured, they put sixty men in a boxcar and, if you fell asleep, three or four guys piled up on top of you. The toilet was in one corner of the boxcar. Not even a bucket; just the floor."[13]

William Shapiro remembered that the latrine facilities in his boxcar were "horrendous and appalling: two simple boxes placed somewhere in the middle of the car. It added to the chaos among the men when someone had to defecate. Urination was generally done against the walls or through the cracks in the floorboards. Some men had no control and wet their pants. The air was putrid and fecal-smelling and made worse by being confined in a very tight space. The

P. Robort Fowler
in 1943.
(Courtesy
Helen Fowler)

stench was unbelievable. . . . It led to loud arguments and fighting between the men as to when, where, and how to urinate or defecate."[14]

The foul smell in the cars quickly became the least of the POWs' concerns. The Allies, who had complete mastery of the air, were keen on bombing German railroad lines and rolling stock. At a thousand feet or so, and at 400 miles per hour, it was, of course, impossible for the pilot of a twin-boom P-38 "Lightning" or P-47 "Thunderbolt" or P-51 "Mustang" to tell if the freight train down below was full of food, ammunition, German troops, or American or British prisoners. As a result, many POWs died tragically at the unknowing hands of their countrymen.

Clifford
Savage,
1943.
(Courtesy
Clifford
Savage)

Richard Lockhart, 1943. (Courtesy Richard Lockhart)

"There had been a nasty bombing of the train in transit," Richard Lockhart said, "and while some boxcars were hit, ours was not. We heard the bombs coming down; you're never sure if they're going to impact you. Nobody said anything; you just hoped for the best."[15]

Jack Crawford, 590th Field Artillery Battalion, 106th Division, also had stark memories of being hit while trapped in a boxcar: "One night when we were in the freight yards, we got bombed. Our sergeant managed to get out the little

Bad Orb, photographed January 2004. (Author photo)

window in the boxcar. I don't know how he ever did it, but he climbed up there and managed to get out and unlocked the door from the outside. I can remember going out in a field. There was like a manhole, and I climbed into that until the air raid was over. Then we got back into the boxcar."[16]

James V. Smith recalled that, on Christmas Eve, "the British bombers came over that night and started dropping 500-pound bombs on us. The rumor was, one of the bombs hit one of our boxcars on the end of the train and killed about thirty-five Americans; I've never had that confirmed. During the day, we could see all these bomb craters all around the train and rail yard."[17]

An official report on the air raid had other details: "Eight men seeking to escape jumped into a field and were killed by an exploding land mine. The German sergeant in charge, enraged that anyone had attempted escape, began shooting wildly. Although he knew that every car was densely packed with PWs, he fired a round through the door of a car, killing an American soldier."[18]

Once the immediate danger passed, the train resumed its eastward journey, but never at a high speed; there was no telling when a bridge or a section of rail, destroyed by a bomb, or a work crew from the Reichsbahn (the German State Railroad), might be encountered. Numerous times the train was rerouted to an undamaged line, but this was old hat for the Germans. As one historian noted, "Laborers were so organized for quick repairs at the marshaling yards that seldom, even after a heavy air attack, did bomb damage interfere with operations for longer than forty-eight hours."[19] Despite the years of being bombed by the Allies, the Reichsbahn system remained a marvel of wartime efficiency—much to the dismay of prisoners on their way to POW, concentration, or death camps.

Peter House commented, "On the 24th, an elderly German civilian brought two buckets of water to each boxcar (for our 64 men). Don't know if this was a nice German or part of the procedure, but it was needed. After dark, several candles were lit and we sang Christmas songs and gave prayers; after all, it was Christmas Eve. Then we settled down for another night of bombing."[20]

The railroad station at Bad Orb. (Author photo 2004)

Aerial view of Stalag IX-B, the POW camp at Bad Orb.
(Courtesy National Archives)

The town of Bad Orb lies about thirty miles east-northeast of Frankfurt-am-Main, at the end of a long railroad spur. On 26 December 1944, the train packed with prisoners stopped on the main line, then reversed and was switched onto a single line of track several miles long, and the train backed into Bad Orb. It was, quite literally, the end of the line.

The scared, starving, thirst-crazed, and half-frozen GIs piled out of the cars and formed up in the railyard of the train station to be counted under the watchful eyes of snarling Alsatian hounds and German guards with rifles pointed menacingly at them. Those who may have glanced up at the signboard on the station wall saw the name of the town: BAD ORB. In German, the word *bad* means "bath." Used in conjunction with a town's name, it means "spa." To the GIs, it meant "bad omen."

Before the war, the town of Bad Orb was an attractive health resort, as it is today, where visitors came to enjoy the curative powers of mineral waters and thermal pools. Tucked into a scenic valley in the Spessart Mountains, Bad Orb is a small, luxurious resort for well-heeled Europeans. During the war, however, Bad Orb meant anything but a pleasant stay at a posh resort; it was the home of

Stalag IX-B, a brutal prisoner-of-war camp that at least one historian called, "the foulest [POW] camp in Germany."[21]

Peter House recalled that once the train arrived at Bad Orb, the POWs were ordered out of the boxcars and lined up in groups of one hundred. "The train left. We stood there in the bitter cold mountain air. I didn't have my driver's mackinaw, gloves, scarf, or wool cap. It was interesting to see a large 'Coca Cola' sign on a building."[22]

After counting the number of prisoners, the Germans led the Americans through the eastern part of town, where Christmas decorations still hung. Technical Sergeant Marion K. Blackburn, a member of Company F, 422nd Regiment, 106th Division, recalled that he and the other prisoners were marched "through crowds of German civilians and soldiers who were crowded on either side of the streets watching us pass. We were halted once so that moving pictures could be taken, and were halted a second time in the center of town where German civilians and soldiers were given an opportunity to look us over. We were hissed and booed. Children threw snowballs at us."[23]

The men were then marched up a tough, eight-percent grade for three miles through four inches of snow to the camp. Once the exhausted soldiers reached Stalag IX-B, the sight was enough to cause the spirits of many to sink. Located atop a heavily forested mountain, the trees surrounding the camp acted like a shield to isolate the prisoners from the outside world and screen the view of the events that happened in the camp from any passersby.

One of the POWs described the camp:

> "I knew it was IX-B, for a sign on the ten-foot-high barbed wire gate said so. The gate opened and we marched through the German area to the next gate, and the next, three in all. Sapped of all energy, we halted in front of a water reservoir whose earthen top edges were 8–10 feet above our heads. A clock tower stood left of the black cinder, muddy road. Six-by-six feet at the base, it rose twenty feet. Four clock faces told the time. . . . The double barbed wire fence was ten or twelve feet high. The two parallel fences were eight feet apart and the space was filled with coils of military barbed wire. Just inside the inner fence on our side was a single strand of barbed wire stretched tight on posts, and in from the main inner fence about twenty inches. The rule was: don't touch or step over the little wire or they would shoot you."[24]

Following the liberation of Stalag IX-B, American POWs pose for the photographer near the clock tower, showing how they carried the large container full of "universal political prisoner soup." (Courtesy National Archives)

Peter House noted, "There was a German Army hospital on the road down to Bad Orb. Its main function was to heal men who had lost a limb. This was the source of our tower guards. It was something to see a man with one leg or one arm climbing the tower ladder with his rifle."[25]

From 1920 to 1939, the hilltop site was home to the Kinderdorf Wegescheide, a nature camp for children; following Germany's invasion of Poland in September 1939, it became a prisoner-of-war camp.[26]

Richard Lockhart, Anti-Tank Company, 423rd Regiment, 106th Division, remembered that the transport he was in arrived at Bad Orb on the day after Christmas, 1944. "With all the air raids en route, it took us about four days to get there. We were the first Americans there, I believe; the Russians, French, and Serbians were already there. The compounds were kept separate from each other, so I have no way of knowing how many in total were there. Not all the Americans came in at the same time. All together, there were probably six to seven thousand prisoners—all privates and PFCs. Except for an American

Protestant chaplain and a Catholic chaplain and a dentist, all the other officers and non-commissioned officers had been sent to different camps."[27]*

Jack Crawford, a member of the 106th's 590th Field Artillery Battalion, recalled that the group hadn't eaten for days. "Once we got to the camp, they had all these old pots lying around on the ground. We used them to get some grass soup that night that was pretty terrible."[28]

P. Robert Fowler, 28th Division, recalled receiving an initial meal consisting of greens, carrots, and sugar beets—and that nearly everyone in his group got sick from it. He also remembered that the POWs received a little potato soup the first week, then only sugar beets and turnip tops for the rest of his four months in captivity.[29]

James V. Smith, Company H, 423rd Regiment, 106th Division, was repulsed by the poor quality of the food. "When we got to Bad Orb, the kitchen was being run by the Russians. They served us a meal of carrots and all kinds of mixed vegetables—beets and carrots and cabbage. I thought: 'That's the worst meal I've ever had.' Later on, I found out that it was the *best* meal I was ever offered there!"[30]

Peter House described the soup as "a great intestinal cleanser."[31]

For the new arrivals, the in-processing procedures began the next day, 27 December. Prisoners lined up before tables at which sat other GIs who wrote down each POW's name, rank, and serial number, plus hometown address so their families could be notified that their son or husband was in custody. Each man was then assigned to a barracks building in IX-B.

Private First Class Owen R. Chafee, of Battery C, 590th Field Artillery Battalion, 106th Division, stated that during the in-processing, "Some men who were ahead of me refused to fill out anything but their name, rank, and serial number. The German officer got mad and called two guards over. The guards hit the Americans with their rifle butts and made them stand outside for three or four hours in the snow. I saw this happen to twenty or twenty-five men." Many of those so treated came down with severe frostbite.[32]

Peter House was one of several soldiers moved to a building to be interrogated shortly after arrival. "There was a man in an American uniform that told me my colonel had told them everything. It didn't sound right. How did he know who my colonel was? A German corporal interrogated me. He was a mean

---

*According to one report, Stalag IX-B at its height held 3,200 Americans (although other reports had the number of Americans at more than 4,000) and 3,300 from other countries. (Foy, p. 148)

SOB. He was very upset when all I gave him was my name, rank, and serial number. He asked my religion. I refused. He asked how would they know what type of service to provide if I died. This seemed reasonable at the time, so I said 'Protestant.' When I refused any further information, he put me outside in the cold in a barbed-wire compound with several others. Don't think we would have lasted long under these conditions. By mistake, someone opened another door and said to leave. We were moved to the top of the camp with the other Americans."[33]

James V. Smith was assigned to Barracks 44. "Barracks 44 was split in two sections. In the middle of the barracks, they had a place for washing clothes; no bathroom or toilet facilities. In each end of the barracks, they had about 500 people. Our bodies basically provided the heat we had during that very cold winter. We would only get two sticks of firewood at night. Each section there had a stove covered with tile, real beautiful things, and it did hold a lot of heat. But, basically, if we had not had all those people, we'd probably have frozen to death. We just had like a sack mattress stuffed with straw; it was very uncomfortable in the beginning, but we soon got used to it. Everybody slept in all their clothes. Any possessions they had, they kept on their body; there was too much danger from somebody stealing it and selling it for potatoes, or something.

"We didn't have any toilet facilities. At the end of the building they had a hole of about six inches in the concrete floor. All these men, with diarrhea and everything else, it was a terrible, terrible situation."[34]

The barracks themselves were in shabby condition, unfit for human habitation. Many of the windows were broken, the roofs leaked, and the electric lights, in those buildings that had electricity, were dim. Mitchell Bard, in *Forgotten Victims: The Abandonment of Americans in Hitler's Camps,* noted that anywhere from 290 to 500 men were confined to each barracks building at Stalag IX-B. One pestilential latrine hole, which emptied into a fly-blown cesspool behind each building, sufficed for an entire barracks; straw was used for toilet paper. Not all the buildings had the appropriate number of bunks; many men were forced to sleep on the cold concrete floors. Justifiably, Bard called Stalag IX-B "the worst of all the POW camps."[35]

There was very little to occupy the POWs' time at Stalag IX-B except for occasional work details, such as cutting firewood in the surrounding forests, digging graves, cleaning out the cesspools, or projects to improve the security perimeter or their captors' living quarters. Because they did not receive the letters and parcels to which the Geneva Convention said they were entitled and were permitted to write only one postcard during the entire time they were incarcerated, the prisoners had little to do but think about food, families, and freedom. Dreaming up escape plans was a full-time activity. About the only entertainment was the frequent overflights by American B-17 and B-24 bombers on their way to strike nearby targets—that, and killing body lice.

Years of use as a concentration camp and then a prisoner-of-war camp had left the buildings crawling with body lice; the barracks, bedding, and blankets were infested with the minuscule, transparent pests the soldiers called "cooties." Thousands of the biting, blood-sucking parasites made nests in the prisoners' hair, armpits, and pubic regions—hatching thousands more nits and causing near-intolerable pain, itching, and discomfort. So intensely did the prisoners scratch themselves that they opened wounds which quickly became infected in the unclean surroundings. The lice brought sheer and constant misery.

One POW recalled that, when the POWs weren't on work details, "We just sat around all day, picking lice from our armpits and crushing them between our fingernails. It was really very boring, except when the American bombers went over, and that cheered us up."[36]

For all forms of life, the search for food is a never-ending endeavor—mammals, birds, insects, fish, and reptiles are on a constant quest for nourishment. When humans do not get enough to eat, they can also become like the lower animals. As their hunger increased, American GIs turned on their fellow countrymen at Stalag IX-B. Joseph Mark recalled, "A guy from my own company called Blackie came up to me one day and asked if he could borrow some bread. I said, 'I don't lend bread.' He threatened me; he said, 'Then I'm going to tell them that you're a Jew.'"

Noting that the human body needs a minimum of 1,700 calories a day just to survive, Mark said, "The Germans had this technique that they used at concentration camps of feeding you a diet of 1,000 or 1,100 calories a day, and if you worked, you died. You didn't die of starvation; you died of some illness, diphtheria, bad dysentery, or something else."[37]

Not surprisingly, food quickly became a burning obsession among the POWs. They thought about food, dreamt about food, and talked about food constantly.

According to Private First Class Dan J. Ferrand, of Company C, 422nd Regiment, 106th Division, even the bread was capable of making the POWs sick: "When everyone got through handling it, after it came out of their dirtiest wagon, it was not fit to eat."[38]

James V. Smith said that, shortly after he arrived in camp, American cooks re-placed the Russian cooks, but with no appreciable change in either the quality or quantity of food. "In the early morning hours, they'd bring in large contain-ers of ersatz tea. At least it was hot and had a slight sweet taste to it. We had this thin soup every day; you were lucky if you found a piece of potato in it."

Every now and then, Allied fighter planes would come over and strafe farm-ers in their fields. "If they killed a horse," Smith said, "we'd have horse meat to flavor the soup that night. But, with that many people, it didn't go very far. Then, at night, we'd get a small loaf of black bread that had to be divided among eight prisoners. That went on for a long time."[39]

Jack Crawford found a way to get a little more to eat. "We were in barracks that were right across from the kitchen. I think the German officers might have stayed there, or close by. Sometimes we'd have work details. For a period of time, I worked on cleaning the German officers' barracks. We were able to get some extra food for that."[40]

Few men received extra rations, however. The grass soup and turnip greens to which the Americans were treated upon their arrival was to be their steady diet. With more prisoners arriving almost daily, the food shortage was bad and getting worse. The overcrowded conditions meant that no one got enough to eat—just enough to keep one barely alive—and the quality of the food was abominable and almost totally lacking in any nutritional value. The bread, for example, was often mixed with sawdust.* Each man rapidly began to lose body weight. A thousand men were forced to eat with their filthy, bacteria-laden hands out of their helmets or tin cans; there were not enough eating utensils, bowls, or plates to go around. The weak tea and ersatz coffee, the only warm wa-ter in camp, was used by many men for shaving purposes.[41]

After a few weeks, the inmates received some small bars of soap and a few ra-zors. James V. Smith recalled, "They also gave one of the fellows in my company some barber shears, so he would cut our hair and charge us two cigarettes—the cigarettes were worth at least ten dollars apiece."[42]

The typical day for the prisoners began at dawn, when they all were required to stand at attention in ranks in the *appellplatz*, or "roll-call square," outside

---

*Often called *Schwartzbrot*, or "black bread," the official 1941 German Food-Providing Min-istry recipe calls for: "50% bruised rye grain, 20% sliced sugar beets, 20% 'tree flour' (saw-dust), and 10% minced leaves and straw." It wasn't just POWs and concentration camp inmates who were served this unappetizing loaf; the general German civilian population also subsisted on it. (*Ex-POW Bulletin,* May 1997)

High-angle view of Stalag IX-B, taken from the clock tower. Note the grave markers leaning against the building at right. (Courtesy www.LoneSentry.com)

their barracks—sometimes for hours on end in the freezing cold—for the tedious, anxiety-producing, and dehumanizing process known as *appell*.

Smith recounted the daily routine that never seemed to vary: "Every morning we'd go out—we didn't actually have a roll call; it was just a head count. They'd start out, *Eins, zwei, drei, vier,* and so on, on up to the number they were supposed to have. If somebody was still in the barracks, the Germans got real upset if the right number didn't come up. We had to do that every morning, no matter how cold it was, or how much it was snowing."[43]

During this twice-a-day routine, camp personnel spent hours counting and recounting the prisoners and often spewing vitriol into their captives' faces; screaming at them for minor infractions; beating them with sticks, whips, clubs, and rifles; threatening them with vicious dogs; humiliating them in any way possible.

In his autobiography, Rudolph Höss, commandant of the infamous Nazi death camp at Auschwitz, noted:

> Every prisoner who lives a sensitive inner life suffers far more from
> unjustified, malicious, and deliberate acts of spite, in a word, from
> acts of mental cruelty, than ever he does from the physical equiva-
> lent. Such acts produce a far more ignominious and oppressive effect
> than does corporal punishment. . . . I grew accustomed to the crude
> language of the junior guards, whose delight in the power they
> wielded increased in proportion to the lowness of their mentality.[44]

The Geneva Convention might as well have been written on toilet paper
for all the force it carried at Stalag IX-B. Besides the food shortage, there was
no change of clothing; the soldiers continued to wear the same uniforms in
which they had been captured. No letters or parcels from home arrived; no
one knew if their families had even been informed of their capture. While
there were an American doctor, dentist, and a number of medics in the camp,
there were little, if any, medical supplies. Sanitation conditions were ap-
pallingly primitive, more reminiscent of the Black Hole of Calcutta than a
civilized nation like Germany. There was also no way to keep clean. At Stalag
IX-B, noted the author David Foy, "The only water supply for a building
housing 160 men was one tap, which afforded only a feeble drip." Dysentery
and its attendant diarrhea were rampant.[45]

One prisoner, Sam Higgins, noted his unsuccessful efforts at keeping clean:
"Monday, I delicately struggle outside on shaky knees to wash my smelly, crappy
clothes in the snow. I am weak from gorging on the Red Cross food last Saturday and Sunday, then vomiting and crapping, sometimes simultaneously. My
stomach aches and my butt is so raw I try to keep the cheeks apart, but the only
way is not to walk. I can't eat anything. I just lie around in pain, feeling sorry for
myself. Time drags on. Finally, darkness and fretful sleep."[46]

Whether keeping the prisoners hungry and filthy was a carefully calculated
part of the Nazis' psychological scheme to degrade and dehumanize the inmates
or came about by accident is not clear. Either way, it was an effective tool to
lower the inmates' resistance to authority. By starving a person and preventing
him from cleaning himself, the captor strips away the prisoner's humanity, dig-
nity, and moral worth, and replaces these qualities with a sense of perpetual
degradation. John P. Sabini and Maury Silver, two social scientists who have
studied the long-term psychological effects of concentration-camp incarceration, pointed out:

The officers and guards of Stalag IX-B. This photo, which was stolen by an inmate from a desk drawer in the camp, is published for the first time. (Courtesy National Archives)

Starvation, along with reducing the economic burden of the slaves to the slave masters, destroys the body's capacity to produce the range of expressions we take as a sign of affective life. Constant hunger, like constant pain, removes the individual from the social world, fixates attention on the internal state, and hence dehumanizes.

Further, the extremes of hunger drive the individual to resort to scavenging through garbage, turning informant, fighting with fellow inmates for a scrap of food (and in the process impeding the development of associations among prisoners necessary to organized resistance). Starvation and constant hunger are extremely effective tools of degradation. . . .

Perhaps the most potent technique of degradation is to make the individual filthy, to make him stink. . . . In modern Western culture the requirement that one remain clean (both of contamination by mud, dirt, and other environmental sources of pollution and, perhaps more importantly, of one's own excrement) is a first and central demand on every child who would be a member of the society. But to do this requires not only a psychological and biological capacity but also social circumstances that make it possible. Baths, showers, and toilets are resources without which it is impossible to maintain the appearance of being a self-conscious, worthy member of the social order.[47]

Not only was such treatment an effective tool for destroying the inmates' capacity to revolt against their captors, but, just as important, it also helped those who were detailed to guard them to feel that the prisoners were less than human ("filthy swine"), thus making it psychologically easier for the guards, whose ability to feel guilt, pity, and compassion was significantly reduced, to brutalize the inmates.[48]

To most of the POWs at Stalag IX-B, the commandant was a shadowy, unknown figure whose name few, if any, of them knew. Some described his rank variously as lieutenant, captain, colonel, or warrant officer; Private First Class Bernard L. Squires, of Company M, 422nd Regiment, 106th Division, described the officer: "He was about six feet, one inch tall, about 200 pounds—a good-sized man. He was about thirty to thirty-five years of age and had a small, thin mustache, dark hair, and a ruddy complexion. He was continually smoking cigarettes. Always had his chest up, had a fancy walk to him, and was a neat-looking soldier."[49]

According to a document in the National Archives, the commandant was an *Oberst* (colonel) named Sieber. Second in command was *Oberst-leutnant* Wodarg; *Hauptmann* (captain) Horn was the camp officer.[50]

While most of the enlisted men assumed that their officers had been separated from them, a number of American officers were evidently incarcerated at Stalag IX-B. Second Lieutenant Edward R. Cassidy of the 110th Intelligence and Reconnaissance Platoon, 28th Division, stated that he was one of 600 American officers in the camp.[51]

Another officer, Lieutenant Colonel Joseph C. Matthews of the 106th Division, recalled that a German officer by the name of Krieger or Kruger "frequented the camp for the purpose of investigating and disseminating propaganda. He spoke very fluent English and I believe that he was at one time employed as a sales manager by the Goodyear or Goodrich Tire Company in Atlanta, Georgia. One of our officers, Lieutenant Colonel Joseph Puett of Macon, Georgia, knew this German officer and identified him."[52]

On 10 January, most of the officers were removed from Stalag IX-B and taken to Stalag XIII-C at Hammelburg; on 25 January, the non-commissioned officers were sent to Stalag IX-A. Only privates and PFCs were left at Bad Orb.[53]

Being locked up behind barbed wire and forced to live in barbaric conditions deep inside enemy territory was bad enough, but no one expected the cruel treatment that was often meted out by sadistic guards.

As part of their basic training, American soldiers had been familiarized with the provisions of the Geneva Convention on the Treatment of Prisoners of War, Article Two of which specifically banned acts of violence against prisoners. One freezing day, Richard Lockhart discovered that the protections supposedly guaranteed by the Convention were nonexistent. Near the end of January, he was on a wood-cutting detail of ten to fifteen prisoners who had been promised there would be extra food for them at the end of the day. "We had been on a near-starvation diet since we had been captured in the middle of December. We had only the clothes on our backs, and many of us had no gloves and had frostbitten feet.

"Out in the deep woods, we were set to work sawing wood for the camp. All of a sudden, one of the guards picks up a heavy piece of wood and begins hitting me several times but, fortunately, not on the head. He then, still saying nothing, began striking two other prisoners."[54] The two other men, Donald Leedom and Arthur Helmbreck, were beaten by their guards with rifle butts and kicked when they fell to the ground when they were unable to carry the heavy load of firewood.[55]

"At this time," said Lockhart, "I thought the guard had gone berserk and was determined to kill us. However, he apparently didn't think we were working fast enough and the beating we took did result in some escalation of sawing. Obviously, if he had hit me in the head with the force he used, I would still be back in those woods and forever 'missing in action.' We did not get any extra food that day—or any other day."[56]

The prisoners were naturally curious about what had happened to their units after they were taken prisoner during the Battle of the Bulge, but information was hard to come by. What they didn't discover for a long time was that Hitler's Ardennes offensive had run out of steam. After decimating the 99th and 106th Divisions and roaring through St. Vith, the gray tide rolled eastward, through

Knocked-out German panzers litter the roadsides near St. Vith—
graphic evidence of the fierce fighting. (Courtesy National Archives)

Malmédy, around Bastogne, and toward the Meuse. It never got there, nor anywhere close to its ultimate objective of Antwerp. The salient that the attack had
created now became a spearpoint that was being broken into small, ineffective
pieces by the hammer-blows of the American First and Third Armies.[57]

Despite the crushing defeat, Hitler made one final effort to save his Reich.
Some seventy miles south of Bad Orb, the final German offensive of the war was
taking shape. And, although it, too, would become a crashing failure, it would
result in more American deaths and more American soldiers being brought to
Bad Orb.

6

CAUGHT IN
A NORTH WIND

IN THE SNOWY hills of Alsace-Lorraine, several hundred miles south of where the Battle of the Bulge was still raging, the curtain was about to rise on the second, and final, act of Hitler's drama to save the Reich.

After landing on the French Riviera on 15 August 1944 in an operation codenamed Dragoon, the divisions of Major General Alexander Patch's Seventh Army began fighting their way northward. The first few weeks went relatively smoothly, with American and Free French divisions chasing General Friedrich Wiese's disorganized Nineteenth Army up the Rhône River valley; at only a few, well-chosen places did the Germans make a stand and offer serious resistance.

As the Allied drive neared the French–German border in September 1944, German opposition became more determined. The Germans, after all, were now fighting with their backs against their borders and were doing everything within their power to keep the enemy out. By October, the fighting in Alsace-Lorraine had settled into a war of attrition, which, little by little, the Allies were winning.

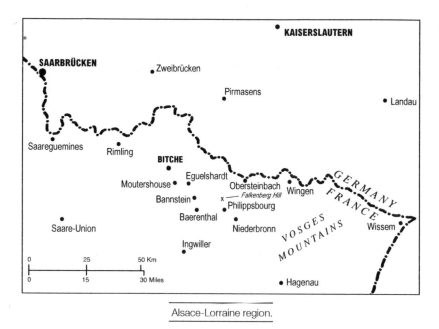

Alsace-Lorraine region.

Here, two new American infantry divisions, the 100th and the 103rd, would see their first combat. Spirits were high. In the official account of the campaign, the authors wrote, "For the 100th, or Century, Division, going into combat for the first time, the prospects seemed less than dismal. The new troops were both nervous and excited, anxious about what the future attack would bring, yet more eager than the veteran soldiers [of the 3rd, 36th, and 45th Divisions, which had been in combat for many months] to show what they could do." The 100th and 103rd Divisions would soon be followed by another, the 42nd.[1]

Private First Class Gerald Daub recalled that, upon landing, his outfit—Company F, 397th Regiment, 100th Infantry Division—was immediately ordered north. "We basically raced up the Rhône Valley until we got to about Baccarat,"* Daub said, "where the German army that we were chasing had prepared positions to the south of the Vosges Mountains. I assumed that they felt that the Seventh Army probably would not be able to penetrate the Vosges, because I don't believe any army had penetrated there before. We were in very mountainous terrain. It was well-treed with evergreens and was very snowy at that time."

---

*About fifty-five miles west of Strasbourg (sixty-five miles south of Saarbrücken).

Four members of a machine-gun squad from Company H, 398th Regiment, 100th Infantry Division, prepare to move out near the Maginot Line, December 1944. (Courtesy National Archives)

On 12 November 1944, Daub's life nearly ended when he was hit in the neck by a sniper's rifle bullet. "The sniper who shot me was about fifty yards away. He was basically aiming at the middle of my forehead. I saw him just about the same time that he saw me, so I fell to the ground and turned my head as I put the rifle stock up to my shoulder to fire. Probably the movement of my head made him miss my forehead but left my shoulder exposed, which was a little better. We both fired simultaneously; I don't know what happened to him. I was hit at the base of my neck and the bullet went down my back and out. Luckily, it didn't strike anything vital."

Daub lay bleeding in the snow for most of that day because his company was engaged in a heavy firefight and medics were unable to reach him. Help eventually came, and Daub was evacuated to an aid station. From there, he went by

GIs of the 398th Regiment, 100th Infantry Division, move down a
wooded lane in Alsace-Lorraine, 17 November 1944.
(Courtesy U.S. Army Military History Institute)

jeep, along with a badly wounded German, to a station hospital in Épinal. "I was
there two or three weeks; the wound was not that bad. At the time, though, the
doctors thought that I was badly wounded, so the Army sent a telegram to my
family telling them that I was severely wounded."

After recuperating, Daub was marked "fit for duty" and given the choice of
either returning to his old unit or being sent to a replacement depot where he
would be assigned to whatever unit needed a warm body. "Well, I was young
and foolish. If I had said that I wanted to go to the replacement depot, I probably would have been there for a week or two before being reassigned. But I told
them I wanted to go back to the guys I know. So I loaded up my gear and
jumped into the back of a truck and, in about an hour, I was back at my battalion headquarters and marched out to where my company was. Everybody was
happy to see me, including my buddy, Bob Rudnick. This was in early December—after Thanksgiving and before Christmas."[2]

During his absence, Daub's unit had been moved farther north to Rimling, a crossroads town just south of the German border, east of Sarreguemines. It was an area the Germans wanted very much to control.

In mid-December 1944, Lieutenant General Jacob Devers's Sixth Army Group had eighteen divisions on the line—two armored and six infantry divisions in Alexander Patch's Seventh U.S. Army, plus three armored and seven infantry in General Jean de Lattre de Tassigny's First French Army. Opposing them was the newly created Armeegruppe Oberrhein's forces: Generalleutnant Siegfried Rasp's Nineteenth Army* and General Max Simon's XIII SS Korps. As the Germans' Ardennes counteroffensive began to bog down, and Patton's Third Army had been pulled out of their positions and trucked north to hit the German salient, thereby relieving the pressure on Bastogne, Hitler saw the Americans in Alsace-Lorraine falling into the trap he had already set for them.[2]

Hitler and von Rundstedt's staff in OB West headquarters at Langenhain-Ziegenberg worked out plans for a large-scale attack by Generaloberst Johannes Blaskowitz's Army Group G that would slam into Allied lines north of Strasbourg, split Patch's Seventh Army, retake Strasbourg, and clear the enemy out of Alsace. Once it was successful, the drive would turn north and strike Patton's army from the rear, thus reducing the pressure on the Wacht-am-Rhein salient. The assault was scheduled for New Year's Eve. Daub and the thousands of other Americans on the front lines in Alsace-Lorraine were about to be hit by the white-hot blast of a north wind—Operation Nordwind.

Unlike Operation Wacht-am-Rhein, Nordwind did not come as a complete surprise to the Allies. Intelligence reports had noted the buildup of German units in the vicinity of Saarbrücken, and Eisenhower correctly surmised that the enemy was preparing to launch an attack against Devers's forces. Plans were swiftly made to go over onto the defensive. With Patton's army now out of the line, Patch's six infantry divisions, covering 126 miles, were stretched to the breaking point. Patch directed Major General Wade Haislip's XV Corps—consisting of the 44th, 100th, and 103rd Divisions—to cover thirty-five miles of front to the west of the Vosges; Major General Edward H. "Ted" Brooks's VI Corps would man the front to the east. The infantry regiments of three divisions—the 42nd, 63rd, and 70th—were rushed up from the south and turned into task forces to plug the numerous gaps in the Seventh Army's lines.[3]

---

*On 15 December 1944, Reichsführer-SS Heinrich Himmler had replaced the less-than-enthusiastic Wiese with Rasp. (Clarke and Smith, p. 485)

Operation Nordwind. (Approximate positions)

Private First Class Morton Brooks, a member of Company C, 242nd Infantry Regiment, 42nd Infantry Division, remembered that it was 8 December 1944 when his "Rainbow Division" (so called because of the rainbow patch they wore on their left sleeve) landed in Marseilles and formed into a task force commanded by Assistant Division Commander Brigadier General Henning Linden. Task Force Linden quickly headed north and relieved the 36th Infantry Division (Texas National Guard) along a thirty-mile front in Alsace-Lorraine.

On the move, Brooks related that his outfit did not encounter much resistance. "We had a Free French unit on the right of us, and I was running a liaison with them for a while. The fighting was just sporadic and it wasn't too serious. You might get strafed or you might see some activity, but nothing too significant."[4]

Late on 31 December 1944, the situation changed dramatically. All hell, as the saying goes, began to break loose. Two thousand men of the 37th SS-Panzergrenadier Regiment of the 17th SS Panzer Grenadier Division, supported by salvos of well-placed artillery rounds, charged through the darkness with suicidal abandon into the lines of the 100th Division's 397th Regiment, which refused to break. At Rimling, however, elements of Simon's XIII

A member of Company I, 242nd Regiment, 42nd Infantry Division, prepares a belt of 30-caliber machine-gun ammunition outside his improvised log-and-dirt bunker, January 1945, during Operation Nordwind (Courtesy National Archives)

SS Korps did manage to penetrate about two miles into the seam between the 44th and 100th Divisions, but were pinched off and the threat was eliminated.[5]

Before the Germans were thrown back, however, Gerald Daub's battalion was in Rimling and was attacked by the 17th SS Panzer Grenadier Division. "We had no tank support at that time and, apparently, we were very anxious for this crossroads. We were so vulnerable that they were able to attack us from both the front and the rear," said Daub.

A Sherman tank of the 781st Tank Battalion stands guard on the outskirts of Wingen, France, during the Germans' Operation Nordwind. The GI helmet, destroyed jeep, and burning truck in the distance attest to the heavy fighting. (Courtesy National Archives)

The Germans had no air power to speak of and were loath to leave their tanks exposed during the day. When a panzer broke down, they pulled it out and would leave their infantry behind to hold the terrain. Daub said, "We would go from house to house and roust out their infantrymen and either shoot them or, more often than not, they would surrender. That went on for several days."

Daub was sent on a patrol with a scout from the first squad, a soldier by the name of Howard Hunter. The two were ordered to go up to the northern edge of Rimling and observe any German movement into the town. "Our instructions were to report back to company headquarters and tell them what was coming that particular evening," Daub said. "We picked a very nice house that commanded a bend in the road where we could see right up to the top of the little hill the town was on."

Toward evening, a German armored reconnaissance unit with several tanks approached the town. "The first tank had infantrymen all around it, dipping and dodging and coming down the street, heading toward the house Howard and I were in. Howard and I fired at them and they fired at us. As we stood there, the tank—we were on the second floor of the house—rumbled right up to the house and put the muzzle of the gun in the window where we were standing. I sort of touched the muzzle as I turned around to talk to Howard. If I were smarter, I might have dropped a hand grenade down the muzzle, or maybe it would have been dumber—I don't know."

Daub and Hunter bolted down the stairs and dashed out of the house. "That part of the town was on a hillside, so it was terraced, and we jumped right into a group of German soldiers. Howard swung his rifle butt at the nearest German and the two of us ran into the first house that we came to. It was my thought, and I'm sure his, too, that we would just go through the house and out the back and head back to our company headquarters."

Unfortunately for Daub and Hunter, the farmer who owned the house had done a very good job of boarding up all the windows and doors, and once the two got inside, there was no way out. "We went to the furthest place in the house, which was the kitchen, and we heard the Germans coming in after us. There had been a lot of shelling in town and so there was a lot of grit and sand on the floor; we could hear their boots. It was dark and the house was boarded up, so we couldn't really see. As they came down the hall toward us, they were throwing hand grenades into each room. Finally, they came to our room."

The two Yanks had turned over a very heavy wooden kitchen table and were taking cover behind it. "They tossed the grenade in and we got down behind the table, and the table just bounced and nothing really happened to us. Howard said, 'I think we'd better surrender.' I recall saying to Howard, 'Not me, Howard—I'm Jewish.' So Howard didn't surrender; he stuck with me.

"They threw another grenade in, and then we heard what we knew was a machine pistol being cocked at the door; that table was not going to resist the bullets. I said to Howard, 'Howard, discretion is the better part of valor—I think we better surrender.' So we threw our rifles out onto the floor, and we yelled 'Kamerad!' and walked out toward them. They grabbed us and dragged us out the door and searched us. We were prisoners of war."

Leon Horowitz,
photographed
in 1943 at the
University of Indiana.
(Courtesy Leon Horowitz)

The soldiers took Daub and Hunter back to the tank, where a badly wounded German was lying in the street. "They ordered us to pick him up and put him on the tank. It was a Panther tank—a big tank with ridges across the front, and we picked him up and set him up above the ridges, and the tank commander told us to get on the tank. So we got on, and the tank backed up, turned around, and headed out of town.

"As we proceeded along the ridgeline, this wounded German soldier was groaning and screaming for his mother. The screaming stopped and I said to Howard, 'I think this guy is dead.' I think the Germans knew it too, because they stopped the tank and ordered us off, and I thought surely they were going to shoot us now."

The tank commander told the two Americans to take a shovel from the back of the tank and dig a grave for the dead soldier. "The ground was frozen as hard as concrete," Daub recalled. "At that time of year it was very hard to dig a fox-hole—or anything else. The two of us scraped at it and chipped at it and they finally said, 'That's enough,' so we just rolled his body into it and threw some snow on top of it. We didn't know what was going to happen next, but they ordered us back onto the tank and drove off to where they were camped, just on the other side of the border in a little farmhouse. They put us in the barn and interrogated us." The next day, the Germans brought in the rest of the company, along with Daub's friend, Bob Rudnick.[6]

Leon Horowitz, a soldier from Brooklyn and another member of Daub's Company F, 397th Infantry Regiment, 100th Infantry Division, was also taken prisoner at Rimling. He quickly faced a moral dilemma that confronted all of the soldiers who were Jewish: "When I was captured, one of my soldier mates advised me to throw away my dogtags. In those days, your religion was imprinted on your dogtags so that, if you were killed in action, they would know what kind of burial service to give you. I threw away my dogtags shortly after I was captured. In retrospect, the Germans would have quickly suspected that anyone who didn't have dogtags was Jewish."[7]

The 42nd Division was not spared any of the fighting. Morton Brooks, Company C, 242nd Infantry Regiment, 42nd Infantry Division, recalled, "We were moving toward Germany and I guess the Germans were making an attempt to recapture Strasbourg, and they hit us with an overwhelming force."[8]

The division fought back hard. A citation his unit was later awarded hinted at the ferocity of the fighting:

The First Battalion [of the 242nd Infantry Regiment, 42nd Infantry Division] was occupying a front of four thousand yards when it was attacked by three regiments from the 21st and 25th German Panzer Divisions supported by heavy armor and artillery. Ordered to hold this position at all costs, the battalion withstood repeated onslaughts of enemy flame-throwing tanks, self-propelled guns, and infantry. Time after time, small detachments of the battalion remained steadfast after their positions had been overrun by hostile tanks in order to stop the foot troops that followed. Cooks, clerks, mail orderlies and supply personnel fought side by side with riflemen, completely disregarding their personal safety. In spite of loss of over five hundred officers and men, the battalion tenaciously held its position in the face

Two soldiers of the 100th Infantry Division's 397th Regiment stand watch with their water-cooled .30-caliber machine-gun in a foxhole near Rimling, France, January 1945. Note one soldier is wearing a white parka and the other a white helmet cover to help them blend in with the snowy terrain. (Courtesy National Archives)

of overwhelming odds for more than fifty-two hours until relieved, exacting a heavy toll of men and equipment from the enemy. The courage and devotion shown by the members of the First Battalion, 242nd Infantry Regiment, are worthy of emulation and exemplifies the highest traditions of the Army of the United States.[9]

Brooks said that he was lucky to be alive. "I was in a forward foxhole. Part of our company—a couple of our squads and the rest of the fellas who were in the town of Hatton—really were blasted away. Most of the company was wiped out and so, in a way, I was fortunate that they had overrun our positions during the night. We were really cut off. Our own artillery was beginning to fall on us, and our phone lines were cut, so I was asked to reconnect the phone line. I took off and was following the line. I got back to a bunker and found some of our fellows cowering in there; they had experienced a lot of shelling during the night."

While Brooks and the other soldiers were trying to determine what they were going to do, a sergeant looked out and saw a Tiger tank coming up the road. "He said we've got to surrender, which I didn't want to do, but that was pretty much it. He was concerned, and rightly so, that they would just put the muzzle of the tank's gun into the entry of the bunker and we would be killed."

Brooks noted that the Germans came out of the woods and set up a machine-gun across from his bunker, then ordered the Americans to come out with their hands up. "We came out and were kept in a trench until their units moved ahead. Then we were marched back to a farmhouse. All of us who were captured at that point—about fifteen or twenty of us—were held there for a couple of days. They interrogated some of us and got our names, rank and serial numbers, and they tried to get some more."[10]

Like the 106th Infantry Division that had been hard hit near St. Vith, the 70th had been raided during its training for thousands of partially trained soldiers to replace battle casualties in overseas divisions. Like the other units in Alsace-Lorraine at the end of 1944, the 275th Regiment of the 70th Division was on the line in the vicinity of Philippsbourg, Schwarzenberg, and Falkenberg Ridge as part of Task Force Herren. As the 70th was moving to attack on New Year's Eve, it ran headlong into the German 256th, 257th, and 361st Volksgrenadier Divisions launching their own part of Operation Nordwind. The fierce fighting in the snowy hills would soon be known as the "Battle of the Bitche Salient."[11]

Company B, 275th Regiment, 70th Infantry Division, was moving forward near the Falkenberg Ridge when it came under intense enemy fire. Private First Class Tony Acevedo, a medic with Company B, had been on a patrol and was about to return to Philippsbourg, when the patrol was told that Philippsbourg was occupied by the Germans. "So we were to head toward a hill called Falkenberg Hill. I got word that the company commander, Captain William Schmidt, was seriously wounded inside a cave there."

The company was ambushed and Acevedo recalled that some of the troops around him began to panic during the ambush. "As a medic," he said, "I encountered fellas who were shell-shocked and scared, and some who even wanted me to baptize them."

When Acevedo reached Falkenberg Ridge, he saw that another medic had been killed while he was taking care of Captain Schmidt. "I continued to bandage Schmidt's wounds. We're up to our waists in snow and the Germans are surrounding us with tanks. We had already been bombarded by our own planes to keep from being captured, but the bombs were getting too close."[12]

Norman Fellman, also of Company B, has his own memories of the events leading up to the surrender. "Company B was about twelve kilometers outside of Philippsbourg when the ambush occurred. Our battalion was ordered to hold the whole range of hills. One of the hills that we were on was the Falkenberg. Nobody was keeping us much up to date as to what we were doing. We were cut off; we had lost communications and had sent out patrols. The patrols would go out and we never heard from them again; we didn't know if they got through or not.

"Our captain was wounded the first day we were on that hill. We lost some officers and that was the beginning of our casualties. We had scooped out foxholes as best we could in the rock, and we were pretty much out of ammo. The Germans came around with flame-throwing tanks at the base of the hill. The Germans evidently decided to bypass us initially and had gone around us and were cleaning up when they came back to get us.

"There was an overhang there on the hill—almost like a cave, but not quite. Our wounded were all in that area, back in a corner section. We only had rations enough for one night, and anything that wasn't eaten after that first night on the hill we pulled for the wounded, which were beginning to build up." Fellman and his unit were there for nearly a week with no food. Water came from melted ice and snow.

Running low on ammunition, and with no hope of rescue, Fellman noted that his surrounded unit was confronted with three choices—none of them good: "We could freeze to death, we could starve to death, or we could surrender; the decision came down to surrender. We tried to damage our weapons as best we could to make them inoperable, and then we surrendered. I was only in combat itself for a few weeks, from the middle of December to the fourth of January. Then it was all over for me."[13]

Tony Acevedo recalled, "The Germans came up and we had to give up. I was forced to take off my boots, which were no good; we were in slush. We were not equipped for the winter. We had to wear several pairs of socks just to be comfortable. So we went down the slope barefooted to where the German trucks were."[14]

Before the march to captivity, Fellman noted, Company B was formed up and the wounded were evacuated. "We were then marched to a railhead, a few days' marching. My first encounter with a rifle butt was while going past a

Interior of a boxcar that was used to transport POWs.
(Courtesy U.S. Army Military History Institute)

bridge abutment; there was an icicle hanging from it. I was dry and thirsty, so I stepped out of line and grabbed the icicle and got my first introduction to the fact that we weren't free to do what we pleased anymore."

The Americans were taken to a railhead and were packed into boxcars. "They probably had cattle in them at one time, because they weren't very clean," Fellman said. "We had between sixty to eighty men to a car. It was freezing. The only guys who had any heat were the ones in the middle. Once the doors closed, they didn't open; we were in these cars for about four or five days—I don't remember exactly. If you had to go to the bathroom, you used your helmet—your steel pot—but there was no place to empty it.

"We sat in the railyards in Frankfurt for awhile. We were strafed and there were hits taken, but whether it was our planes or somebody else's, I don't know. We lost some guys."[15]

Gerald Daub remembered that the group of prisoners he was in was "taken to the nearest rail line, each given a loaf of bread, and put into boxcars with some other Americans that had been captured. The boxcars were locked and wired shut, and we went on about a week's journey to Frankfurt-on-Main. When we arrived at Frankfurt, it was night, and I think it was the Royal Air Force that bombed the railyards while we were sitting there in the boxcars. One of our officers, Lieutenant Rabinowitz, was killed in the bombing and strafing. He was in a different boxcar; nobody in my boxcar was injured, that I can recall. We went on to Bad Orb."[16]

What neither Fellman, Daub, Acevedo, Brooks, nor Horowitz learned until much later was that Operation Nordwind had turned into a complete disaster for the Germans. Although the battle raged throughout the month of January, the Allies held the line and threw the Germans back with heavy losses; total Seventh Army casualties for the battle came in at 14,000 dead, wounded, or missing, while the Germans lost 23,000 men.[17]

Nordwind was Germany's last major counteroffensive of the war. But while Germany was fighting to stave off defeat, the Americans captured during Operations Wacht-am-Rhein and Nordwind were soon fighting for their very lives.

—⁄⁄⁄⁄—

Once the train carrying him and several hundred other prisoners reached Bad Orb, Gerald Daub recalled, "We were marched through the town and the local people were very angry. We were marched to this very large prisoner of war camp called Stalag IX-B. The barracks that we were assigned to had a great deal of the 106th Division in it already. We were in a very large stone barrack; there were no beds or bunks—just straw on the floor. I think the building probably was an old stable. At that time, we thought the food and living conditions were pretty bad, but we really didn't know what was to come."[18]

During the in-processing procedures, the Germans seemed inordinately interested in the new prisoners' religions. Morton Brooks recalled, "When we were processed, they had American soldiers doing the processing and they asked about religion. This was not something we had to provide, but they said, 'Look, we were told that we had to get it,' and that was it. I wasn't going to hide who I was, so I gave it."[19] He had no idea what was in store for those who identified themselves as Jewish.

As more and more prisoners piled into Stalag IX-B, the camp administration became concerned that, unless something was done, the *lager* would burst at the seams. Late on the night of 27 January 1945, the lid blew off.

Nearly crazed by hunger, two American privates by the names of Sparks and Leondosky decided to raid the camp's sole source of food. Everyone who was there has some version of what transpired. Martin Hagel, a private first class with Company I, 422nd Regiment, 106th Division, said, "They broke into the prison camp's kitchen to obtain food. A German guard discovered them in the kitchen and Private Sparks hit this German guard with an ax, splitting his skull open. The German guard was discovered later and his life was saved."[20]

James V. Smith noted, "They broke into the kitchen. There was this old guard, probably in his late seventies, and they beat him up and cut him up with a hatchet, of all things. That was a Saturday night. The next morning, when they normally let us out to go to church, they took us outside and lined us up in front of these machine-gun squads. They told us if we didn't report who did that terrible thing, they were going to start shooting twenty of us at a time."[21]

According to Jack Crawford, "The Germans were pretty upset over the incident. They took us outside and lined us up out in the cold for a long period of time. They were trying to find out who did it. A lot of fellows passed out. That was a little nasty."[22]

Norman Fellman added, "They marched us out and put us into this quadrangle in whatever condition they found you sleeping in. If you had shoes on, you had shoes; if you didn't you didn't. If you had time to grab your coat, you got a coat; if not, you didn't. We all slept in our clothes; nobody took off anything, so most of us had our overcoats on because the barracks weren't heated and you did whatever you could to try and keep warm. We were outside in the cold for a little over seven hours. They had machine-guns lined up on us and they said they were going to start taking us down if they didn't find out who broke into the storeroom. That's when I noted the chaplain [First Lieutenant Edward J. Hurley], because he came out and they were able to push the offenders out front and turn them over to the Germans. We were finally allowed back into our barracks."[23]

Richard Lockhart said the camp commandant wanted to find out who the culprits were. "Nobody came forward, so they announced that they were going to take every tenth man and shoot him unless the culprits admitted their guilt and stepped forward. They set up these machine-guns right in front of us. Apparently, the Protestant and Catholic chaplains negotiated with the German authorities at the camp and said that they would look for the persons responsible. They went through and identified two men who were complicit in the incident,

Headquarters building at Stalag IX-B, Bad Orb, Germany.
(Courtesy National Archives)

and they admitted it. We were finally allowed to go back to the barracks. None of us got any food whatsoever that day. I don't know what happened to those two soldiers. From what I have read of other accounts, it is my understanding that they were put into solitary confinement; if they had killed the guard, I think there would have been another consequence."[24]

After the attempted murder, camp life settled into a dull routine that was soon upset by the Russian POWs. James V. Smith related, "They let the Russians roam around in the camp. What we called the potato wagon would come through the front gate and come up the hill toward the kitchen; the Russians would run in and grab potatoes or, if it was loaded with bread, they'd grab loaves of bread. The German guards—they were all old people, or they'd been wounded on the Russian front—didn't stop it."

To halt the problem, the camp administration formed a company of military policemen from the Americans; Smith, at six feet tall and almost two hundred pounds, was appointed to be one of the MPs. "They took my steel helmet and painted 'MP' on it in white lettering," he recalled. "It was our job to keep order at the kitchen and protect the wagons bringing in food. So that meant a knock-down, drag-out fistfight. We noticed that the Russians were taking any bread and potatoes and whatever to this young Russian colonel and he would decide who got what. We finally realized that he was the one we had to beat the hell out of. Which we did, very easily. That was my job for awhile. We stopped the raiding of the potato wagon."[25]

Prisoners continued to be assigned to work details. A new arrival, Private First Class William C. Thompson, from Hialeah, Florida, and a member of Company E, 253rd Regiment, 63rd Infantry Division, who had been captured near Sarreguemines, was sent on a burial detail, but the strenuous work "took more energy in the cold of winter than could be recovered by the extra liter of soup given as pay. The frozen ground had to be pick-axed and lifted out by hand. No thank you! No gravedigging for me!"

Thompson instead was assigned to housekeeping chores—with somewhat amusing results. "I was taken out of the compound to the German officers' quarters, given a broom, and told to sweep down. The commander's quarters were sparsely furnished, containing a rough bunk bed, a dressing stand, and a low chest of drawers upon which sat a plate with half of a spiced walnut cake. Next to the cake was a squatty bottle of brandy. The dust began to settle as I set the broom aside and sliced a small piece of cake. It was delicious. So I took another slice. He'd never miss only two small slices.

"I had never drunk strong spirits, but I poured a glass of brandy and chased the cake down. More brandy. More cake. I was reeling. To cover my crime, I began furiously sweeping the floor but found myself drawn again and again to the squatty bottle on the chest. It was soon almost gone and I was drunk as a sailor. I finally had to lie down on the commandant's freshly made bed. I was rudely shaken awake by an enlisted German guard who was shaking with fright at the sight of a drunken, lice-infested POW sleeping in the captain's bed after having consumed a cake and most of his fine brandy.

"I soon found myself on the operating end of a bucksaw, cutting logs for firewood. I had difficulty keeping the saw blade taut and was receiving a tongue-lashing when I was saved by the flyover of a thousand-plane raid. The sky was filled with contrails, and P-47s weaved back and forth.

"We were all looking up. I told my guard, 'All is *kaput*—you're going to lose.' He said, 'When, for God's sake, when?'"[26]

Stalag IX-B also held several black American soldiers who had been captured during the two German counteroffensives. As Private First Class Fred G. Koenig, of the 422nd Regiment, 106th Division, remembered, "It was some time in January or February 1945 that a Corporal Schultz, a German guard at IX-B, beat up a colored American soldier. I witnessed this assault. The colored soldier was called 'Shorty' and came from Baltimore." Shorty's crime was walking past a group of German guards without saluting. Schultz stopped him and said something in German which the American did not understand, so Schultz hit him several times with a bayonet scabbard, knocked him to the ground, and kicked him. "Shorty was a bloody mess," said Koenig.[27]

James V. Smith remembered that he was moved out of Barracks 44 and into the MP barracks in front of the kitchen. "There, for their own safety, we had three African-American soldiers. The camp commander suggested that we put them in the MP barracks for their own protection. He said, 'We've got a lot of fanatical idiots.' Which was an understatement. He was afraid that if we didn't keep them in there for their protection, some German might do harm to them."[28]

Just as the prisoners were beginning to accept their fate at Stalag IX-B and wait out the war in the camp, a startling order came down that would significantly change the lives of hundreds of the American inmates.

7

THE LAST TRAIN
TO BERGA

DURING *APPELL* ON Thursday, 18 January 1945, the Germans running Stalag IX-B announced that all Jewish prisoners would be required to identify themselves the following day for the purpose of being moved to a segregated barracks. This order was met with no small measure of fear and incredulity. *After all, we're American soldiers, not civilian Jews rounded up in the ghettos of Europe,* seemed to be the common thought.

"We got the order that all Jewish prisoners were to fall out the next morning and bring their things with them," said Leon Horowitz. "We didn't know what the significance of that order was. We had heard a little bit about the Nazi extermination of the Jews in Europe, but we couldn't conceive that this would be carried out against American soldiers."[1]

To some soldiers, such as Richard Lockhart, admitting to the camp authorities that one was Jewish was tantamount to signing one's own death warrant. He said, "You're only supposed to give name, rank, and serial number. Anything else is cooperating with the enemy. I understand people who say 'I was born a Jew and I will die a Jew,' but why would they do that while in the hands of the

Nazis? Was it done as an affirmation of their culture and religion? Was it done out of naïveté? Did the Jewish soldiers think that, because they were Americans, this would somehow protect them? It defies understanding—I don't think the Germans had the Jews identify themselves because they were doing a term paper or some sociological study on the prisoners in Stalag IX-B."

Lockhart said he never believed in giving the Germans anything. "I didn't like being captured in the first place and, in the second place, I wasn't going to give them anything more than what I absolutely had to give them. When I was first captured, they wanted all our money turned in, on threat of death. I put my money in the lining of my jacket; I wasn't going to give it to them."[2]

Norman Fellman remembered, "The word came down that the Germans knew that a percentage of the GIs in IX-B were Jewish and they wanted all the Jews to step forward. I don't know whether they were ignorant of the fact that those of us who still had dogtags would have an 'H' stamped on them for 'Hebrew,' or a 'C' for 'Catholic,' or a 'P' for 'Protestant,' but they didn't look at the tags. When we had signed into the camp, all the clerks were American and they wrote down everybody as 'Protestant.' The Germans didn't like Catholics very much, either, so nobody was listed as Catholic or Jewish; everybody was 'Protestant,' but the Germans knew that wasn't so."[3]

Peter House recalled the German explanation: "They said that this was proper under the Geneva Convention because it was done in Germany. After all, didn't we separate blacks from whites in our own army? Again, it sounded reasonable."[4]

That evening, discussions in the barracks raged about whether or not the Jewish soldiers should comply with the order. Some felt that to voluntarily identify oneself would be committing suicide, while others argued that the Germans might shoot everyone if the Jews did not step forward. Some Jews believed the Germans would never dare harm Americans no matter what their religion, and said they would comply, while some of the non-Jewish Americans begged their Jewish comrades not to step forward.

Gerald Daub recalled, "I believe that Hans Kasten, our 'Man of Confidence,'* gave the order to all of the barracks leaders that the Jewish soldiers should not step forward and be separated, and so, the next day, we did not."[5]

---

*A soldier elected by his fellow prisoners to be their spokesman or liaison with the German camp administration. In German: *Vertrauensmann*.

Leon Horowitz said, "There were some like myself who said to themselves, 'Yes, I'm Jewish; I'm not going to deny that—I'll fall out in the morning.' There were others who rationalized and said, 'Well, I was born Jewish, but I wasn't reared Jewish, and I don't identify as Jewish, and I don't know if I should or should not fall out.' And there were others who said, 'I'm just not going to do it; I'm going to deny that I'm Jewish.' The reaction ran that gamut."[6]

The next morning, the Germans gave the order but were very angry when the American Jews failed to comply. The Germans had another meeting that day with Kasten and the barracks leaders and laid down the law. Said Daub, "The barracks leaders were told again that tomorrow the Jewish prisoners *must* step forward; I recall being told this by my barracks leader, who also was in my company and platoon. I was told that, when we're ordered to step forward, step forward—and he knew that we were Jewish. The next day, when the barracks were opened again, we stepped out and the street was lined with very formidable-looking German troops. After formation, the order was given again for the Jews—the *Juden*—to step forward. I looked at Bob Rudnick and Bob looked at me and the two of us stepped forward together."[7]

Norman Fellman noted, "Maybe because I had more pride than brains, I decided to step forward. Most of the other Jews also stepped forward, and we were segregated to another barracks."[8]

Eighty to a hundred Jewish GIs gathered what few belongings they still possessed and were moved to the former officers' quarters, renamed the Judenbarracke.

According to Leon Horowitz, "Those of us who did fall out were marched to another barrack in a separate barbed-wire enclosure—a kind of a ghetto within Stalag IX-B. In this barrack, we had even less food than we had been getting. We had less firewood for the one potbellied stove and we had harsher work details. We had to go out and chop down trees for firewood, most of which the Germans took for their own barracks. Many of us developed symptoms of non-freezing cold injury that I suffer from to this day. Non-freezing cold injury is prolonged exposure to cold, which affects the nerves and blood vessels, particularly of the extremities."[9]

Gerald Daub and the other Jewish POWs were ordered to step out of the formation and gather in a group. "When the formation was dismissed," he said, "we were taken to a separate barracks, which was no different than the rest of the barracks. In fact, it was better in a way because it had bunk beds—wooden bunk

122   GIVEN UP FOR DEAD

beds—and there were just Jewish-Americans there. Basically, we got the same food. The Germans were a little less willing to be pleasant to us. They stood us out and counted us longer or whatever, but basically it was the same as what we had been accustomed to. The main difference was that this barracks had a barbed-wire enclosure around it; we could go out and walk around the barracks but we couldn't communicate with the other prisoners. We were kept separate."[10]

The Jewish prisoners were not in their new home for very long. At the beginning of February 1945, Oberst Sieber, the *kommandant* of Stalag IX-B, received an order from higher headquarters at Stalag IX-C, located at Bad Sulza. Sieber was to ship 350 prisoners by rail to a labor camp at Berga-an-der-Elster, a rural village of 7,000 inhabitants located some 125 miles east of Bad Orb and fifty miles south of Leipzig. Whether Sieber was told specifically to send the Jews is not known; what is known is that he selected the Jews who had identified themselves and had been moved to the Jewish barrack, along with non-Jewish "undesirables" or "troublemakers"—men who had smarted off to their captors, disobeyed camp regulations, tried to escape, or otherwise had been a nuisance—and others randomly chosen just to reach the 350 quota figure.

Sergeant Howard P. Gossett stated, "We knew about two days prior to their removal that [the Jews] were going to be taken away. Our 'Confidence Man,' at the request of several of us, went to the Germans and told them these American Jews were as much American as any of the rest of us and were fighting for the same thing, and requested that they not be removed. The Germans paid no attention to this request."[11]

Gerald Daub recalled that the Germans explained to the POWs that they were opening another camp for Americans, "because Bad Orb was like a reception center, in a way. It was a general camp and there were contingents from many different armies in it—French, Poles, British, a lot of British. So they were opening a new camp just for Americans and they were randomly selecting barracks to go there. The first barracks that was selected 'at random' just happened to be the Jewish barracks. I believe that men who had committed minor crimes had been separated before and were also kept in a barracks, and I believe that the barracks leaders were told to select the men who they thought were troublemakers. The rest of the shipment was just filled out with names of people that the Germans thought sounded like they might be Jewish. They might have even

WESTERN UNION

War Department telegram sent to Stella Mark, informing her that her husband was reported "missing in action." (Courtesy Joseph Mark)

been selected because there were a lot of Italian men who may have been Catholic. In any event, we had nothing to pack because we basically slept in our clothing; we were afraid somebody would steal our boots, or whatever, if we took them off."[12]

Some people were plainly panicked by the order. James V. Smith recalled the story of a Jewish POW he identified by the initials "R.J.," who had somehow avoided being moved to the *Juden* (Jewish) barrack. "Shortly after the Jewish soldiers, or American soldiers who looked Jewish, were segregated, I got word that R.J. wanted to see me. He had managed to convince the Germans that he was not Jewish but a farmer from Alabama. While R.J. had escaped being segregated, he was trying not to attract any attention to himself. I found him sitting on a lower bunk in another barracks. He wanted me to tell him everything I knew about farming in Alabama. I told him about when they planted, when they harvested, and what the products were: cotton, corn, and soybeans. He managed to survive and made it home to Cleveland."[13]

About this time, the families of the prisoners learned that their loved ones were guests of the Nazi government. Normally, the Germans notified the International Red Cross, which informed the War Department, which then sent telegrams to the next-of-kin, telling them that their loved ones, who had previously been reported as "missing in action," were now prisoners of war. No other information was provided—no indication of where the POW was, or what his condition might be.

Stella Mark, who had met Joseph at the Brooklyn Navy Yard and married him shortly before he was inducted in 1943, recalled, "I wasn't aware that he had been captured by the Germans for a long time. I read about the Battle of the Bulge in the newspapers, and I had gotten a telegram from the War Department telling me that he was missing. I applied to the Red Cross to see if they knew anything, but they didn't. I really didn't know what had happened to him for months after the Battle of the Bulge. I finally got a postcard from him telling me that he was in Bad Orb, but it didn't say much. At least it gave me the hope that he was still alive. I knew that he wasn't missing anymore, but he wasn't in a good situation.

"We had been married just before he went into the Army, about three weeks before he left. We didn't have our own apartment; I lived with my parents in Manhattan and I visited his mother on weekends. I really didn't know where Joe was until he was liberated in April." She continued to write to him in the hope that the letters would be forwarded, but they never were.[14]

Tony Acevedo recalled learning later about the anguish that the War Department telegram caused in his family: "My parents lived in Mexico but my mother had a sister in Pasadena, my aunt Carmen. In case of an emergency, if something ever happened to me, like I was missing in action or something, I gave the Army her address so they could report it to her. At that time, my stepmother happened to leave Durango to bring my brother, who had infantile paralysis, to be treated by the doctors at the children's hospital in Los Angeles. My stepmother was at her sister's house when someone knocked at the door and said, 'This is Western Union.' She answered the door and received the message that I was missing. She became ill right there when she found out that I was missing in action."[15]

At Stalag IX-B, it came time for the 350 prisoners to be sent to Berga. Norman Fellman recalled how the 350 were chosen: "The Germans needed a work detail of about 350 to fill a job at another camp. They wanted to do that with

Jews but they couldn't find enough. So they went down the line; if you looked Jewish or if your name had a Jewish sound to it, they pulled you out. If you looked Catholic or they assumed you were Catholic, you were also pulled out. Of the 350, only about a third were actually Jewish; the rest were either Catholic or they were troublemakers in the camp—people they caught stealing and whatnot. As it turned out, there were eighty to a hundred Jews."[16]

Peter Iosso and Tony Acevedo, both Catholics, found themselves selected for the transport to Berga. Iosso noted, "In early February 1945, 350 of us, includ ing all the known or presumed Jewish-American soldiers, were rounded up to be shipped to an *Arbeitskommando* [work detachment] in Berga-am-Elster in eastern Germany. Why Gentiles like me made up the other half or so of this group I could not understand, except perhaps to complete the number needed. We all had one thing in common, though: we were all 'undesirable.'"[17]

The Germans had skillfully relocated millions of Jews from the ghettoes of Europe to the extermination camps with a simple ruse: They told the Jews they were being resettled in a place that would be far superior to the cramped, squalid quarters in which they had been living. Fearful, desperate people will of ten cling to the slightest flotsam of hope that their captors are telling the truth. Thus it happened for the American POWs at Stalag IX-B; Tony Acevedo, for one, had heard rumors that the living conditions at Berga would be far superior to Stalag IX-B: "They told us that this place would be a place of life and glory with basketballs, games, hospitals."[18]

With this tiny scrap of hope buoying them, on 9 February 1945, the 350 selectees were marched down from the camp to the Bad Orb *bahnhof,* where a line of boxcars awaited them. They would not see their buddies and fellow POWs— Lockhart, Smith, Crawford, Kline, Savage, and hundreds more—again.

Incredibly, some of the Jewish soldiers were left behind at Stalag IX-B, either by their own or their buddies' efforts at deception or by sheer luck. Leon Horowitz described an incident that prevented him from being sent to Berga—an incident which may have saved his life: "One night we were told that the next morning everybody should fall out again with all of their possessions. We didn't know what that was all about. Having been working out in the cold without adequate clothing, I had been coming down with a cold and terrific coughing. The next morning, when they took the Jews out of the barrack, I was so sick, I collapsed unconscious on the barrack floor. What had happened was, as I now know, I had developed pneumonia and I had a raging

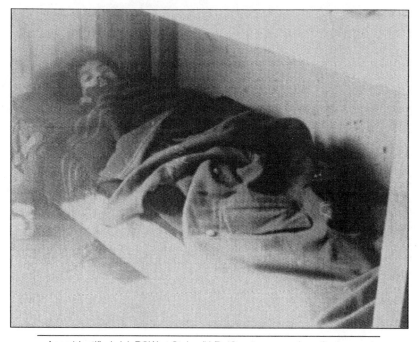

An unidentified sick POW at Stalag IX-B. (Courtesy www.LoneSentry.com)

fever; I was literally unconscious. Everybody thought I was dead. They even sent the burial detail for me. Fortunately, they noticed that I was breathing, although shallowly, so they took me to the *krankenhaus* [hospital]. In this *krankenhaus*, we had two captured American doctors and four or five corpsmen [medics] but they had no medicine; any medicine they might have had when they were captured was taken away. So they just put me on a cot. They didn't even have aspirin for fever; they just put cold cloths on me. They really thought I was a goner. But I fooled them; I recovered. Later, they took me out and showed me the coffin with my name on it.

"What I had is known in medicine as the 'crisis of pneumonia,' where your fever goes so high that you begin to hallucinate. I remember the hallucination to this day, because I was screaming, 'Get the elephants off my chest! I can't breathe!' With pneumonia, fluid accumulates in your lungs and it's like drowning. Breathing is extremely difficult. But the good Lord watched over me and I did survive. The *Juden* barrack was empty at that time, so they sent me to another barrack."

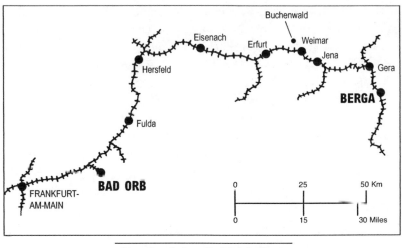

The rail route from Bad Orb to Berga.

When Horowitz was in the *krankenhaus* and regaining his strength—he weighed only eighty-five pounds when the camp was finally liberated—a choir that had been organized by the Protestant chaplain came through the hospital. "They sang hymns and some of the popular songs of the day. That buoyed me up. I felt spiritually lifted. I had sung in a choir in my synagogue when I was a teenager. I felt that, if this choir was able to do for others what it did for me, maybe I could do this for some of the other guys in the camp. So I went to the Protestant chaplain and I asked him, 'Do you think it would be all right with God if I joined your choir and sang Christian hymns?' He said, 'I think it would be very much all right with God.' So that's what I did. I learned to sing 'The Old Rugged Cross' and a few other hymns, and it was good for me because it was a diversion; we didn't have anything else to do in camp."[19]

The train headed east, with sixty or seventy men to a car. As before, there was no food or water, and the only sanitary facilities was a bucket in the corner. As virtually everyone had dysentery, the bucket was soon full to overflowing.

According to Gerald Daub, "Some men managed to hold on to their steel helmets, which was a very good thing because you could use it in the boxcar to pee or poop in, and then use it to pour the stuff out under the door because there was no toilet facility. The boxcars were very unpleasant. They had packed so many people in there, you couldn't lie down; you'd take turns just trying to scrunch down on the floor. Bob Rudnick and I did that for each other."[20]

No one knew where they were headed, but rumors and guesses were rampant. Some said it was a death camp, some a concentration camp, others just another miserable POW camp like Stalag IX-B. Some held out the hope that it would better than Stalag IX-B. They had no idea that they were on their way to Berga-an-der-Elster, which one author has described as having "the highest mortality rate of any camp where POWs were held."[21]

Not only did the American prisoners have to worry about where they were being taken, they also had to worry about whether or not they would make it there alive, for Allied aircraft continued to strafe or bomb trains at will without knowing the nature of the cargo.

Morton Brooks recalled, "It took us about four or five days to get from Bad Orb to Berga. We were hit the second or third day by aircraft. The boxcar I was in wasn't hit too bad, but there was one boxcar where a lot of people were hurt and killed as a result of the attack. They sounded like bombers of some kind or another. I'll tell you—I never realized that I could crawl into a helmet.

"There were no sanitary facilities, so it really was a miserable trip. They had given us a small piece of bread and a drink of water before we left. That was it for the entire trip. Some died en route, I think—just crushed. They had problems breathing; they didn't make it. There were about seventy people in each boxcar. You couldn't lie down to sleep, so you just propped yourself up against the next guy and tried to sleep that way."[22]

Eastward the train crawled, across rolling farmlands, past heavy stands of trees, past the cities of Schlüchtern, Fulda, Hersfeld, Eisenach, Neudietendorf, and just south of the sprawling Buchenwald concentration camp.

From their rolling prison cells, the American prisoners could not see Buchenwald, one of the largest of all the notorious Nazi camps, hidden behind trees in the distance. It had been established in July 1937, on the Ettersberg Hill, outside of Weimar, and most of the early prisoners were persons Hitler's regime considered to be political opponents of the state—including homosexuals, Gypsies, and Jehovah's Witnesses. Once public persecution of the Jews became widespread after Kristallnacht, in November 1938, Buchenwald became home to 10,000 Jews who had been rounded up from across Germany.

At its height, just before the end of the war, more than 80,000 men, women, and children were incarcerated at Buchenwald. The starving and mistreated prisoners were forced to work in a nearby stone quarry, camp workshops, and a giant armaments factory. Periodically, prisoners too sick or weak to work were

Corpses piled outside the Buchenwald crematorium.
(Courtesy National Archives)

euthanized at killing centers set up at Bernburg and Sonnenstein, or were killed at Buchenwald, either in mass slaughters or as the result of inhuman medical experiments, their bodies incinerated in the camp's six oven *krematorium*, Even as the American POWs rolled past, the camp was being used as the final destination of evacuation transports from Auschwitz and Gross-Rosen.[23]

In addition to the main camp, the Buchenwald authorities also controlled over one hundred subcamps. One of those subcamps was located at Berga-an-der-Elster, some fifty miles to the southeast.[24]

And it was to Berga-an-der-Elster that Tony Acevedo, Morton Brooks, Gerald Daub, Norman Fellman, Peter Iosso, Joseph Mark, William Shapiro, and the 344 others from Bad Orb were heading.

8

BERGA

ORIGINALLY, THE AMERICAN prisoners thought that Berga would be just another dismal POW encampment—with conditions no better and no worse than they had already endured at Bad Orb. They soon discovered otherwise.

The train from Bad Orb arrived at the Berga *bahnhof*, located on a high embankment along August-Bebel-Strasse, on 13 February 1945. The unloading from the boxcars followed the familiar routine: orders being shouted in German by armed guards, the barking of dogs, the quick inspection of the foul cars to see if anyone inside was dead or feigning death, the usual roll call. The POWs then were herded at bayonet point down a ramp at the south end of the station and sent marching along the street. Almost directly across from the station was a large concentration camp that held a thousand gaunt European political prisoners—European Jews—dressed in the traditional blue-and-white striped uniforms.

To Norman Fellman, the faces of the political prisoners staring as the Americans trudged by burned themselves indelibly into his psyche. "There were these civilians packed in there with their striped pajama-type uniforms," he said. "They were packed against the fence—there must have been a thousand of them. They were deathly silent, not a sound out of them. Skinny human beings

The railroad station at Berga-an-der-Elster. (Author photo 2004)

The site of Berga One, the political prisoners' camp, across from the railroad station, as photographed in 2004. The original camp has been demolished; in its place stands a farm machinery manufacturing facility. (Author photo)

One of the barracks at camp Berga Two, circa 1945.
(Courtesy National Archives)

with huge eyes. Their eyes were the most dominating feature—just watching us in total silence. I will never forget it—the saddest eyes I've ever seen in my life."[1]

Gerald Daub, too, was haunted by the looks on the faces of the inmates in the camp Berga One: "I was really shocked; it was a place filled with all these political prisoners and they stared at us and we just marched by them."[2]

The Americans continued marching southward, out of town, toward the hamlet of Lula. The road steepened until, after about a kilometer, the group reached a small, barbed-wire enclosure made up of four or five wooden, tar-paper barracks—a hilltop camp unofficially called Berga Two. The bedraggled men were herded into the compound, given a burlap bag filled with straw to act as a mattress, and assigned to a barracks building.

At first, the prisoners were relieved to find that their new home had many features the old one at Bad Orb lacked. Peter Iosso thought the situation "seemed to be promising—a new compound situated on a hill in a rural area; six large rooms with the smell of freshly cut lumber, with new triple-decker beds and bedding; new eating utensils; a new outdoor sheltered latrine; water, even if transported in a big wheeled tank from town, for personal hygiene and laundry; tea in the morning; a thick potato soup at noon. That impression [of better conditions] did not last, however."[3]

Overcrowding quickly became the first problem. Morton Brooks recalled that there were two men per triple-decker bunk, "with maybe sixty people in the room that we were in. There were 350 of us in this compound—350 of us in five buildings."[4]

William Shapiro added, "None of us had the slightest clue as to what was in store for us."[5]

What was in store for the 350 American POWs at Berga was to augment the thousand political prisoners who were being used as slave laborers to dig a series of seventeen mine shafts or tunnels into the *Steinberg* (Stone Mountain) on the bank of the Elster River. None of the prisoners at the time knew why the tunnels were being dug, and so speculation was rife. Some prisoners thought the tunnels were going to be used as underground manufacturing facilities for various types of armaments.

Norman Fellman explained that the prisoners "were to dig into the mountain a certain distance—fifty meters or so—then open out laterally both sides and wind up with an underground facility, an underground factory. They had some of those already built and, although it was late in the war, and I'm sure the German generals knew that the war was lost, they were still building these places."[6]

Morton Brooks said that, for each POW, "the purpose for the tunnels was a matter of interest. We thought it was some kind of industrial project that they were trying to hide in the mountain. About fifteen years ago, I saw a documentary on TV about POWs. One of the fellows who was in our group was on the program—the producer had gotten him to go back to the site at Berga. I remember the hair rising on my body when I saw him talking at that spot. I inquired later on to see what he had learned and he told me that it was an atomic power plant. There were uranium mines nearby,* but I don't know if the Germans were really working on the bomb. I remember reading that one of the Germans' top physicists was not interested in fulfilling Hitler's wishes for an atomic bomb, but was interested in atomic power. Apparently, the plan I had heard something about may have been a heavy water facility, because the Allies had destroyed the one in Norway."[7]

In actuality, however, the tunnels were to be a bomb-proof oil-shale production facility. The mysterious project was code-named *SS-Führungstab Schwalbe V* (SS-Command Swallow Five) and overseen by two SS lieutenants named Hack and Heieck. The commandant of the two Berga camps that supplied the labor for the project was fifty-nine-year-old Ludwig Merz, a former schoolteacher from Haardt, near Neustadt in the Pfalz region; his right-hand-man initially was a sergeant by the name of Kunz.[8]

---

*Near Auw, about twenty kilometers north of Berga.

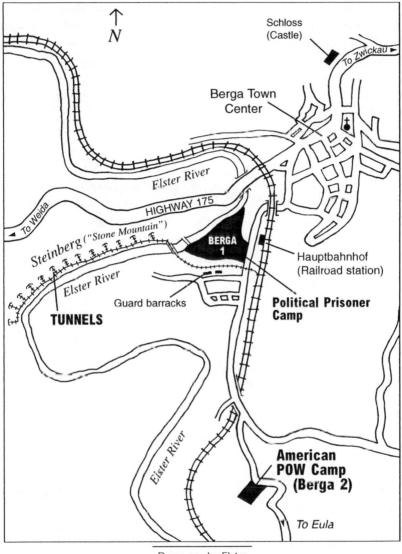

Berga-an-der-Elster.

William Shapiro remembered that, shortly after arrival, the POWs were assigned to their individual work details. "You were selected for a particular job by the Arbeitskommandoführer [Kunz]. My International Red Cross card identified me as a medic. It was the most important factor in the selection of my particular work detail, and it was the ultimate factor in my survival. There were nine medics in the group and we were assigned to the food detail and to remain in the barracks to attend the sick men. The remainder of our group were to become slave laborers, working in two twelve-hour shifts every day of the week for forty days straight. They worked in slave tunnels, not unlike numerous other tunnels in different sites in Germany where underground armament factories were being constructed."[9]

Peter Iosso sensed the Americans were in for a bad time the first day they were led to the tunnels. "They marched us through the town, where hostile people had gathered to spit at and curse us as we headed to the work site."[10]

To Gerald Daub, the thing that left the biggest impression on him were the political prisoners that the POWs joined at the worksite. "The morning after we got there, we were marched out of the barracks, over a bridge on a stream, divided into little groups of ten or twelve, and were dropped off at these seventeen tunnels. Our guards basically disappeared for the day; I guess they guarded the general area but not us or that tunnel in particular. There was one German miner foreman, whatever you want to call him, who was in charge of us, and we were totally his slaves. He could do anything to us that he wanted.

"I remember walking through the worksite and seeing these gangs of political prisoners, working and looking like they were starving and dying, which they were. They were falling and being beaten by their own foreman to get up to work again. It was my impression of Dante's *Inferno*, like my vision of hell—a totally hellish place. Apparently, we took over for people who had just worked so hard that they couldn't perform anymore."

Daub was picked to drill holes in the rock face of the tunnel. "The drill was very big; it had a bit that was six feet long. I'm not a tremendously big guy, by the way. The thing would vibrate. I mean, I could even feel the thing vibrating even after I was done drilling. I worked with the foreman and I would hold the pneumatic drill up to the face of the rock wall and he would point out where I should put the drill.

"That first day, we worked one twelve-hour shift, and that shift was all American GIs. The political prisoners took over for the next shift, and we were marched back to the barracks. We all got back to the barracks that night or morning, whatever it was, and grumbled about the fact that this wasn't a very appropriate place for soldiers to be working, that it was hazardous work, and it was not healthy, and it was dangerous besides, and that we shouldn't be there.

The worksite at Berga. The Elster River is on the left; note the bridge over the river leading to camp Berga One. The tunnel entrances are not visible among the trees; the wooden structures held explosives for blasting. Photo taken after U.S. Army units secured the area in April 1945. (Courtesy National Archives)

A lot of people complained about it to Hans Kasten, our 'Man of Confidence,' who then complained to the commandant. As I recall, we said we were not going to go to work the next day; it was obviously a big threat."[11]

Peter Iosso remembered the short-lived prisoners' revolt: "The next day when they came to take us to work, we refused to go outside and protested that the work violated the Geneva Conventions. The German guards with bayoneted rifles entered and rousted us out, kicking and hitting many with the butts of their rifles—the first of many occasions they did this to make us move faster."[12]

Daub added, "The guards open the barracks doors and they're outside with these vicious German shepherd dogs. I think that Kasten got the impression that they were going to sic the dogs on him. We were all threatened that if we didn't get out of the barracks and get to work, the dogs would be turned on the barracks. So we all got out and marched off to work and really didn't give them any trouble after that. I mean, we went to work every day."[13]

Kommandoführer
Erwin Metz,
photographed in
1946. (Courtesy
National Archives)

In early March, three prisoners—including the "Man of Confidence" Hans
Kasten—escaped; Arbeitskommandoführer Kunz was sacked and in his place
came a brutal, sadistic World War I veteran named Erwin Metz.[14]

Metz, fifty-two, had been a bank clerk in Stuttgart before being drafted into
the Wehrmacht in January 1944. As a sergeant in Landeschützen (Home Guard)
Battalion 621, Metz had come to Berga to be in charge of work details performed by the political prisoners. When Kunz was relieved of his duties, Metz
moved "up the hill."[15]

Medic William Shapiro recalled that Metz, who would become every
POW's nemesis, "was a middle-aged man, not an SS trooper, who somehow

avoided being in the Wehrmacht or fighting on the Russian front. He was in the National Guard. "He was a heavy-set man in his late forties or early fifties, wore glasses, had a pointed nose, about six feet tall, and weighed about 200 pounds. He had a distinctive voice that you knew who was talking when you heard it. I have heard that other POWs described it as a 'Donald Duck' voice."[16]

Another POW said that Metz had a habit of always ending a sentence with "*Nicht wahr?*" ("Isn't that true?")[17]

Shapiro continued, "Unquestionably, in Berga and on the 'death march' later, Metz's cruel, indifferent, oppressive, and deliberate actions caused the deaths of many of the POWs and added to our indescribable sufferings. . . . We were the *Untermensch*—slaves, undesirable humans with whom he could do as he pleased without regard to any sense of humanity."[18]

Putting prisoners to work was nothing new for the Nazis. POWs from other camps across Germany were sent to work in rock quarries, steel mills, and military supply depots, or worked at hauling military equipment, building roadblocks and fortifications, repairing railroad tracks and bomb damage in cities, picking up unexploded American bombs and artillery shells, and digging graves.[19]

The inhuman treatment at Berga never ceased. William Shapiro witnessed a number of lynchings while on the daily ration details to the political prisoner compound at Berga One; "I saw many hangings in the courtyard not far from the entrance gate, near our kitchen waiting area. At different times, as we waited [to pick up] our rations, I saw two, three, or four persons . . . hanging from ropes from a broad beam supported at each end by angled beams of wood. It was there! In front of us! Out in the open! . . . We came to accept this as part of [Berga One's] physical appearance.

"I had no idea of the why, what, or who of these public hangings. But every time that I saw a hanging, I was frightened, lost, felt defenseless, and intimidated. I looked away, kept very close to myself and tried to prevent making any slight movement or expression which would involve me with this scene. I saw, but I did not want to know. I did not want any of the SS troopers to notice my observation of the hangings. All of us observed, made no comment to each other, and remained silent. I just wanted to get out of there without being part of the horrible scene. When there were hangings, it appeared that we all had a sense of relief when we started pushing our wagon back up the hill. . . . Even our guards failed to make any comments nor [did they engage] the SS troopers in conversation. They accompanied us through the gate, remained silent, and observed these events as if this was not their business—a common response of not becoming involved in order to protect yourself."[20]

One of the "political prisoners" at Berga One was a twenty-two-year-old German Jew from Mannheim named Ernest Michel. He had been arrested by the Gestapo in September 1939, shortly after Germany's invasion of Poland. His only crime: being Jewish. Separated from his parents, he somehow managed to avoid the fate of millions of other Jews and stayed alive for over five years despite being interned in concentration camps, slave-labor camps, and extermination camps, including Auschwitz.

Michel recalled that Auschwitz was evacuated in January 1945 as the Russians were closing in on the death factory. "There were 60,000 people that were left there," he said, "and half of them died in the cold and freezing weather in January 1945; we eventually wound up in Buchenwald in late January 1945. In late February or early March, I was sent to Berga with two other friends of mine, Honzo Munk from Prague and Felix Schwartz from Vienna. We were there because we were Jewish. There were about 2,000 prisoners in my camp and, as far as I recall, almost all were Jewish. The largest number of Jews came from eastern Europe. Polish, Romanian, Czechoslovakian, Hungarian, et cetera. German Jews were in the minority.

"After we began to work in the tunnels, we learned that there were American-Jewish POWs who were in a separate camp. I remember the situation in the camp itself was pretty horrific. Food was very minimal. I had typhoid fever, and we had lice all over our bodies, so it was pretty terrible. There were no gas chambers in Berga, but there were other killings. There were quite a few people who died."[21]

The dangerous, debilitating, unrelenting work in the tunnels went on twelve hours a day, day after day, week after week, without so much as a food or water break. The prisoners—both American and political—were forced to work with no protective clothing or equipment of any kind; the GIs labored in the uniforms in which they had been captured. There were no helmets, safety shoes, gloves, or dust masks; injuries were commonplace. Hungry, thirsty, slate-dust-covered men operated like automatons, barely thinking, barely reacting to the blows from the foremen who harangued them and beat them with rubber truncheons when they felt they weren't working fast enough, or who suspected that the slaves were deliberately sabotaging the project.

Morton Brooks recalled, "Our work shifts were at least ten or twelve hours every day. I was amazed at how quickly our energies were drained and, of course, there was the combination of the dysentery, which I guess almost all of us experienced, and the limited food that we were getting. It was estimated we got only around four to six hundred calories a day. And the work—you're in there drilling and shoveling and pushing the carts out, and sometimes there were accidents.

"In the shaft that I was in, there was a civilian overseer who was particularly brutal; he had a sadistic streak. He carried a rubber hose and a pick-ax handle, and he never hesitated to use them on anybody he thought wasn't working hard enough. We weren't interested in being very helpful to them and we didn't work as rapidly and as hard as they wanted us to, so I was often beaten across the back and the neck; some people got it even worse."[22]

Norman Fellman recalled that the POWs' twelve-hour workday. "Some guys started at noon and worked through, and some guys started at midnight and worked through. It was around the clock. We would drill holes in the back of the rock, in the face of the wall in the tunnel, with these big, pneumatic drills. They would drill fifteen or twenty holes at a time, maybe more. Some of the guys remember them having dynamite, but where we were we only had gunpowder, and some of our people made the gunpowder 'sausages.' They put eighteen or twenty of those in the holes, and then they would run fuses to all of the holes. We would all get out of the tunnel and they would blast. Before the dust had settled, before the noise had stopped echoing, we were forced back into the tunnels. Nobody had protective gear of any kind. You'd breathe that air; you'd breathe that shit."[23]

Gerald Daub noted, "The air was just totally filled with stone dust. Everything coated with it, including your lungs filled with it. And we had no bathing facilities, so you can picture that, after a day or two, we just looked like cement statues walking around."[24]

Not everyone worked in the tunnel shafts. Morton Brooks recalled that "Some got assigned to details like hauling lumber or railroad tracks, things like that. I was in the mine on a pneumatic drill, drilling holes into the rock wall. Then the German explosives expert would come in and set the charges and they would blast it. Then we'd shovel the rock into the mining cars and dump it into the river."[25]

In 1950, Tony Acevedo sketched his memory of German brutality while prisoners were on a work detail carrying a rail at Berga. (Courtesy Tony Acevedo)

Norman Fellman's job was to load the broken rock into open mining gondola cars. "Once they were loaded, we would push them out to the river's edge. We would flip a lever on the side and the gondola's body itself would roll and dump the rock along the river's edge. Sometime in the morning or early evening, the Germans would come and spray paint the rock so that it wouldn't look new or fresh from the air; we were constantly overflown by the Allied air forces. By then, the German air force was nothing, and we were being overflown by our bombers, sometimes continuously. At night, when our bombers were going over, the Germans draped tarps over the face of the tunnels to hide the light and we would work right through."[26]

Even when the long workday ended, the harassment did not. William Shapiro observed, "The return to the barracks was often marred by indifference and uncaring, long waiting periods until our guards arrived to march us back to the barracks and our bunks. Even after this torture, there was a further delay of the much-deserved rest because they had to stand in line for the evening count

American soldiers
who came upon
Berga in April 1945
inspect one of
the tunnels.
(Courtesy
National Archives)

of the prisoners. These repetitive, disruptive, inane counts increased our suffering. . . . Outside the barracks was a field, called the *Appellplatz,* on which we would line up to be counted by tens. We would stand in the cold, freezing weather for countless hours. Endless and repeated counts were often used as a form of punishment for contrived infractions of the so-called rules or as opportunities for [Metz] to harangue us. A common, torturous act was to be forced to stand outside of the barracks in the damp, windy, and bitter cold weather after a workshift in the tunnels in order to be counted again and again before receiving the night's food rations.

"Finally, the rations of a bowl of rotted potato or turnip-top green soup and a slice of hard, grainy, black bread was the meager 'reward.'" Shapiro called the luke-warm liquid the "Universal Political Prisoner Soup."[27]

The strenuous work, starvation rations, cold and damp weather, and body lice all conspired to ravage the prisoners' health and strength. Already thin and weak from their previous incarceration at Stalag IX-B, the GIs at Berga were reduced to near-skeletons. "Our diet was anywhere from a seventh to a tenth of a loaf of bread a day," recalled Norman Fellman, "depending on the size of the loaf, and two cups—one in the morning and one at night—of a greasy liquid that sometimes had something floating in it and sometimes it didn't. That was our diet, and it began to take a toll on us."[28]

Tony Acevedo added, "Customarily, they would give us a hundred grams of bread per week, if it was available. And that bread was usually made out of sawdust, ground glass, ground sand, and camouflaged with barley. We got some watery soup sometimes. They would tell us it was flavored with extract of cooked rat or cat."[29]

Peter Iosso remembered a nightly routine. "Bread distribution and eating became rituals that lasted two hours; you would try to make that tiny piece of bread last as long as possible. Then, after an hour's sleep, we would wake up scratching our lice bites and remove our clothing to crush the nits in the seams so that they wouldn't be disturbing us during the night. Some people developed pretty bad sores from scratching their bites. Some of them, I think, lost their lives to disease that came from those infections. Then, at six A.M., they had us out for differing counts and gave us tea of some kind, which at least was warm."[30]

For years, Tony Acevedo had nightmares about the terrible conditions: "White lice. Oh my God, I'll never forget it. I can still feel them running up my back, my hair. We tried to shave our faces with glass. We tried using broken glass to shave as much hair as we could off of our faces to prevent the lice. We didn't have any soap or water. We could get nothing. We were never provided with soap at all."[31]

It didn't take long for the POWs to begin dying. The first officially recorded death was that of George "Buck" Rogers, a former University of Colorado English professor and a private first class in Company L, 423rd Regiment, 106th Division. According to one account, Rogers was seriously ill with pneumonia and requested that he be excused from work in the tunnels. Enraged, Metz pulled Rogers out of his bunk, hit him several times until he passed out, then threw a bucket of cold water on him; Rogers died within an hour.[32]

Medic William Shapiro described the POWs' worsening health conditions: "After being in Berga for about two weeks, the men had numerous diseases such as dysentery, dehydration, advanced emaciation, large ulcers on feet and hands, leg edema, pneumonia, and probably tuberculosis. Many times we were not sure

Interior of a lice-ridden barracks at Berga Two. The burlap bags stuffed with straw served as mattresses for the prisoners. (Courtesy National Archives)

of the diagnosis, but we certainly knew when someone was close to death. . . . Impending death was all around me."

Shapiro also recalled one prisoner's unusual suicide. Shapiro had treated a large ulcer on the man's foot with sulfa powder, but gangrene had already set in. "This was a self-inflicted, desperate act of creating a wound with a rock so he would not have to return to the tunnels," Shapiro said. "He was so despaired, resigned, and he gave up. In effect, he killed himself."[33]

Pleasures at Berga were nonexistent. About the only pastime in the barracks, while waiting for sleep to come, was talking about favorite foods, exchanging verbal recipes, and discussing which particular food a prisoner would have for his first meal when he got back home. Then the prisoners drifted off to sleep. Some recall that, from different parts of the barracks, intermingled with the moans and hacking coughs and nightmare shrieks, came the soft sounds of crying.

"Most men had slate dust in their lungs," remembered William Shapiro, "and were forcing up globs of mucus in order to breathe. This cacophony of coughing sounds would continue for hours. Intermittently, there would be sudden, very hurried sounds of someone jumping off the bunk, racing to the latrine to prevent the explosive diarrhea from covering himself or his clothes."[34]

There was one more sound: The deep, gurgling rumble of hundreds of stomachs that weren't getting enough to eat. It sounded like men being strangled.

No matter how badly the Americans were treated, the political prisoners down the hill at Berga One were treated even worse. As William Shapiro on the ration detail observed, "My food detail of eight men, who assembled every morning about 4:00 A.M., picked up the two guards who accompanied us on our walk down the hill to [Berga One]. At that time of year, it was very dark, cold, damp, and often the blowing winds of February and March made our trek on snow, ice, or slush very treacherous and difficult. I was miserably cold and unbelievably uncomfortable, suffering in silence, but not a whisper of complaint because I knew the alternative. . . .

"When we arrived at [Berga One], the large entrance gate would be opened by *Capos* [prisoners detailed to work as police] or special privileged political prisoners. At the time, I had no knowledge about certain categories of prisoners but I saw that there was a difference in the behavior and the so-called authority of certain prisoners. They were dressed differently and looked better fed. . . . On the inner aspect of the front gate were SS troopers in black uniforms with the *Totenkopf* [Death's Head] insignia on their lapels. They had large German shepherd dogs on leashes at their side. It was a frightening sight every time we entered the camp.

"We would push our wagon to a kitchen area on the left, just inside the gate. We would stand there and wait until our Marmite cans were filled by young boys wearing the blue/black and white striped pajamas of the political prisoners. I did not know at the time, but I know now that most of them were Jews. They all wore hats and would remove them prior to bowing, then stand at attention before addressing an SS trooper or Capo. They scurried around quickly and looked very busy to complete the job of filling the food containers. It was as if they feared being struck by the closely observing Capos or SS guards. The Capos had batons, as did SS troopers who were not carrying rifles."[35]

Morton Brooks noted that the Americans only mingled with the political prisoners at the worksite latrine. "If you had to use the latrine, sometimes they would let you go and you would have the opportunity to talk to them. They had a terrific grapevine; you could learn what was happening in the outer world. It was a very mixed group—Polish, Russian, you name it. I remember someone—I think he was an Englishman who was captured in France—who was there. I know that we weren't sure who we could trust. You never knew when someone was a 'plant' by the Germans, so you had to watch what you said."[36]

With men dying daily from disease, infection, and worksite accidents, the thought of being killed while escaping evoked little fear in many of the POWs. The brutal conditions and omnipresence of death naturally caused every GI to think about escape—and for some to actually attempt it. Those who escaped and were recaptured faced retribution upon their return; one POW recalled escapees being forced to stand outside the barracks at night and then sent off to work a twelve-hour shift in the tunnels without food or sleep.[37]

"A few men tried to escape from the worksite," recalled Peter Iosso, "only to be captured and returned to the camp on display with bullet holes in their temples as an example to the rest of us."[38]

One such was a prisoner named Morton Goldstein. On 20 March, Goldstein, a member of the POW food detail, had slipped away while going down the hill to Berga One to pick up breakfast, but had been captured in a nearby town. Kommandoführer Metz had gone to retrieve Goldstein, but Goldstein made a run for it and Metz shot him in the back. His body was left to decompose outside his barracks for three days as a warning to others of the consequences of escape.[39]

"There were some fellows who tried to escape," said Morton Brooks, who also recalled them being brought back. "A few of them were dead; those who were not killed got the job of cleaning out the latrine. I wasn't involved in any of the escape attempts. I didn't have the feeling that an escape would be successful. You're surrounded by Germans in an area that you're not familiar with; I didn't see that escape was possible."[40]

Norman Fellman noted that, at the beginning, he and others had made plans for escape. "The guys that I was with were able to put together bits and pieces of food to give to those guys to help them sustain them, at least so they could do it."[41]

"Most of the men who escaped were brought back," recalled Gerald Daub, "and usually they were treated a little worse than everybody else. They got another assignment, like cleaning the latrine or something like that. When Kasten and [Joseph] Littell escaped, which was early on, they didn't come back, and we were hopeful that they got away. But the people who escaped really made it a lot harder on the people who stayed behind. When someone escaped, and before we were allowed to have dinner and go to bed, we had to be counted. The Germans always pretended that they just couldn't believe that the count was not right, and so they would just count and recount—remember it was very cold and we were very hungry and very thin—so that was, in a sense, a form of torture, just to stand out there to be counted interminably for hours.

"In the film,* Kasten said they crawled under the wire; they would have had to crawl under two sets of wire, as I recall it. He said that they were just lucky at the time they escaped that there was an air raid going on. In Joseph Littell's book, he said they went into a German tavern to get food, and a German officer walked up to them and asked them for their papers. Of course, they didn't have any, and were arrested."[42]

Morton Brooks remembered, "You would try to get through every day. It was like routine. When you got up, you were taken outside, lined up, and identified yourself by number. They checked off the prisoners and they marched us down to the mines. If anybody said that they couldn't go, that they weren't feeling well, Metz said he was a doctor and he would make the determination. There was no hospital at the camp; we had a few medics who did what they could—they might have had some medication that hadn't been taken away, but I don't think that they had very much. On occasion, some sick people were taken down to a medical facility in the town, but not many. I remember a fellow prisoner [probably David Young] dropping to the ground, and he got a pail of water thrown in his face, but he didn't get up, so they carried him back into the barracks. The medics took care of him as well as they could."[43]**

Stanley Cohen, the Acting Man of Confidence after Kasten's escape, recalled that, early one morning, he was informed by Young's barracks leader that Young had been delirious the night before. Cohen told Metz that Young was in no condition to go to work that day, but Metz ordered two POWs to hold Young up while he threw a bucket of cold water in his face. "Young flickered his eyelashes and gave no other indication of his consciousness," Cohen reported. "[Metz]

---

*The 2003 PBS documentary *Berga: Soldiers of a Different War.*

**According to testimony at the post-war trial of Erwin Metz, this incident occurred on 19 March 1945.

bent down and touched Young's head. He said, 'It is warm. You can let him stay in today.' He said to leave him on the floor until he regained consciousness and then help him back to bed. I left a medic, Tony [Acevedo], and returned to my bed. Ten minutes later, Tony came and reported Young's death."

Cohen also described the beatings that were often administered by the German mine supervisors, specifically one that led to the death of fellow-inmate Jerry Cantor: "Cantor was a very slow-thinking, methodical person, and his death was indirectly caused by beatings received while at work—beatings instigated at the hands of the foremen. The men in the tunnels were afraid of these foremen." A tall, heavy-set foreman named Reifling "started the system of hitting men with a rubber hose so as to leave no marks and still convince them to work a trifle faster. Cantor was very slow and came back beaten up day after day. In an attempt to work faster, he scratched himself in innumerable places with rocks and stones in the mine. His scratches became infected. He was not permitted to refrain from going to work until his arm was so swollen as to make work impossible. The official cause of death was blood poisoning."[44]

As the terrible conditions at Berga took their toll, many of the POWs turned inward, just trying to stay alive, and cut off contact with their buddies and fellow prisoners. Medic William Shapiro noted that there was very little interactive talk among the POWs and that "The men were all consumed in caring for themselves. They were half-starved, exhausted, had different types of wounds, illnesses, and pains which involved them with their respective misery. They sat or lay on their bunks tending to their own needs. There was cold water for washing, but many men were not interested in washing at any time. They appeared totally detached from their surroundings, did not talk to others, and functioned in isolation. . . . Food would activate them into a frenzy, but after the distribution of the food, they would go off, climb onto their bunks, and disassociate themselves from the other men. . . . I would learn the beginning signs of the 'giving up' syndrome—the desire for peace and death."[45]

As a medic, Tony Acevedo also tried to save his fellow prisoners, but often without success. "Some of the fellas died in my arms," he said. "I tried to feed them but they wouldn't eat. All I had was my prayer book and my faith and the will to live."[46]

9

THE END OF HOPE

WITH ESCAPE OUT of the question, it wasn't long before some of the prisoners began fighting back in the only way they could: sabotage.

Gerald Daub quickly discovered how to slow down the tunneling operation: "I would try to break the bit of my big, pneumatic drill, because that would stop the operation for a time while the foreman got another drill bit. If he thought I was doing that on purpose, he'd get angry and poke me."'

Norman Fellman discovered another way to hamper the operation: "We found that, after we loaded the gondolas, if all of the heavy rock in these gondolas was on the side nearest the river and all the light stuff were opposite, when we flipped the lever, the centrifugal force would carry the whole gondola off the track, over the edge, and into the water. That would slow the work down and the Germans would go nuts—screaming and hollering—and everyone in sight would get a beating with rubber hoses and rifle butts to the head. I heard a guard say that the trouble started when the Americans arrived, because they had never had that problem before. We were 'screw-ups.'"

Another way to sabotage the project was to manufacture defective explosive charges. Fellman said, "They had prisoners make these gunpowder sausages. That was stupid, because somehow every tenth or twelfth one would have some glob of mud or some dirt mixed up with it; the explosions would never go off evenly and the Germans would go nuts. This was our only way of fighting back."[2]

The guards at Berga were not uniformly cruel, and a few, once in a while, even displayed a slight touch of humanity. "The officers and the non-commissioned officers were SS," noted Fellman. "The actual guards, many of them were Volksturm—the 'peoples' army.' They were older men, and every one of them had had a relative who had been killed in action. They had been told it was done by Americans shooting up hospitals, or bombing hospitals, and so on. In other words, they were convinced that we were committing atrocities."

On occasion, however, Fellman encountered guards who would sneak him an extra bit of food. "But if another guard came around and saw him, the same guy that was offering me the food would start beating the hell out of me. They themselves were scared to death of the SS guards. I don't believe that they had a hell of a lot more to eat than we did. Their food might have been a little bit cleaner, but they weren't very well fed, either. Yeah, there was some humanity if you got one of them alone by himself, but two together—they would be afraid that one would squeal on the other and you caught holy hell."[3]

Gerald Daub, on the other hand, could not recall any moments of kindness by the guards. "The friendliest they were, was just to talk to you just before they dropped us off at the mine. Once in a while, a guard might ask where you were from and what was going on in the world. That was it."[4]

Eventually, the brutal physical and mental beatings each prisoner absorbed began to wear away at the men. According to Norman Fellman, "We had what you might call an 'education in progress'—not a formal education but a practical education in psychology, in a way. Your first intention when you got to Berga was to survive the week. After you've been there a little longer, you began to just try and survive the next day. Toward the end, your only goal was to survive the next hour.

"You could—and this is something that haunts the survivors to this day— you could be talking to someone during the morning and that guy would die sometime during the day. They would stack his body like firewood right where the chow line was, and you could walk by it, and not be moved and not even look at it; it could have been pieces of wood, not human beings. The only thing that mattered was to live another hour."

Somebody once asked Fellman if he ever reached a point where he thought he was ready to die. "I can tell you as a fact that anyone who ever had that thought died. It never occurred to me that I wouldn't make it home. It just never occurred. It just wasn't an option."[5]

The daily psychological devastation was compounded by the physical—the beatings; the scarcity of food; the lack of water; the choking dust of the tunnels; the thousands of lice that inhabited each prisoner's body; the raging dysentery that sapped each man of strength; the long walk to and from the worksite every day; the colds and bronchitis brought on by the cold, damp, dusty conditions; the sense of isolation and abandonment that came from being cut off from loved ones and the rest of the world.

At night, when the prisoners staggered back into camp after twelve hours of hard labor, there was another problem to be faced: the assault on the olfactory organs. The stench in the barracks was overpowering—sweat-soaked wool uniforms; bodies that had gone unwashed for months; rotting, unbrushed teeth; festering wounds; clothing impregnated with urine and feces. No one who was there has ever forgotten the smell.

Apparently, very few outsiders knew of the existence of Berga. Only once did a representative from the International Red Cross visit the camp—but without doing anything to make the POWs' lives better. William Shapiro carried bitter memories of that visit: "I recall speaking to the International Red Cross representative on the one time that he visited our camp on the hill. I asked for some paregoric, which I knew was used in the treatment of diarrhea. I can still visualize this tall man in a military uniform, walking into our barracks, looking about superficially, and indifferent to my request. I have often spoken of this episode when I returned home. It was my feeling that he was a Nazi sympathizer. Obviously, at that time, and until the recent disclosures of the nefarious relationship between the Swiss and Germans in World War II, the truth was not known to me. I now know that my feelings at that time may have been correct. We did not receive anything through the International Red Cross and, to this day, I continue to harbor undiminished animosity for the IRC and the Swiss."[6]

The soldiers' families back home may have received word that their loved ones had been captured, or were missing, but the prisoners, thrown into the hell-hole of Berga had, for all intents and purposes, vanished from the face of the earth. Although many wives and fathers and mothers still clung to hope that their husbands or sons might be alive, the grim truth remained that many had been given up for dead.

Joseph Mark said quietly, "It was tough on our families back home."[7]

Dan Goldin, after his rescue, April 1945. (Courtesy National Archives)

To stay alive—and sane—many of the prisoners supported each other, each encouraging the other to make it through another hour, another day. Norman Fellman found strength in the friendship of a fellow captive named Dan Goldin, who had been a grocer in Richmond, Virginia, before the war. "He was an older fellow. I say older; he must have been in his twenties. He was married. I don't know how he got into the service, because he had one or two children. He was like a father figure to me. I remember him that way. We bunked together. He would talk to me and try to keep me straight. I believe that if it wasn't for him, I don't think I would have gotten through it. I was at my end a number of times. I remember him talking to me. I don't remember his words or what we said; I just remember him talking to me. He kept me going."

At one point, however, Fellman almost gave up hope. "All of us had dysentery. In the camp outside our barracks, they had like a vat—a big, round, low-cut barrel—that we used for a latrine. I remember sitting over that thing, so bloated that I thought my stomach was going to explode. Metz came by and he ordered me to go inside into the barracks. I told him, '*Nein*,' that I wasn't finished. He pulled out his Luger and he put it to my head and he cocked it and he told me again to go in. I told him, 'Go ahead and shoot, you son of a bitch; I'm not moving.' I didn't care. I really did not care whether he shot me or not. The normal reaction if someone puts a gun to your head is, something is wrong with you if you're not terrorized. But I just did not care. He put his gun in his holster and walked away. He didn't do anything—go figure. It gave me a little sense of triumph."[8]

Norman Martin, a POW from the Bronx, testified about the escape of one prisoner: "Private Israel Cohen was a soldier who was with me in the work camp at Berga; we were working building an underground factory in the side of a mountain. On or about the 28th of March 1945, Private Cohen made an attempt to escape from Berga. He was apprehended and brought back to the camp. When he was brought back, he was severely beaten. He was first struck and knocked to the ground, and then he was continually kicked in all parts of his body until he was unconscious. He was in very bad physical condition after this beating." Martin reported the person who carried out the beating was Metz.[9]

With little to lose except their lives, which many of the prisoners now regarded as worthless, escape plans began to be formulated in earnest. The men studied the barbed wire; wondered how long it would take to cut through the multiple strands; calculated how long it might take to dig a tunnel from one of the barracks under the wire to freedom outside—or if anyone even had the strength for such a mammoth undertaking. The prisoners furtively glanced up at the guard towers to see if the guards established any sort of pattern to their scanning of the compound, and tried to calculate how long the floodlights that illuminated the compound would be turned off when Allied air raids flew overhead and hit cities nearby.

Despite the overwhelming odds against it, some prisoners did manage to get away, even if only briefly. Joe Mark described his escape attempt: "At some point in March, I realized that Berga was a death camp—our guys were dying every day from overwork and starvation rations. I myself weighed about eighty-five pounds then, down from one-thirty-five." He recalled that Hans Kasten and Joseph Littell had earlier escaped from Berga. "But one or two were later caught and 'shot while escaping,' and their bodies were brought back to impress us with the dire consequences of trying to escape.

"Nevertheless, conditions were so reprehensible that it was a question of whether you died obediently in the Berga work camp, or whether you might be shot and killed escaping. It seemed no greater risk to try and break out and get away. It was unwise and courting disaster to openly oppose the Germans, but I would literally spit with determination not to buckle under their heartless and savage treatment and die like a dog without offering at least some token resistance.

"There was a fellow American that I remember as 'Kaplan.' He was a responsible and intelligent man who was a history teacher from Boston. He and I began to hatch a plan for escape. On the appointed morning, I awoke all excited and primed for the great escape. As luck would have it, Kaplan came down with dysentery, a rather too-frequent ailment among us Kriegies, and he was too sick to go. It never occurred to me to go alone, and so I was terribly disappointed."

Other prisoners had known of the plan and, once Mark was at work in the tunnel, two GIs, Charles Morabido and another whose last name was Bokanic, approached him and said they also had a plan, and would he like to join them? "I knew that these two were 'bad medicine.' They had made a previous escape attempt that had failed because it was poorly planned and executed. The fact was that they were escaping only to find food. They were, I must say, even though they were fellow Americans, two rather irresponsible characters. But I was so eager to go that I fell in with them."

Mark and his co-conspirators began secretly assembling a pitiful escape kit: a map from a small address book, a few matches, and some extra pieces of bread.

"From our crummy little map," Mark noted, "we knew we were somewhere between Dresden and Leipzig. The Americans were too far away, and so were the Russians."

They decided their best option was to head southeast, toward Czechoslovakia, where they hoped to find some friendly Czechs willing to hide them. "The secondary plan was to make enough distance between us and the Berga camp and to come under some other POW camp's jurisdiction," Mark said. "Any other POW camp had to be better than Berga.

"Our plan was to pretend that we were on a work detail and march out of the tunnel area past the guards. Only sheer desperation would lead me to buy into such a lousy escape plan. I grabbed a wheelbarrow to make it look good, and we started making our way out."

An elderly guard, who had been, according to Mark, "an unusually nice guy," was on duty at the worksite. When he stopped the trio, Mark waved at him and said, *"Holz tragen,"* meaning they were on a detail to get firewood. "He could have shot us—and another guard perhaps would have—not that I cared particularly if he did. But he didn't shoot—miracle of miracles—and we walked right the hell out of that miserable death trap. So this idiotic plan proposed by two devil-may-care soldiers—with the help of a little acting on my part and a kindly, old guard—worked!"

The trio hid until dark in a nearby woods and heard the Germans conducting roll call. Once the guards became agitated about the numbers not being correct, they took off. Mark told his companions about his plan to head for Czechoslovakia, and they agreed—as long as they could get some food along the way. He and Kaplan, his original escape partner, never thought of foraging for food. "But that's all that my fellow escapees had on their minds. They had no resolute desire to escape— only to eat."

The group soon came to a farmhouse. The farm must have been visited by previous escapees, for in front hung a sign which, when translated, meant "Whoever plunders gets shot." The sign did not deter Bokanic and Morabido in their quest for food. Entering the walled courtyard, the three men found a door that led to a storeroom with barrels filled with potatoes. Mark and Bokanic filled their pockets; Morabido had disappeared.

"I asked Bokanic where Morabido was and he said that Morabido went to milk a cow. Believe it! Soon, we heard the noise of cows mooing, then lights went on in the farmhouse. A farmer with a lantern came into the storeroom to

look around. Bokanic and I were crouching low in a corner behind some barrels. I held my breath, and soon the long shadows cast by the lantern spread out
and the farmer left."

Once the coast was clear, Mark and Bokanic dashed from the storeroom, out
the gate, and ran for cover to wait for Morabido. Five minutes passed and then a
shot rang out from the direction of the farm. "We surmised the worst—Morabido was caught, shot, and killed. We took off and found an abandoned sort of
[railroad] line shack, about the size of a large privy. We had to get indoors to
make a fire at night and not be seen while baking our potatoes, which we did.
My matches enabled us to make this fire, and we baked the potatoes all night
and ate every one of them. We were literally starved, so it was an easy feasting. I
still have a fondness for potatoes."

The two remained in the shack until the next evening, as it was dangerous to
travel by day. Mark noted the setting sun and the position of the north star so he
could navigate in the dark. "We walked most of the night, sometimes on a de-
serted road, sometimes through fields, but generally south. No food except for
some oats that we got somewhere. Another day passed in the woods, and that
night Bokanic spied a pile of potatoes buried under a pile of earth. I knew it was
a stupid move to go near that pile, as it was out in an open field with some
houses nearby. But my hunger overcame my better judgment, and Bokanic had
no sense of caution at all.

"Well, that's where we got caught. After approaching the pile of potatoes and
before we could dig any, I noticed a ring of Germans approaching us on all
sides. They were coming slowly in a crouch with arms outstretched. We should
have run for it, as none of them had a gun, but I couldn't make that out at night.
As it was, I almost got us loose. I told them that we were French volunteers laborers—'*Je suis un Français, et mon ami aussi, je travaille à* . . . (some nearby
town).' They almost believed me, but as we began to walk away they saw, even in
the dark, the big 'K' for Kriegsgefangener painted on the back of my coat, and
that did it."

The civilians marched Mark and Bokanic into town and lined them up
against a stone wall. "I knew enough German to overhear their plan for shooting us 'while escaping.' The strange thing about my impending end was that I
didn't give a damn. We had been in such rotten straits for so long that it didn't
much matter anymore whether I was dead or alive. So there I was, cracking

some oat hulls from my pockets and eating oats. Dying was of no great consequence, but being hungry was."

One of the elderly Germans who had captured him came up to Mark to see what he was eating. When Mark showed him, the farmer expressed his belief that oats were only fit for feeding to swine. "I replied in German that we weren't fed as well as swine. He didn't answer. In the meantime, the *burgermeister* [mayor] showed up and talked them out of shooting us, insisting that we be returned to—guess where—Berga! So we hadn't managed to get out of Berga's control. After three days, we were recaptured, and our escape was for naught."

The Germans loaded the two Americans into a truck with a nervous old German guarding them. "He had a rifle that he kept cocked, and the road was very bumpy. He was one of those that would have shot us when we were lined up against the wall in the village, and he would have still liked to finish us off. He couldn't quite make up his mind; being German, he had a natural tendency to follow the order to deliver us to Berga alive—and he finally did."

The two escapees were returned to their captors. There, lying under a blanket at the base of a wall of one of the camp buildings, was Morabido's lifeless body, a bullet hole in his chest.

Mark realized that he and Bokanic were in big trouble if their escape was tied to Morabido's "plundering" at the farm, and he explained the predicament to Bokanic A German noncom "badgered Bokanic about knowing and escaping with Morabido. Bokanic had a bad reputation with them because of the previous escape attempt. The soldier drew out a handgun and held it to Bokanic's head and said, 'Admit that you escaped with him.' Bokanic looked at me, and I stared right back at him—and then he flatly denied escaping with Morabido. It was a tense moment, and I must give Bokanic credit for not buckling, although there was no other way out. The German put his gun away."

Mark and Bokanic were removed from the camp and taken away by train to Greiz to be court-martialed. "A German colonel, through an interpreter, asked us about how we escaped and where we were going. I lied all the way. What really got to the colonel was when I said that our plan was to go east to join our Russian allies. I understood enough of his German to know that he called us all kinds of names, that the Russians would tear our tongues out, and so on. The translator gave a much milder version of the colonel's remarks. These Germans were really scared of the Russians.

"Our escape ended ingloriously. The court-martial verdict was to put us on bread and water, and every morning we had to carry the 'honey buckets' out into a field to empty them. Since our ration was only bread anyway, it was no big deal. They couldn't punish us by taking much away, because they didn't give us much to begin with."[10]

———

The American prisoners, wracked by hunger, thirst, and disease, continued to die. The stronger soldiers did what little they could to keep their fellow prisoners alive, but it often wasn't enough. It often took two buddies to keep up each other's spirits. Gerald Daub recalled that he and Bob Rudnick did their best to keep each other going. "You could just see somebody give up; they would be dead the next day," Daub said. "The night before it happened, you could just tell who would be dead the next morning. I wanted to go home and go back to college and see my family—that was my goal. I didn't lose sight of it for a minute."[11]

Morton Brooks recalled that he had been working in a tunnel with a fellow soldier who was a Christian Scientist. "He kept saying to me that 'you just have to believe that you'll be okay; you just have to think good thoughts,' and that sort of thing. He said that—until he was really depleted by dysentery, then he changed his view. I just knew that I wanted to get back home, so I avoided picking up any potato peelings I saw on the ground or egg shells that some guys took and licked to see what kind of nutrients that they could get; I tried my best to avoid becoming ill.

"I know the lice and the dysentery weakened me tremendously. I remember one time when one of the fellows took somebody else's socks and I yelled at him and went to hit him. My blow was like a powder puff; I realized that I really had lost a lot of strength. I didn't even have the strength to hit the guy. So I just tried to do what was necessary to get through, from day to day."[12]

Tony Acevedo sensed that the group was at the end of its rope. "We were at the point where we just didn't know what to do. We knelt on the floor, praying to God."[13]

If there was one thing that kept many of the men from giving up, it was the fervent belief that, each day, the Allies were coming closer and closer to Berga. Acevedo could tell that liberation was near just by the sound of planes overhead.

View of the bridge over the Elster River, taken from near the site of the last American barracks at Berga. (Author photo 2004)

"The United States was sending thousands of airplanes to bomb Germany as much as they could." Although Berga itself was not bombed, Acevedo remembered the terrific concussions felt in camp by bombs that fell on nearby towns. "I'm telling you, those 'block busters' that they used, you felt the bombs would tear the hinges off of our windows and doors."[14]

Norman Fellman also hopefully noted the increasing size of the raids. "Sometimes it would take about forty-five minutes to an hour for the planes to go over because there were so many of them, and that sound always made us feel good."[15]

Morton Brooks recalled an air raid "where our armada passed close enough so that we could see them. I remember how happy we were."[16] Although he didn't know it at the time, he had witnessed the massive, 800-plane air raid on 13 February 1945 that reduced Dresden to scorched rubble and left anywhere from 40,000 to 140,000 dead.[17]

According to Tony Acevedo, some of the *Volksturm* guards were Austrian. "When they saw our planes up above, they would make the sign of the cross and ask God to save them.[18]

—✺—

Winter melted into spring, and the farm fields around Berga turned green. But, despite the almost daily overflights of Allied bombers, no liberators appeared to assault the town or break down the barbed-wire fence of Berga Two. Shortly after the killing by Metz of Morton Goldstein on March 20, the prisoners in Berga Two were moved to a large, warehouse-type building across the river from Berga One.[19]

Peter Iosso noted, "We were moved to another building, older and dirtier, across the river from the big prison for the political prisoners, and closer to the worksite. Although we had usually kept pretty much to ourselves, the severity of our living conditions made us more and more distrustful of each other and uncommunicative. We had descended to the lowest level of human existence."[20]

A few of the POWs at Berga received a brief-but-welcome reprieve. Four of the medics, including William Shapiro, were given permission to escort eight very sick men to a British POW camp for treatment. The twelve Americans, along with two "surprisingly helpful and friendly" guards, were loaded into a truck and driven to a railroad station where the group boarded a regular civilian train, rode overnight, and detrained near Stalag IX-C, northwest of Weimar. Not everyone made it; one of the sick soldiers—Edward Gorinac—died en route.

The POWs at IX-C were British soldiers who seemed to be robust, adequately nourished, and not suffering from mistreatment. William Shapiro recalled being in a state of wonder at the conditions: "There was an entirely different look and feel. There were noncoms as well as privates. The men were orderly, dressed in a variety of their army uniforms which appeared clean, not ragged nor torn. The British POWs appeared well-fed and were walking leisurely about the open field as we entered the gate. This was in sharp contrast to how we appeared and what we were permitted to do in our Berga camp. We had no free exercise time out in an open field. . . . We were approached by a British Sergeant Major Browne, who directed some men to relieve us of our burden of unloading the sick American POWs. . . . I did not see our sick men [again]. . . . We assumed that they were taken to the Stalag hospital."

During their short stay in the camp, Shapiro and the other three medics were treated like kings. They were powdered with DDT to kill their lice, and allowed to shave and take hot showers. Their uniforms were returned, deloused. They were also introduced to something Shapiro had never seen before: the Red Cross parcel, which contained wondrous goods. The four medics were given two parcels to share between them.

"When they gave us this life-saving, wonderful gift, I knew how important it was for me and how I had to protect it. . . . It was vastly more food and goodies than any one of us had seen in three months of starvation. . . . We were giddily happy; we ate and tasted everything. I could not fully encompass this tremendous good fortune. . . . Prior to this glorious moment, none of us had been aware of American Red Cross parcels for POWs. We did not know how to get them, who was to get them, how often and how many POWs were to share a parcel. The British told us that it was part of the Geneva Convention to supplement the diet of POWs. A fantastic revelation! We also were told that they had a supply of these food parcels stored in this camp. Unbelievable!"

Shapiro and the other three medics explained to the sergeant major the desperate plight of the Americans at Berga. "He promised that a truck-load of parcels would be sent from Stalag IX-C to Berga," said Shapiro. "Until the time that we left Stalag IX-C to return to Berga, we continued to remind him of our urgent need for food parcels and medical supplies."

Refreshed and renewed, the four medics were escorted back to Berga, lavishing American cigarettes on their guards who had treated them without brutality on the journey. Shapiro noted, "That trip to Stalag IX-C was the lifesaving respite which nourished me and prepared me for the horror of the next five weeks."[21]

On 23 March, the nature of the work at Berga unexpectedly changed for the Americans. "We had shifted from working in the tunnels to a work detail in a forest carrying logs from the woods to the side of the road," noted Joseph Mark. "Even though we were in very poor physical shape, the change from the darker tunnels to the light of the forest was like an elixir for us, a reprieve. The sights and sounds of the trees and birds brought back memories of a more familiar and friendlier world we had known."

Mark said that whenever he thought of death, one of his singular regrets was that he would never again see a tree. "I wondered if that thought was due to Joyce Kilmer's line during another war about never seeing 'a poem as lovely as a tree.' But I believe that the main connection is that a tree is such an important essence of life on this planet. Our close association with trees is taken for granted by most of us.

"It was while I was in the German woods at Berga that I found a stand of pussy willows, and I brought a bunch back to our dreary barracks. Pussy willows may seem like ordinary little sticks with tiny balls of cotton here and there. But these pussy willows were familiar to me from back home, and because of this familiarity—a friend in an alien land—they brought hope to my soul along with a tear in my eye. I had a top bunk and I was able to enjoy my freshly acquired gift as I fell asleep."[22]

Near the end of March, the prisoners received another gift: the promised Red Cross food parcels from Stalag IX-C. The parcels, however, were not given out immediately. William Shapiro said that Metz sadistically tantalized the starving men, telling them they would not receive the boxes until they "cleansed themselves, shaved, and appeared orderly. What a brutal blow! More torment! How devastating and incredibly cruel to expect starved, sick, low-functioning, and half-crazed men to comply with this order! A delay in the distribution was, in effect, a new order to further punish us. Make us suffer in order to achieve complete domination over us. Make us beg and twist the demands a little tighter.

"It was almost impossible to even modestly perform to the order. Men could not even walk about because of foot sores, dazed from hunger, exhaustion, and completely focused on getting to that food in the parcel. Few had the necessary razor or even an old, used blade to shave; there was no soap and no cloth or old paper to use as toweling. . . . We had no other uniforms and we all wore the same clothes since the day that we were captured. . . . How could you look orderly dressed when you were in rags—a stained, fecal-smelling uniform?"

Shapiro noted that there were repeated delays in the distribution of the parcels. "It was obvious that Metz was tormenting us, using the parcels as a reward for some action or other by the men. . . . Eventually, on 26 March, Metz allowed the distribution of one Red Cross box to be divided among four men. Despite our torment, this was welcomed by us. However, I know that he kept many boxes intended for our use and gave them to the twenty-five guards and many others."[23]

There was yet another reprieve. On 1 April, Easter Sunday, everyone was given a day of rest—their first day off after forty continuous days of labor. William Shapiro sarcastically remarked, "It was principally because the civilian engineers and gang bosses of the tunnels suddenly became 'holy.'"[24]

Any thought that the brutal treatment of the slave laborers would suddenly end, however, was quickly dispelled. On Monday, 2 April, the prisoners were back at the worksite, being beaten by their foremen, working just as hard as ever, and wondering who would arrive first to relieve them of their misery: the Americans, the Russians, or the Angel of Death.

10

TOTENMARSCH

BEYOND BERGA, SIGNIFICANT military developments were taking place, with the Russians, British, and Americans squeezing Germany on all sides. On Monday, 2 April 1945, American forces reached Stalag IX-B, the mountaintop POW camp at Bad Orb.

The night before liberation, the barracks doors were left unlocked, and the searchlights on the guard towers remained dark. William Thompson said, "We opened the door after dark to find the yard filled with POWs milling around. 'The guards are gone,' someone said, 'at least most of them are.'"

A kindly old guard the prisoners called Schmidt, a farmer in civilian life, entered Thompson's barrack. "Schmidt said that the staff had fled but he wanted to stay. The war was over for him. We took him and put him back in a far corner. We covered him up in a blanket as he had done so many times for our own sick. He snored like a lion as German tanks and infantry climbed the hill beyond and passed our nervous compound, heading down into Bad Orb. Along about midnight, they roared back up and retreated into the night. From Bad Orb below came a steady sound of tank guns and 105s [howitzers].

"Some time after midnight, the *clink, clink, clink* of infantry could be heard moving through the woods outside the wire and on the road. It was pitch black.

American and British prisoners react with joy as their liberators free them from captivity at Stalag IX-B (Bad Orb), 2 April 1945. (Courtesy National Archives)

Not a spark of light. We didn't know whose troops they were but we knew their nerves were on hair-trigger alert and the slightest out-of-place sound would result in a barrage of fire. We returned to our barracks and kept quiet. If we should come under heavy fire, I had planned to crawl across the yard to the latrine. . . . It was the only ready-made foxhole available.

"The firefight in Bad Orb continued until dawn. Three Shermans squeaked and clanked up the hill road. They halted just below the crest, listening, turrets turning left and right, then up a little more. Finally, they took the bit and roared up the final stretch to the first entrance gate opposite the beer hall for off-duty guards. *BLAM!* The first gate went down. *BLAM!* The second gate flattened under the tank tracks. *BLAM!* The third gate went down and we were free at last! Damn, those tanks were beautiful in the morning sun. A jeep sped past the lead tank, carrying a colonel chaplain. The driver, unbelievably, was an old acquaintance of mine from Boy Scout days. He drove right past me. Didn't see me and probably wouldn't have recognized me if he had. We were scarecrows in dirty uniforms. . . .

"Behind the jeep came three Shermans, loaded down with supplies of delicacies that only tank outfits can carry—live geese-a-honking, live pigs-a-squealing, cartons of 10-in-1 rations in case they got hungry in the night—a deli on a half-track."

The starved men charged the food-laden vehicles and stuffed themselves with everything edible. A Red Cross truck then drove into the compound. Thompson said, "Two hard-working young ladies began handing out real coffee and doughnuts. The rich food reactivated our diarrhea to the extent that the compound began to resemble a duck pen as dozens of POWs were hit with a call so acute they dropped their pants and puddled up in full view of the doughnut wagons. To their everlasting credit, those dedicated ladies never flinched.

"We introduced Schmidt to the officers who were setting up a control unit. We told of his efforts on our behalf. He was paroled that first day and delivered in a jeep to his wife on their still-intact farm. . . . He was a decent man."[1]

James V. Smith recalled that the liberators began moving out the prisoners who were the sickest and those who had been wounded. "They moved them out

Sick POWs are removed from the infirmary at Stalag IX-B.
(Courtesy National Archives)

by ambulance for several days. Since I was one of the healthiest ones in the camp, it was about ten days or close to two weeks before I got out. They took me to Fulda, which had been a big German air base. They had a Red Cross tent set up there, and they gave us shaving equipment, toothbrushes, toothpaste—this type of thing.

"Later, we were deloused. We had to throw away all of our old clothes; they were full of lice. On some of the warm days in March, we had been able to take off our shirts and pick the things off, but you never get them all. On the morning after I arrived at the camp in Fulda, a C-47 came in loaded with 55-gallon drums of gasoline. They unloaded the gasoline and then loaded us on the plane and flew us back to France to a place called Camp Lucky Strike [near Le Havre]. After a few days there, they started feeding us a lot of eggnog to try and get us to regain some weight. All of us had lost a tremendous amount of weight. I probably weighed around 210 to 220 pounds when I was captured; when I came out of there, it was probably close to 150."[2]

Jack Crawford recalled, "We could see the fire [in Bad Orb] from a distance, and you could hear the gunshots. The Americans came up to the camp on tanks. One of the GIs gave me a can of chicken soup—it was really good."[3]

Not wanting the Allies to discover the enormity of their monstrous crimes against the Jews and others, the Nazis were evacuating the concentration camps and death factories. Suddenly, the roads of Germany were crawling with living skeletons in striped uniforms.

The evacuations had begun as early as mid-January 1945, when the death factory of Auschwitz, in Poland, was quickly emptied and its 60,000 surviving inmates forced to march toward Wodzislaw. Anyone who fell behind was killed by the SS guards; over 15,000 never made it to Wodzislaw. Once the survivors reached their destination, they were packed into boxcars and transported to Buchenwald, Dachau, Flossenbürg, Mauthausen, and other camps inside Germany; on 27 January 1945, Soviet troops entered Auschwitz to discover 7,000 deathly ill prisoners and the grim evidence of mass murder.

Throughout January, other camps were evacuated by the Nazis. From dozens of camps came tens of thousands of weakened prisoners, suffering from the wintry conditions and the brutal treatment of their SS guards. For example, some 5,000 prisoners from Stutthof, in northern Poland, were herded into the freezing waters of the Baltic Sea and machine-gunned to death without reason.

In late March and early April, thousands of inmates were evacuated from Buchenwald and its sub-camps. Some evacuees were marched northward, toward Hamburg, while others were taken east, toward Chemnitz and Theresienstadt. The Third Reich had spent many years and expended billions of Reichsmarks to build the camps and use the efficient German railway system to transport millions of people across Europe for the sole purpose of killing them. Now those who had been lucky enough to survive the camps were sent on foot to wander the roads under armed guard in order to keep from falling into the hands of those who might save them.[4]

On the third of April, the door of their barrack opened and the American prisoners at Berga were rousted out for what they thought would be just another miserable day of hard labor and brutal treatment. But this was to be no ordinary day.

After *appell,* the prisoners marched—not toward the worksite, but out of town, under the watchful eye of a handful of German guards overseen by Hauptmann Merz and Kommandoführer Metz.[5]

"When we were captured, the U.S. Army was at Germany's border," Gerald Daub recalled. "We felt that we were definitely winning the war and so, after a couple of months had gone by, we knew the American army must have gone on the offensive again, and soon they would be approaching us. But we had no idea how close they were until the Germans marched us out, and then we felt that we were probably marched out of the camp, not to save our lives, but just to get us out of the camp because the Americans were getting close. The American army entered Berga just a few days after we left."[6]

When the march southward to Bavaria began, there were 280 Americans who started out; twenty-five of the original 350 had died at Berga or were "shot while escaping"; another twenty-five had been taken to hospitals. Another twenty had escaped from the camp, their whereabouts unknown.[7]

No one had any idea where the group was going. All anyone knew was that they were heading south. After being confined for so long, the road march should have been a tonic for the men's spirits. All around were signs of spring: green grass, budding trees, twittering birds, fragrant air, farmers working their fields behind horse-drawn plows. Escape from the meager guard force in this open country seemed possible, yet no one had the strength or will to try. "The Germans had about four or five who watched us—not a large number," said Morton Brooks. "They really didn't need a large number."[8]

The city of Plauen, through which the POWs marched.
(Author photo 2004)

The men were in no shape to make this march, let alone escape. William Shapiro realized, "None of us . . . had any idea how destructive this march would be to our group. All debilitated, exhausted, emaciated, sick, maimed, and cowered soldiers. It was simply walking—no strenuous work in the tunnels, no lifting heavy rail ties, no moving of rail track for eight hours daily. This was a walk at a slow pace, interrupted by a break every hour and one half in order to defecate, urinate, or just sit down along the gutters of the road. Simple!"

But Shapiro added, "We were totally unprepared for the horrors that we would encounter—the profound despair, the inability to continue to take another step forward, the discovery of dead buddies each morning, and the wanton, gross murder along the roads."[9]

The straggling line of POWs plodded through the hostile stares of citizens in the bombed-out center of Greiz—an old, baroque city with a castle looming high above the Elster River—then Plauen, then Hof, where ten marchers died. Each day, when the wilting prisoners asked their guards where they were going, the answer was always the same: "To the next town."

Although the city of Hof, near the Czech border, was only thirty miles from Berga, some of the soldiers could go no farther. Norman Fellman recalled that, near Hof, his infected leg swelled, causing his boot to burst. "During the night, we were in a barn. I tried to get up the next morning but my leg was full of pus; I couldn't walk, so they found a cart that had an old horse pulling it. This cart was 'V' sided—narrow at the bottom and wider on the top. It could probably hold eight or nine people comfortably; they piled twenty-five, thirty guys in it. More than once the guy on the bottom suffocated. So you played Russian roulette everyday as to how they loaded you."

At some point during the march, the horse pulling the "sick wagon" disappeared; the POWs were drafted to pull and push it—an almost impossible task for men who could barely walk. Fellman said, "There was a fellow that I knew—a guy named Greg. He talked about his brothers and family at home. His head was in my lap; he was disabled somewhere along the line. I don't know what his problem was, but he's talking about giving up, that he couldn't take it anymore. I talked to him for hours, trying to give him all the reasons why he should live—his family needed him and his brothers needed him and so on, and somewhere during that conversation, he passed away. I don't know how long I talked to him after he was dead."

Liberation came quickly for Norman Fellman. The column of POWs had become strung out even before the group reached Hof, and he and several comrades "were liberated on the road in the vicinity of Hof by elements of the 90th Division. I was taken to a field hospital and, after a day or so, was flown to Paris to a hospital where I remained for a period of time."

Fellman was unable to articulate exactly his joy and emotions at finally being liberated: "I don't know if I could ever explain it, and I don't know that I could ever make someone else understand it. You almost have to be in the similar situation. It was overwhelming, it really was. Some of us let go of all of our restraints, messed ourselves up. All the restraints that we had in trying to stay alive and to be able to move, to be able to watch out for yourself, all gave way. We had no idea how bad we looked until we saw [the liberators'] eyes when they saw us. We felt like we were lepers. They certainly didn't try to make us feel that way. But we were about as close to being skeletons as we could be and not be one."[10]

The rest of the group, perhaps stronger and able to walk at a faster pace, was forced to keep marching farther from the liberating arms of the 90th Division. Norman Martin recalled the death of a prisoner named Israel Cohen while on

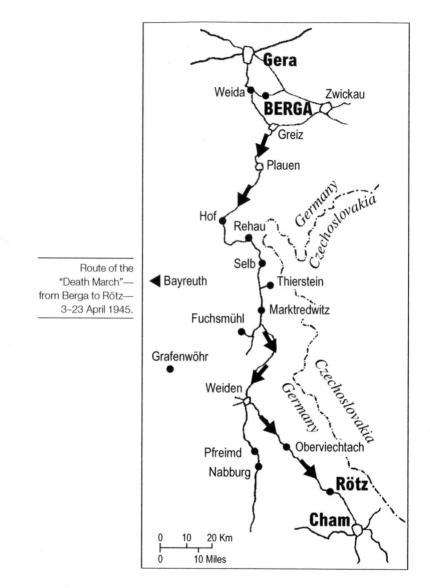

Route of the
"Death March"—
from Berga to Rötz—
3–23 April 1945.

Gera

Weida Zwickau

BERGA

Greiz

Plauen

Germany *Czechoslovakia*

Hof

Rehau

Selb

Bayreuth Thierstein

Fuchsmühl Marktredwitz

Grafenwöhr

Weiden

Czechoslovakia *Germany*

Pfreimd Oberviechtach

Nabburg

Rötz

Cham

0   10   20 Km

0   10 Miles

the march: "Private Cohen had considerable difficulty in maintaining the pace of the rest of the men. About the seventh of April, he collapsed from exhaustion. . . . He was put in a manure wagon, which was used as a sick wagon. He was the first one in the wagon and, during the day, more men began to fall out from exhaustion and illness. Private Cohen was on the bottom of the cart and as each man would collapse, they would be thrown on top of Private Cohen. Toward the end of the day, there were many men piled on top of Private Cohen. When I saw him, he was dead, and from the position in which he was lying, he must have died from suffocation from all the men being placed on top of him. . . . His face was a picture of agony, and from the position of his body, he looked as if he had been struggling to get air. . . . We protested to Metz that the conditions were in violation of the Geneva Conference and he told us that *he* was the only Geneva Conference available."[11]

While on the march, Gerald Daub handed Joe Mark a small bag of potatoes he had picked up somewhere along the way. "He asked me to take it," Mark said, "because he couldn't carry it anymore. I was not a leader, but I was twenty-three years old and a senior member, as opposed to Gerry and most of the others, who were eighteen. I took the potatoes and hung the bag on the wagon loaded with the very sick so that, later, we had access to the potatoes.

"We would stop in barns at night for rest. One guy killed a chicken. We couldn't make a fire, so I ate the white meat raw but, even starving, I couldn't swallow the dark meat."[12]

On 9 April, south of Hof, Peter Iosso said the group "reached a town that had somehow become free of federal control. Although we didn't understand the words, body language told us that the *Burgomeister* was chewing out the *Kommandofiihrer* [Metz], probably about us. Fifty of our sickest were taken to a hospital; the rest of us stayed in a clean barn. For the two or three days we stayed there; they gave us slices from freshly baked family loaves and boiled potatoes."[13]

On 12 April, a German officer rode up to the group on a motorcycle and informed the POWs, in perfect English, that President Roosevelt had died. William Shapiro recalled, "He said, 'It is a sad day for Germany.' I did not understand nor appreciate what he had meant by Roosevelt's death being a sad day for Germany. Many years later, I presumed that he was frightened of the Russian advance and political takeover. . . . I remember that we all began to cry and this, superimposed upon our existing anguish, brought us to hopeless despair. After all this suffering, I thought there was no hope, no chance for liberation. I was lost—did not know where I was, what was going to happen to me. I remember some sort of makeshift memorial service that we had for President Roosevelt."[14]

The village of Thierstein. (Author photo 2004)

A week after the American POWs left Berga to wander the roads of Bavaria, the political prisoners who had remained behind finally were marched out of their compound. Ernest Michel recalled, "The camp was evacuated on April 11. The reason I remember it so well is because the following day President Roosevelt died. The camp commander announced that 'the war-monger Roosevelt is dead and now Germany is going to turn it around and win the war.' The only American names I knew at that time were Franklin Roosevelt and Eisenhower. Don't forget—we had no access to news. We just heard it through the grapevine. Those were the only two names I knew."

To "celebrate" Roosevelt's death, the SS shot ten prisoners. "We were walking at that time," Michel said, "marching through a small woods, and they shot them in the woods. The shooting of prisoners went on about every other day. My friends—Schwartz and Munk—and I knew what was happening and we decided that the only way to avoid getting shot was to escape; we didn't want to be shot and killed. So, on April 18, we escaped. Even the SS has to sit down and relieve themselves. During one of these periods, while walking through some woods, we decided to slowly move to the back and into the woods, into lots of small trees. That's how we escaped."

The trio spent the first three days and nights moving through the dense forests, hoping not to be seen, sleeping in the daytime, and walking at night. "We were going in a westerly direction, because this is where we knew the Americans and the Allies were coming in to Germany. But we were starving; the only thing we had to eat was grass and the bark of trees and maybe a rotten potato. We were literally starving."[15]

—⁓—

The POW group rested until 13 April. Peter Iosso called the five days of rest "the only bright or redeeming event of my whole POW experience."[16]

One of the German soldiers later reported that an order reached the group, an order "to set the POWs free in the various villages and to bring the troops across the Danube. It [Battalion 621] was ordered to reach the city of Wörth." Then, on 13 April, a Major Otto of battalion headquarters ordered Merz and

Thierstein town cemetery. (Author photo 2004)

Marienkirche (St. Mary's Church) in Fuchsmühl, near the hospital to which some of the sick POWs were taken. (Author photo 2004)

Metz to disregard the order to set the prisoners free.[17] The parade of death staggered through Rehau, Schönwald, then onto the high tableland near Thierstein. But the POWs began to drop at an alarming rate—some from exhaustion, some from disease, some from the savage beatings they received at the hands of their guards. Eight men died and were buried at Rehau. At Thierstein, a week later, four Americans were buried in a common grave in the town cemetery beneath a cross inscribed in German, "Here Lay 4 American Prisoners of War 15 April 1945."[18]

When the group reached Fuchsmühl, Kommandoführer Metz allowed a group of the most seriously ill prisoners to be taken to the town's hospital. They received no medical care and slept on straw.[19]

Close on the heels of the POWs was the 357th Regiment of the 90th Infantry Division. The regimental historian wrote,

> At Fuchsmühl, 33 Americans were found lying in straw bunks. To describe their condition would be to play upon the imagination of the reader. They had been forced to work long hours in salt mines [*sic*] on a ration that was a disgrace to humanity. At the time of rescue, most of these men had declined to the point where they were unable to move from their bunks. . . .[20]

Day after day, mile after mile, the pitiful column plodded southward, uphill and downhill, struggling to put one foot in front of the other, with the stronger GIs helping support the weaker ones, continually spurred on by their captors with the promise that they were just going as far as "the next town."

At some point during the march, Captain Merz was replaced by a Captain Hahn, but the lives of the POWs did not change appreciably.[21]

According to Peter Iosso, the group "dragged ourselves over the roads of eastern Germany, covering fifteen to thirty kilometers per day and spending the nights sleeping in barns or open fields. One whole day we slogged through freezing rain. Food was an uncertain commodity. Some days we got none. Others, the group got random numbers of loaves of bread at hastily set up points of distribution."[22]

———

On 22 April, their courage bolstered by their desperate hunger and because they spoke fluent German, the political prisoner trio of Michel, Munk, and Schwartz dared to approach an isolated farmhouse near Lindenau and knocked on the door. "This was the one area in all of Germany that was never occupied," Michel noted. "Not by the Allies, not by the Russians—nobody. A woman came to the door. I covered my arm with the tattooed Auschwitz number, and the others did, too. We told her we were on a work detail and were bombed out by the Allies, and could we get something to eat? She closed the door and we thought that was the end of it. Then she came back with some milk and bread and sausage. That was the first food we had. As a result, the three of us stayed in that area; each one of us worked on a different farm. It was April and the German farmers

Tony Acevedo's 1950 sketch of the "death march." POWs are pushing and pulling the "sick wagon," while being followed by small, remote-controlled "Goliath" tanks. The bodies of dead political prisoners, murdered by their Nazi guards, line the roads. (Courtesy Tony Acevedo)

obviously needed hands to help work the farms, so each one of us stayed at a separate farm in the same neighborhood, and they left us alone. They gave us something to eat and let us sleep in barns, but at least we got food. That was a lifesaver."[23]

⎯⎯⎯⎯

As the endless kilometers passed step by agonizingly slow step, the ordeal of the American POWs began to take on the character of the fruitless labors of the mythical Sisyphus. The elderly *Volksturm* guards that accompanied the column were suffering almost as much as the POWs. But the guards had rations and water to sustain them; the prisoners were fed only when they stopped for the night.[24] During the march, Kommandoführer Metz, ever eager to prolong the suffering of the prisoners, forbade compassionate German civilians from giving food to them.[25]

The POWs began to make out a large body of political prisoners moving along the highway a few miles ahead of them. Soon, the lovely spring landscape began to reveal its incongruous horrors. The road climbed a rise and, as the Americans struggled uphill, they noticed up ahead what looked like odd bundles littering the ground. As they got closer, the bundles became clumps of gaunt corpses carpeting the road, sprawled in ditches, and hanging limply from barbed-wire fences. Each one had a bullet hole in its head. They were the political prisoners the POWs had been following.

Gerald Daub remembered, "As we approached this hill, we saw a few prisoners lying by the side of the road in these atrocious pleading and praying and frightened positions—all shot. I didn't hear any shooting or see the incidents.

Today, the route of the *Totenmarsch* (death march) is pastoral and bucolic, offering no hint of its previous horrors.
(Author photo 2004)

We just saw them lying there dead and it was very grotesque, I mean, just the way they were lying there in these grotesque positions. Somebody asked the guards what had happened and they said American planes had strafed them, but we knew that was not true because all of them were shot in the head. It seemed as though we marched all that day, and practically all we saw were these bodies along the side of the road."[26]

Medic William Shapiro was aghast at the sight. "During my five months of front-line combat, I had witnessed many instances of gore—dismembered and blown-apart bodies. Dead soldiers were a common sight. But this scene on the 'Death-March Road' was significantly different. . . . As we approached a steep hill, I saw the most gruesome, cruel, barbarous, inhumane acts that I have ever seen in my entire life. As we climbed the hill and caught up to where we had seen the political prisoners in the distance, we saw on each side of the road hundreds of dead Jews. Most of them were in the kneeling position, many on their side in a fetal position and all were dead by obvious gunshots behind the head. Many heads were blown open by the force of the shot, and the brains were splattered about. It was ghastly. It was indescribably frightening. It was unspeakable. It was so shocking to look at the very recent, awesome destruction of human beings. The murder was, presumably, because they could not continue the march up the inclined road. . . . What was in store for us? Is this the manner in which it will all end? The horror of it reflected onto me and my overwhelming despair. After all the suffering that these Jews had encountered, so close to freedom, their inability to climb the hill resulted in instant death.

"I was exhausted and just dragged along, fearful of stopping until we were told that it was time for a break. I became an automaton. As we continued to walk through them and past them, we came to another group of political prisoners in similar positions. As we ascended the steeper part of the hill, there were more and more victims. You became immune to the sight. You expected it. It was walking into a hell. The 'trees' lining the sides of the road to hell were dead Jews. I could never imagine anything as macabre as this massacre. As we were catching up to the civilian prisoner march, we began to hear the firing of machine-guns and burp guns in the woods a short distance from the road. We could not see the Jews, but we knew what was happening in those killing woods among the pine trees which blocked our view."[27]

Joseph Mark was stupefied at the scale of the crime: "We passed a section where I saw dead Jewish concentration camp victims lying in the road every few

Steep road near Oberviechtach, climbed by the POWs.
(Author photo 2004)

feet, for over a mile. I thought maybe they were Hungarians, but I'm not sure. The Germans were marching them somewhere. They were just concentration camp victims in striped suits from other camps, and the SS just shot them in the head. Our guards gave us a little special treatment as soldiers, because they knew there were German soldiers that were POWs in the U.S., and they marched us as soldiers."[28]

Tony Acevedo was equally appalled. "Up ahead, the Germans were slaughtering the Jews from another camp. They were slaughtering old people, young people, women, children, everyone. We saw people hanging from the barbed wire fences on both sides of the highway, hanging down, slaughtered by the machine-guns of the Germans."[29]

To Peter Iosso, the march "was like a descent into hell, spiritually and physically. Death and thoughts of death were ever present. We saw huge masses of political prisoners in open fields, some being shot for breaking ranks, the others with little hope for a better fate. As a matter of fact, for two whole days we walked on a road lined on both sides, at about three-foot intervals, with dead political prisoners who had neat bullet holes in their heads. We wondered where we were headed and whether we'd ever get there and, if we did, what good it would do. There were rumors of ovens." On 19 April, Iosso managed to drop out of the column but was captured and spent a night in a local town jail; he was returned to the group by wagon the next day.[30]

The 357th Regiment of the 90th Division, still trying to catch up with the American POWs, also found the evidence of German atrocities. The regiment's historian noted,

> The unburied bodies of the ones who were unfortunate not to be able to walk any farther were seen all along the roads. Many had been shot in a group and shared a single uncovered grave. Many thousands of British prisoners of war were also liberated. Some of the chaps had been taken at Dunkirk and had been with the Germans for five years.
>
> The sight of these liberated prisoners of war and slave laborers from other nations wrung pity and pride from the hearts of all, and brought to everyone's mind the real reason why America was fighting this war. The deplorable condition of these unfortunate people brought stark realization of the true value of democracy and its worth to freedom-loving people.[31]

The scene of wholesale death was the last straw for Morton Brooks; he had had enough, and decided he would rather perish while escaping than be shot like a helpless animal. "This friend of mine, Sam Fahrer, and I attempted an escape; we just dropped back until we were trailing and it was getting dark and the guard in the back didn't seem to be that concerned about us. We eventually took off into the woods, but we didn't get away for long. Fahrer tried to go up and get some food from a farmhouse but the farmer came out with a gun and we were taken into a town and put into a kind of dungeon. I guess they found out where we came from and we were returned to the group."[32]

The death march continued to take its toll on bodies that were seriously weakened by disease and malnutrition. Men continued to die on the route to nowhere. "I didn't think I could live much longer," Joseph Mark admitted. "Like

A roadside crucifix along the "highway of death." A grotto like this one gave Joseph Mark hope for liberation. (Author photo 2004)

a few more days, at most. I weighed about eighty-five pounds and I could feel the ligaments I was walking on."

An unexpected scene then caught Mark's eye. The state of Bavaria is predominately Catholic, and most of the villages have roadside grottoes—graphic depictions of a suffering Christ on the cross. Mark said, "I was so moved by the sight that it brought tears to my eyes—and I'm a Jew! I have nothing to do with Jesus! In a land of Nazis and Hitler, the sheer humanity of Jesus got across to me—it was the only humanity that I saw in all the time that I was a prisoner.

Approaching Rötz from the direction of Neunburg.
(Author photo 2004)

Then, as we rounded the turn after seeing this statue, there were two buxom, Bavarian women cutting large slices of black bread and handing them to us." The act of kindness enabled him to carry on with renewed hope that the group would soon be liberated.[33]

On April 20—Hitler's birthday—the guards from Berga were relieved by a new set of guards. Kommandoführer Metz was also relieved, but the march and its attendant agonies continued. Joseph Mark said, "They changed the guards because some of our guys had it in for the guards. These were new guards and they made us a thick soup, which the Germans call *dicke zuppe*. At Berga, the soup was so thin, I used to wash my socks in it."

In spite of the hearty soup and kinder treatment, Mark felt that everyone had reached the limits of his endurance. Somehow, in one of the most amazing feats of human resilience, the group of survivors had managed to walk 300 kilometers in three weeks. "About the twenty-second of April, we wound up off the

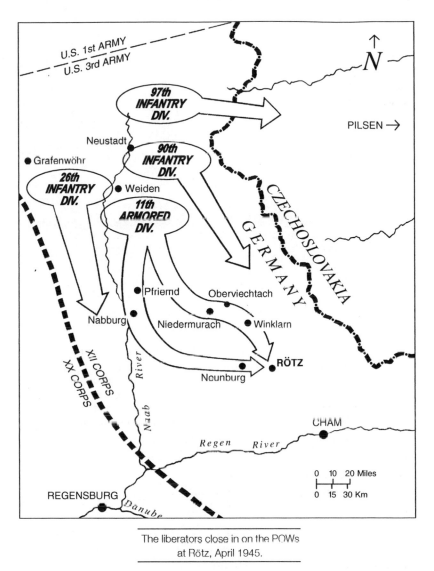

U.S. 1st ARMY

U.S. 3rd ARMY

N

97th
INFANTRY
DIV.

PILSEN →

90th
INFANTRY
DIV.

Neustadt

Grafenwöhr

26th
INFANTRY
DIV.

Weiden

11th
ARMORED
DIV.

CZECHOSLOVAKIA

GERMANY

Pfriemd

Oberviechtach

Nabburg

Niedermurach

Winklarn

XII CORPS

XX CORPS

RÖTZ

Neunburg

River

Naab

CHAM

Regen   River

0   10   20 Miles

0   15   30 Km

REGENSBURG

Danube

The liberators close in on the POWs
at Rötz, April 1945.

road at a barn that was up in the hills near Cham.* There we just fell into a slush of cow urine. At that point, you just didn't care. You just wanted to die."[34]

On the night of 22 April, the POWs were resting in the barn, their sore and blistered feet bleeding, their spirits at their lowest ebb. All seemed hopeless; death seemed near. Morton Brooks recalled, "We had been bedded down in a

Some of the surviving POWs identified this barn, located on the northern edge
of Rötz, as the one in which they were held the night before
their liberation. (Author photo 2004)

barn for the night along the road; we were exhausted. We had been marching for
three weeks. We decided that, when the Germans tried to get us up in the morning, we would not move.

"The next day, we heard the guards say, '*Raus! Raus!*' The word went through
the barn: 'Don't move,' and we just laid there. A couple of minutes later, we
heard some shots and the guards took off. After about ten or fifteen minutes of
quiet, one of the fellows looked out the back end of the barn. We were on a hill
and it sloped down from the back and he saw American tanks coming up the
road, and some of our fellows shouted, 'Americans!'"[35]

---

*The group had reached the town of Rötz, a few miles north of Cham.

11

LIBERATION

LIKE THE LEGENDARY Civil War Union General William Tecumseh Sherman who blazed his way across Georgia, the Sherman tanks of Major General Holmes Dager's 11th Armored Division, nicknamed the "Thunderbolts," were blazing their way southward down the *autobahns* and backroads of eastern Bavaria. Occasionally, a booby-trapped roadblock or small crews of Germans armed with *panzerfausts* and automatic weapons attempted to slow the drive, but without much success. The division had already taken Bayreuth, Grafenwöhr, and Weiden, and was on its way to Cham and then Linz, Austria.

At 0100 hours on 23 April, Combat Command A of the 11th Armored Division took 490 Hungarian troops, who had aligned themselves with the Third Reich, prisoner at Pfreimd. Before daylight, some 800 Hungarians had agreed to surrender at Nabburg, and another 1,200 of the enemy near Oberviechtach gave up without a fight.[1]

Besides capturing the enemy, the 11th Armored had also become well-versed in rescuing large numbers of Allied POWs. On 2 April, the division had liberated 400 POWs at Grimmenthal; 570 at Meiningen on the 5th; 2,000 at Weiden on the 22nd; and another 1,160 Americans and Russians at Winklarn and Niedermurach on the morning of the 23rd.[2]

In addition to prisoners of war, the Thunderbolts also found evidence of Nazi atrocities along the way. Major James Q. Simmons, Jr., the 11th Armored's acting division surgeon, reported, "All along the road [to Cham], thousands of former inmates of German concentration camps were encountered in all states of nutrition. They had been marched from one camp to another southward to keep them from being liberated by the Allies. Dead and dying were all over, some from starvation and hundreds from being shot by their SS guards. These people were of all nationalities, including German (mostly Jews)."[3]

Another member of Combat Command A wrote, "On resuming our drive toward Cham, we saw our first evidence of German atrocities. The roadside was littered with the bodies of political prisoners for miles back, victims of Nazi brutality. Those too weak to march were shot where they fell. Tears came to our eyes when those poor, starving, wretched individuals came begging for food at the side of our vehicles. We gave them all we had, which wasn't much, and they returned thanks by kissing our hands. I will never forget that scene and others to follow for as long as I live."[4]

Receiving reports that additional POWs could be found east of Neunburg, Task Force Wingard of Combat Command A struck out for the village of Rötz.[5]

At 1526 hours, Combat Command A's radios crackled with the news: "160 US PW near Rötz." The task force had found what was left of the 350 Americans who had been transferred from Bad Orb to Berga and had set out on their 300-kilometer march to nowhere three weeks earlier.[6]*

Gerald Daub recalled that on 23 April he, Joe Mark, Bob Rudnick, and another soldier named Jack Bornkin were sleeping late in a barn. "When we woke up, the guards seemed to be in great confusion. One of us suggested that perhaps this would be a good time to try to get out of there.

"But Jack Bornkin didn't get up; he was just lying in the straw, making gasping noises, unable to communicate at all. There were some poles in the corner of the barn and one of the three of us suggested that we make a stretcher for Jack. We buttoned Bob's overcoat over the poles and told the guard that Jack was very sick and we wanted to get him out of the barn and

---

*After taking the Americans to Cham, the 11th Armored Division continued on and discovered even greater horrors on the road: some 16,000 starving inmates that had been marched from Buchenwald and Flossenbürg; the division then liberated the concentration camp at Mauthausen. (G-3 Journals, 11th Armored Division, 1 April–8 May 1945, National Archives)

The city of Cham.
(Author photo 2004)

take him to this little hut that was over on the side. He said, 'Yeah, yeah, okay, go ahead,' which was not like our former guards at all. So we took Jack to this little hut and put him on the floor. It was a candling hut for goose eggs. We found some goose eggs in the hut and we tried to feed one of them to Jack but he just wouldn't suck it."[7]

Suddenly, a strange sound was heard. Joseph Mark said, "We heard a rolling of thunder and machine-guns in the distance. What we heard was the rolling of American tanks. There was a little rise in the road and you could see the tops of the tanks coming toward us. The Germans tried to force us to get up and get out and follow them, but one of our fellows was near death and we couldn't move at all. What the Germans wanted to do, more or less, was to use us as a shield. But then they took off."[8]

William Shapiro, lying in the barn, was numb—and near death. "I believe that I was in that twilight zone before death that I had observed in some men in Berga. I do not believe that I was sick with any disease except severe weight loss, intermittent diarrhea, exhaustion, and lice infestation."

A Sherman tank rolled in front of the barn but, in his delirium, Shapiro thought that it was a German panzer. "I saw the white star on the side of the tank, and then some men started to shout and scream that they are Americans. It was after some time, just sitting there and hearing the commotion, that I realized that I was liberated. My mind was blank and I was not functioning."[9]

Gerald Daub opened up the door to the candling hut and saw, heading for the barn, an American tank. Behind it was a jeep flying a Red Cross pennant; it, too, stopped in front of the barn. "I ran over to the jeep and the medic said, 'We have been looking for you guys,' or words to that effect. They apparently knew that we were around and the reconnaissance group was trying to find us. I said we had a very sick guy in the hut, and the medic said okay, and he went to the hut. He also said, 'We have plenty of food in my jeep; help yourself.' I did that; I think they were some K-rations. The medic went up to the hut and when he came out, he said, 'He's dead; there's nothing you can do for him.'"

Daub went back to the hut and told his buddies to go to the jeep and get some food. "I took Jack Borkin's ring from his finger—it was a gold, high-school graduation ring; when I got home, I managed to get in touch with his family. I think his family was from Detroit but he had a sister in New York, and she came to my house and I gave her the ring. So April 23rd was both a good day and a bad day."[10]

Joseph Mark also recalled the moment of liberation. "We all thought that Patton would rescue us, liberate us. It's a funny thing about war. Patton was kind of a crazy guy, and he was the one we expected would rescue us—not Bradley or Eisenhower. Sure enough, Patton's tanks came down the road to where we were in this barn.

"One of the German guards had a bicycle, and I took the bicycle out of his hands and rode across the field toward a tank; the tank stopped, I told him that I was a prisoner. One of the guys at the tank picked me up like a feather and I wound up on top of the tank. They gave me a loaf of bread and a Luger. I will never forget—there was a lady nearby with a jug on her shoulder that was full of milk—raw milk—and she offered it to me and I drank it and I'm telling you, I thought I was going to die. Luckily, we wound up in a hospital and they flushed the milk out."[11]

Another prisoner, Philip Dantowitz of Peabody, Massachusetts, heard the shouting but thought, "I had heard that cry before and it never came true. So, when I heard this, I thought it was just another hoax. But I got up out of the high loft where I had been hiding, looked out the window and saw a German guard on his knees surrounded by soldiers and prisoners."[12]

William Shapiro walked out of the barn into a bright, sunny day. "I saw many tanks roll by. Soldiers were hanging over the turrets and throwing food and chocolate D ration bars at us. I picked one up and had great difficulty opening the package. A jeep pulled up and the driver told me to get in. I remember sitting alongside the driver, mumbling, and trying to chew on the chocolate bar; I do not recall any extended conversation. He knew that I was in the 28th Infantry Division by the shoulder patch on my field jacket. I knew that he was part of the 11th Armored Division and subsequently, I learned that this was part of Patton's Third Army. I did not cry, nor shout, nor jump about as some of the others did. I recall seeing several of my buddies sitting on the side of the road with all kinds of food and stuffing it into their mouths. They were shouting and eating at the same time."[13]

Morton Brooks said the liberating soldiers "loaded us up on whatever vehicles they had—tanks, half-tracks, or whatever. They were headed for the town of Cham and this is where we were taken. They took over a civic building, and in this large room they set up stretchers. They took our clothing and they burned it or disposed of it in some way. They sprayed us with DDT and administered to our needs as best they could. There were about a hundred and forty* of us left."[14]

According to Gerald Daub, "Bob Rudnick and I—and I believe Joe Mark, also—got into that medic's jeep and he took us to a German hospital, which had nuns with big, starched hats. I was deloused with kerosene, if I'm not mistaken. They then told me to get into a bed. I remember that that bed was monstrously high; I could hardly climb into it. I got into the bed, but I recall nothing. I don't know if I was in that bed for an hour or a day or a week, although I think it was probably less than a day."[15]

William Shapiro was also taken to the same hospital. He was guided into a large room where all of his clothes were removed and discarded. There was one cherished item that he would not relinquish—his International Red Cross card. "We were thoroughly dusted with DDT in every conceivable place except our mouths. We were not shaven and, after some time, I remember being placed into a shower. They gave me two army blankets, but no underwear, nor pajamas."[16]

---

*The "official" count by the 11th Armored Division was 160.

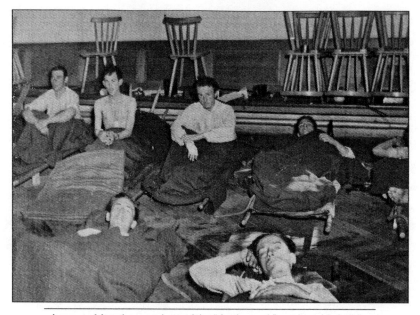

A group of American survivors of the "death march" rest in a civic building
in Cham, shortly after their liberation in Rötz by the 11th Armored Division.
Gerald Daub is sitting up in the back row, second from left;
Peter Iosso is lying on the stretcher, top right.
(Courtesy Gerald Daub)

Once they were deloused and cleansed, Gerald Daub said that a team of
Army medics "examined us and tagged us and took us to a town hall or some
kind of public building in Cham by ambulance, and we were put on stretchers
on the floor. Some of us were photographed. When we were taken to this town
hall or public building, Bob Rudnick was found to have double pneumonia. He
was taken away immediately; he was probably on his last day or two. I did not
see Bob again until sometime in mid-summer, like July or August.

"There were two or three of us who were able to sit up; the rest were just sort
of lying on the stretchers. They could not get off. I had a compulsion to find
some of our rotten guards, but it was a couple of days before I could even stand
up or go to the toilet." Daub was taken to the airfield at Cham and flown on a
two-motored American hospital plane to a station hospital in England. "The
plane was full of stretchers, two or three tiers high."[17]

William Shapiro said that some of the liberated men soiled themselves while on the stretchers. "This may have been the result of their dysentery or from gorging themselves with great quantities of different foods since the morning of liberation. I do not believe that I had any accident since I did not eat very much that first day. I was dazed, exhausted, listless, and probably disinterested in my surroundings. I do not recall any care by any nuns, but they were present in the room. Either that day or the following day, I was debriefed by a soldier asking me many questions and recording my answers. Shortly thereafter, I was allowed to write a letter to my parents."[18]

Medical personnel attend to emaciated and ill American POWs in Cham. From foreground to background, the prisoners are identified as Pvt. Winfield Rosenberg, Pfc. Paul Capps, Pfc. James Watkins, Pvt. Alvin Abrams, and Pfc. Joseph Guigno. (Courtesy National Archives)

Joseph Mark refused to stay in the field hospital. "I had a thing about going to bed during the daytime; I associated going to bed in the daytime with dying, because that's what would happen at Berga." Instead, he roamed the streets of Cham, picking up souvenirs and knickknacks for his buddies in the hospital. "I would come back like Santa Claus, with a big bag of Nazi knives and things. During one of those trips, I took a bath in an ex-colonel's house because I still felt dirty and lousy. I dressed up in a Bavarian costume with those shorts and a hat with a feather, and a mandolin. When I got outside, a Russian—the Russians were roaming freely in the town, in the liquor stores and taverns, drinking and so on—and he wanted the mandolin. I let him play it and he played the mandolin so beautifully, I finally gave it to him."[19]

On 25 April, Norman Fellman was approached by an Army officer from the Military Intelligence Service and informed that he would need to sign a "Security Certificate" before he would be discharged. The document read:

> Security Certificate for Ex-Prisoners of War
>
> 1. Some activities of American Prisoners of war within German prison camps must remain secret not only for the duration of the war against the present enemies of the United States but in peacetime as well. The interests of American prisoners of war in Japanese camps require maintenance of the strictest security on the activities of American prisoners of war in German camps. The interests of American prisoners of future wars, moreover, demand that the secrets of this war be rigorously safeguarded.
>
> 2. I therefore understand that under Army Regulations and the laws of the United States, during my military service and later, as a civilian, I may not reveal, discuss, publish or otherwise disclose to unauthorized persons information on escape from enemy prison camps or evasion in enemy occupied territory, clandestine organizations among prisoners of war, any means of outwitting captors or of promoting intelligence activities within prison camps.
>
> 3. The authorship of articles or stories on these subjects is specifically forbidden and military personnel are warned that they will be held strictly accountable for the communication of such information to other persons who may subsequently publish or disclose such material.

> 4. I understand that any information suggested by the above
> mentioned categories is SECRET and must not be communicated to
> anyone other than the agency designated by AC of S [Assistant Chief
> of Staff], G-2, War Department, or the corresponding organization
> in overseas theaters of operations.

Without giving it much thought, Fellman signed the document; curiously, not everyone who was held at Stalag IX-B or Berga was required to sign such a form.[20]*

Morton Brooks remembered that the medical staff at the hospital tried to give him blood transfusions, but his veins were so constricted, they were unable to get the needle in. "I was taken to the field hospital near Bayreuth and flown to England on a hospital plane. I really couldn't eat. I remember the day they tried to give me a C-ration, which was cheese with bacon. I tried to take a bite and I couldn't. I guess that saved my life because I understand some people tried to get some food down and they killed themselves. If I put anything near my mouth, I would gag. They put me on a liquid diet in England."[21]

Norman Fellman, who had been liberated earlier at Hof and then hospitalized, said, "They sometimes gave us more food than we could really handle—rich food, too rich for us to digest. What went in came out. It was tough. They wanted to give us an injection, and there was no place to put the needle; it was bone. You do like you do a dog—you pick up the skin and slip it under the skin and the bone. I used to feel sorry for the guy from the blood lab; he had to give me a needle and he didn't know where the hell to put it."

Fellman was taken to a nearby Army mobile hospital. "I had lice bites all over my body and had the beginning stages of gangrene in my leg from infected bites. They treated us the best that they could and they flew us to a hospital in Paris. When I got to Paris, I guess the wounded were coming in faster than they could handle them, and the chief medical officer of the hospital said that my leg had to come off; they couldn't fool with it. This lieutenant said to this doctor,

---

*The reasons for requiring some POWs to sign this document remain cloudy to this day. Dr. Patricia Wadley, national historian for the American Ex-Prisoners of War organization, who has studied POWs for years, believes that a secret agreement made at Yalta in February 1945 between the United States, Britain, and the Soviet Union regarding repatriation of POWs holds the key, but as of 2004 the text of such an agreement has not become available. (Author correspondence with Dr. Wadley)

'You know we have this new medicine, penicillin, that is working miracles; I would like to try it on this fellow.' I was lying there in the bed, listening to these two guys and they may as well have been discussing some kid in China. It didn't matter; I just wanted them to go away and leave me the hell alone.

"Finally, the lieutenant persisted and the colonel was getting upset and he said, 'I'll give you three days, and if that leg isn't better, it comes off,' and he stormed off. They were giving me twenty thousand units of penicillin, twenty-four hours a day, every two hours around the clock. Today, if you get a shot of penicillin, it's half a million units or more, but in those days they were still experimenting with the dosage; I thought it was a miracle. They saved my leg. They would irrigate it with a penicillin solution and you could just watch those holes clean up. I had a series of lice-bite holes in my leg and they were all connected. They would put a wash in one and it would come out the other one. You could actually watch the wound heal."

Men began to realize that their families probably knew nothing about what had happened to them. Conversely, they also realized that none of them knew what had happened to their families during the past five months. Norman Fellman's mother had had a nervous breakdown before he went into the Army and he was not sure whether she was even still alive. "I had written a number of times, but I had no letter, no contact," he said. "The Red Cross had wired their chapter back in Norfolk, and they had inquired on my mother's health because I wanted to know if she was alive; I wanted to know what her condition was before I communicated with her. I wanted to know what to say."

Fellman recalled the hospital dietitians asked him what food he missed the most. "For some reason, it was eggs. They asked, 'How would you like them?' I said I want them every which way you can make them—two of each. So I got a dozen eggs. One was fried, one was turned over white, boiled soft, boiled hard— I ate every one of those eggs and, in an hour, every one of them came back out. There was a special diet after that. And vitamin pills. You couldn't have gotten better treatment anywhere."

With his leg healing, the Army flew Fellman and a number of other sick and wounded soldiers back to the States toward the end of May on a specially equipped C-47 "Dakota" hospital transport plane. "Everybody on the plane was on a stretcher; none of us could walk. They flew us first to Lisbon, where we refueled, and then they landed in the Azores. There were about eighteen patients and a flight nurse and an attendant.

"We were over the Atlantic and I'm looking out the window, thinking all kinds of wonderful thoughts, and I see this brown liquid begin to wash over the glass. I'm puzzled, so I call the flight nurse and say, 'What the heck is that?' She pulls the curtain shut and goes running into the cockpit where the pilots are and, the next thing I know, they feathered the prop on that engine and did a one-eighty and we were heading back to the Azores on one engine. We sat there for eight hours, long enough to put a new engine on. The other engine had been shooting oil. If they hadn't turned around, there would have been a fire; we would have all gone down."[22]

Peter Iosso recalled that he came back to the United States after spending some time in a field hospital and then a station hospital in England. "They made an effort to restore us physically," he said. "They fed us maybe five times a day. In no time I went from ninety pounds to 168 pounds. I was bloated. In that condition I returned to the United States. I got a ninety-day furlough. The purpose of that was to make us human beings again and have us readjust to civilized life—the food, family, and friendship."[23]

Joseph Mark reported that he was shipped to a hospital in Rheims, where the valise full of Nazi souvenirs and other mementos that he had picked up in Cham disappeared. "I was there a few days and they gave me a leave in Paris. There was nothing really wrong with me, other than the fact that I weighed just eighty-five pounds; I normally weighed only a hundred thirty-five then, so I wasn't down too much.

"Nothing was going on in Paris, nothing was working. Finally, they sent me to Camp Lucky Strike, which was the staging area in France for soldiers going back to the States. I got on a liberty ship, and ships were crashing into each other on the ocean because of a fog. It took two or three weeks to get home."[24]

Tony Acevedo remembered, "We wound up in New Jersey. I'll never forget it, it was just a dream. We came down the plank and here was this big sign: 'Welcome Prisoners of War,' and here was the Red Cross receiving us. We didn't have a penny to our name and they asked us for five cents for a chocolate bar. Coffee was five cents. That was the Red Cross for you."[25]

───✸───

Ernest Michel, the political prisoner who had been hiding out on a farm, recalled the significant date of 7 May 1945. "I remember distinctly, on May 7th, I was building a fence; I had a two-by-four in my hands. The farmer's wife came out to the field and she told her husband, 'Der Krieg ist vorbei'—'the war is over.' We stayed on the farms—I needed food. I was down to eighty or ninety pounds and it was the only way I could think of to eat and get my strength back. I stayed at that farm until the end of May 1945, long after the war was over. I never saw any Americans; I never saw any soldiers."

Michel had given no thought to what he would do if he survived the war, but now that the reality of peace began to sink in, he was filled with a desire to return home. "By the end of May, I must have gained twenty or twenty-five pounds. I was eating like it was going out of style. I decided I wanted to go back to Mannheim to find out if anyone in my family had survived. When I told the farmer's wife I was leaving, she said, 'Why don't you stay here? You can work here. We'll take care of you.' I said 'No, I must find out what happened to my family.' So she packed me a little package—sausage and bread and so forth—and I walked toward the west.

"I walked for two days and on the road I came across a black American GI in uniform. Evidently, he didn't speak German and I didn't speak much English. So he looked at me and pointed for me to go over to the side where there were maybe fifteen or twenty German soldiers. They wanted to talk to me but I didn't want to give away who I was." He pretended to be hoarse and unable to talk.

"A few hours later, the Americans sent me to a German POW camp. I was interrogated after maybe two days in that POW camp, never saying who I was or what had happened to me. I was evidently the only non-soldier in that camp. I always kept my Auschwitz tattoo covered; I was afraid for anyone to see that. I was interrogated by a German-speaking GI who was obviously born in Germany because he spoke without an accent. He never looked up—'Name? What unit are you with?' I said, 'Look, I have no unit. I was in the camp.' 'What camp? An army camp?' I said, 'Auschwitz.' He looked up and said, 'What?! What are you doing here?' I said, 'They told me to be in this camp. I didn't know where else to go.'

"Then he took me out and brought me to the officers, and that was where I spent the first day, telling them who I was and what had happened to me. From there, they gave me a motorcycle and I went back to Mannheim. It took me several days, obviously. But I learned how to ride a motorcycle."

When Michel reached Mannheim, he found the city on the Rhine in ruins. "There was nothing left. My parents had been deported from Mannheim in

Morton Brooks (right) and his cousin, Major David Powers,
have a family reunion at Fort Dix, New Jersey.
(Courtesy Morton Brooks)

1940 to a transit camp in southwest France at Gurs. From there they were sent in 1942 to Auschwitz and were gassed there. My younger sister was kept by Catholic nuns in a convent, and in 1942 she was sent by a Jewish relief organization to Palestine."[26]

———~~~———

In mid-June, Morton Brooks was sent to London where he was debriefed and then came back to the States on the HMS *Queen Mary.* "The POWs were supposed to get some priority but we ended up down near the engine room. But at least we didn't have to change places with the fellows on deck. I wasn't seasick on the voyage back; it was relatively smooth. It wasn't like going over on the troop ship."

The *Queen Mary* docked in New York and Morton Brooks came down the gangway a free man. "My parents didn't know I was on the ship. I had a cousin named David Powers who happened to be a major in the Air Force. He was a navigator but was working in New York City at the time. When I arrived at the hospital in England, I sent a letter home to tell the family I was alive. They sent my APO [Army Post Office] number to my cousin who was able to locate the hospital I was in from the APO number. He visited me on the first day I got out of bed. Suddenly, he showed up and I was shocked. Upon my arrival at Fort Dix, an uncle of mine, Major Murray Shorago, who was also stationed in New York, arranged to bring my family to see me at Fort Dix. I believe he was also instrumental in hastening a furlough for me."

Brooks was in the hospital and getting milk shakes every day, putting on a little weight. "I didn't look as bad as I did before; I had begun to look like a human being again. But still I hadn't gotten all of the lice out of my hair; that was something I was working on."

While on recuperation furlough, Brooks reported to a dispensary in New York and then was sent to Asheville, North Carolina. "A recuperation center examined me and put me back into the hospital," he said. "They found something on my lungs. I guess maybe it was dust from the mines, I don't know. Whatever it was, I stayed in the hospital until I was sent up to the medical center and then I was discharged."[27]

Because the POWs did not return as a unit, like most of the other divisions, they were greeted by no parades, no welcoming speeches by dignitaries, no great civic celebrations to commemorate the Allied victory in Europe. Instead, there were quiet, tearful reunions with mothers, fathers, sisters, brothers, and wives. There was laughing and crying and prayers of thanks that those who had been given up for dead were, at long last, home safe and—outwardly, at least—sound.

William Shapiro noted that, in mid-June, his plane to New York made a refueling stop in Newfoundland. As he was deplaning in Newfoundland, he was greeted by Salvation Army workers handing out refreshments. "It was the first time in my entire service overseas that I saw Salvation Army people. They were out in the freezing cold on a dark and windy night to feed us hot coffee and doughnuts. I will always remember the wonderful sight of these volunteers."

The plane reached Mitchel Field at Hempstead, Long Island. Shapiro remembered that everyone on board "had a great feeling of being home; the ordeal was finally over." While the group waited in the terminal to be transported to Halloran General Hospital on Staten Island for further evaluation, Shapiro suddenly realized that he was only about a ten-minute drive from his brother Dave's house in Forest Hills, Queens. He wanted to call, but had no change for the pay phone. Finally, after scrounging a dime, Shapiro called and talked with his sister-in-law. Because he had relatives nearby, Shapiro was able to obtain an overnight pass.

As it turned out, his girlfriend Betty was visiting his parents, and they all drove out to Mitchel Field for a reunion. "I was waiting at the front gate," Shapiro remembered, "and I had a new uniform. I was no longer emaciated, but I was not up to my normal weight as yet. I had no outward appearance of being ill, but I was now almost twenty years of age and probably, in their eyes, somewhat older and different from the boy that left for Europe one year ago.

"I began to run toward them as I sighted them walking through the gate. There was a lot of hugging and kissing and the many repeated '*Tanks, Gut*,' from my parents. I remember sitting in the backseat of Dave's car; Betty and I were holding hands and I was looking out the window, viewing the highway, going to the Bronx, and I truly could not believe that I was going home."

His first night home was a complete blank. "I do not think that I was very talkative. There must have been a lot of looking me over, and certainly I do not recall any talk of my imprisonment." The next day, Shapiro was sent to Halloran Hospital for two or three days, then received a seventy-five-day furlough so he could recuperate at home.[28]

Back in Brooklyn: Gerald Daub (right) and his buddy, Bob Rudnick, four months after their release from Berga. (Courtesy Gerald Daub)

Gerald Daub said he returned to the States on 9 June 1945, spent a short time at Halloran Hospital then, like Morton Brooks, was sent to Asheville, North Carolina. "I went there for what they called 'rehabilitation and reassignment.' Oddly enough, when I was finally examined, I was considered rehabilitated and declared fit for duty and sent back to an infantry division!" The Army sent Daub to Fort Jackson, South Carolina, and assigned him to a division that was scheduled for the invasion of Japan. But the war ended in August, and Daub was ordered to Fort Oglethorpe, Georgia, from where he was discharged in early December.[29]

Norman Fellman's hospital plane landed at Long Island's Roosevelt Field. "My parents were in Virginia; they didn't know that we were coming back. But two of my uncles—my father's brothers—were there to greet me and that was my first contact with my family. The Army flew me from Roosevelt Field to Maguire Army Hospital in Richmond. My mom and dad met me there. My mom just stared at me; she said I was too skinny. She's a mother; you know mothers have to be like that. Fortunately, she was over her nervous breakdown and she was fine when we were reunited."[30]

Peter Iosso reported that, once he arrived back in the States, he was sent to an Army hospital due to a persistent infection in one of his ears. "They were never really able to clear that up," he said. "I had that infection right up until the time I was discharged. They tried antibiotics, nasal sprays, throat sprays, everything. I went to Asheville, North Carolina. That was kind of a vacation at the expense of the government."

The luxury hotel in which several hundred ex-POWs were billeted was run by the Army, and all of the "guests"—privates, noncoms, and officers—were treated equally. "There was no saluting, no preference given to rank—a very unusual experience," said Iosso. "We had our meals served to us in the dining room, and we could play golf and take advantage of all the recreational programs they had going. I was reassigned to the Repatriation Center, in Special Services, Athletic Division, in Asheville. I did that for a few weeks. We took care of the golf course and the gym. We could play basketball and things like that. It was fun, it was fall, it was life in the Smoky Mountains. It was nice, very pleasant.

"While I was there, a bill was passed that any ex-prisoner of war could ask out of the service—a 'special convenience of the government' discharge. Well, I took advantage of that. I was discharged on the fourth of December 1945. Then I went home with my three hundred dollars mustering-out pay. I didn't have a hell of a lot of imagination at that time. I thought I'd probably go back to work in the factory.

"My sister told me that my mother and father were very worried when they got word that I was missing in action. My mother cried quite a bit." Iosso and his father had had some disagreements before he went into the service. "He may have been wishing that we should have had a more harmonious relationship; my sister told me that every once in a while, while I was missing, my father would hit his head against the wall.

"When I got home, I was warmly received; we had a small party. But the greeting they gave was kind of low key, because my two older brothers were still in the service. I was allowed to leave the Army early because of that special type of discharge."[31]

As soon as Joseph Mark arrived in New York, he saw his wife and mother and family. "Stella didn't know what had happened to me; they didn't know I was a prisoner until very late. They got a telegram saying I was missing in action, that's all. MIA. It wasn't until I was practically liberated that they learned I was a prisoner, so that was a very happy homecoming."

Mark received a thirty-day medical leave and was assigned to Lake Placid, New York. "The war with Japan was still going on, so this corporal there said that he was going to send me down to Camp Fanin, near Tyler, Texas, to train infantry, and I said, 'No, I'm not going.' I told him I thought I had done enough already. I said, 'Corporal, do you know how you train infantry to go on a ten-mile hike?' He said no. I said, '*You go on a ten-mile hike!*' I told him I can't walk like that anymore. So he took me in to see this major, who apologized for not sending me to someplace in New Jersey, near where I lived. I spent a short time in Camp Lee, Virginia, and the war finally ended; the atom bomb was dropped on Japan, and I was discharged right away."[32]

For Tony Acevedo, the road home to his family in Durango, Mexico, was especially long. "When I left the United States, a friend of mine who happened to be a disc jockey in Guanajuato, Mexico, knew the secretary to the owner of the radio station. Her name was Maria Dolores. I met her by phone; I was supposed to marry her when I came back from Europe. The Army gave us a ninety-day leave and we were advised by a psychiatrist, 'Don't make the mistake about getting married or going to work or going to school. You're going to rest. Take your time. Remember, this is something that you're not aware of, you're not having any capabilities of civilian life at this moment.' So the idea was, I was going to go visit my parents and visit Maria Dolores. I went to a surplus store in El Paso, Texas, and got some little presents to take with me. I was looking good, with my uniform and stripes and all."

While he was doing his shopping, a man came up behind him and covered his eyes and said, "Who do you think this is?" The voice sounded familiar. "It was the ex-governor of the state of Durango, who was a partner of my father. He was on a campaign tour for the next president of Mexico.

"Then he says, 'What are you doing? Where are you going?' I say, 'I'm heading for Durango to visit my parents.' So he says to the reporters, 'Take note of the son of Engineer so and so,' you know, like the way they describe your title in

Tony Acevedo with his father, Francisco, stepmother, Maria Luisa, and two-year-old brother, Agustin. Photo taken in July 1945 in Durango, Mexico. (Courtesy Tony Acevedo)

Mexico. He says, 'I want you, Mr. Acevedo, to be free on that train. If you need any help, let me know or let the conductor know.' So we hugged each other and said good-bye."

Acevedo went across the border to the Juarez station and paid twelve dollars for the trip to Durango. "The train started and the conductor came by and asked for my documents. I said, 'The only documents that I have, sir, is my uniform, but if you have any problems, please go see the ex-governor in coach so and so. A few minutes later, he came back and says, 'Sir, this train is at your disposal.' The governor must have told him, 'Look, don't bother him.' So everybody inside that coach where we were sitting kind of looked at me and says, 'Oh, my God—who is *he*?'"

On the train home to see his parents and marry Maria Dolores, Acevedo met another young woman—"Chita" Martinez—who happened to be the neighbor of one of his buddies. "I got her address and phone number, but when I got to Durango, all hell broke loose. My father asked if she and I got acquainted, if we got 'chummy' there. He was angry. Then he said, 'Son, take the car and take your friends out for a ride, get reacquainted with them.' I said, 'But, Dad, I cannot drive.'

"Then he blew his stack. He says, 'What! Why can't you drive? Doesn't the Army provide you with a car?' I said, 'No. You follow orders. You just don't pick up a car from the Army and just drive yourself to anywhere you want to go. You follow orders. You just can't take a car because you want to.'

"And then he got real pissed at me. He said, 'How come you let yourself be captured? That's kind of cowardly, don't you think so?' Then I said, 'Dad, you know what I think? You're way off beat.' We got into a big fight. I says, 'Dad, you don't know nothing about war. I know that your Mauser rifles back in your day were very highly pollutant. But I'll tell you one thing—I don't think you ever swallowed more gunpowder than I did. Your powder was nothing but just a fog. You'd choke to death if you smelled the powder of our ammunition.' I laid it down. So I got up, packed myself, and came back to the United States. I left Maria Dolores hanging. Then, five months later, I married Chita Martinez—the gal that I met on the train."[33]

World War II was well and truly over, but a new, "cold" war had begun. The Soviet Union took control of Poland, Czechoslovakia, the eastern half of Germany, and more. To use Winston Churchill's phrase, an "'Iron Curtain' had descended over Europe," and, for half a century, Berga and its terrible secrets lay hidden behind that curtain.

And the soldiers who had been incarcerated in Berga would soon become, in a very real sense, casualties of that new, "cold" war.

12

AFTERMATH

WHAT BECAME OF the others—the Germans who were responsible for the mistreatment and death of American prisoners of war at Berga?

In September 1946, the war-crimes trials of Captain Ludwig Merz, the head of the slave-labor work force at Berga, and Sergeant Erwin Metz, the overseer of the POWs, were held at the former concentration camp at Dachau, outside Munich. Both men were represented by defense counsels. During the course of the month-long trials, some sworn depositions from American ex-POWs were introduced, but no Americans were called to the courtroom in Dachau to testify. In fact, very few of the ex-POWs even knew that the trials had taken place until many years later.[1]

On 25 March 1946, six months before the trials began, Charles Vogel, a New York lawyer and the uncle of one of the POWs who died on the death march from Berga, offered his services to Major Clarence L. Yancey, in the War Crimes Office of the Judge Advocate General:

> My nephew, PFC Bernard J. Vogel, was one of those who perished among the 350 American prisoners of war that were taken by the

A former guard at Berga being questioned by two officers from the
5th Armored Division. (Courtesy National Archives)

Germans to the work camp at the Berga mines. . . . My nephew perished on that [evacuation] march.

I will be only too happy to help secure evidence from the survivors so that the Germans who caused this mistreatment may be
brought to trial. Can you advise me if that has yet been done?

I have in my possession a list of sixty of those 350. I know more
than sixty survived, and it should be easy to secure an accurate and
complete list of the survivors, obtain their statements, and work up
the necessary evidence for the prosecution. Of the sixty names, 28
have addresses. Seventeen of these are in the New York area. If you
will send me a letter stating that any affidavit or statement which I
forward to you will be considered in connection with a prosecution, I
am sure that I will have a fairly better chance of obtaining coopera-
tion, and time will be saved. I will make it my business to see each
and every one in the New York area, and will devote my evenings to
that purpose until that is accomplished. . . . [2]

Vogel's offer of help evidently was ignored by the War Crimes Office.

At their trials, both Merz and Metz proclaimed their innocence, saying that because of the general conditions of deprivation that existed throughout Germany during the final months of the war, the prisoners could not expect better food or living conditions than what they received.

Ludwig Merz said that he tried constantly to improve conditions in the camp but was prohibited from doing so by his superiors at Stalag IX-C at Bad Sulza and by SS Lieutenants Hack and Heieck, in charge of the Schwalbe V project. He also noted that, on his infrequent visits to Berga Two, the POWs had the opportunity to complain personally to him about the conditions and none ever did. In fact, Merz claimed that he was always in trouble with his superiors because he was regarded by them as being "too lenient" with the slave laborers. He said that the reason he was relieved of command on the "death march" was because he had not been tough enough on the Americans.[3]

For his part, Sergeant Erwin Metz argued that he, too, had gone out of his way to provide for the health and welfare of the POWs under his care. He claimed that it was *he* who had had a new barracks building constructed adjacent to the work-site so that the Americans would be spared the long walk to and from their camp and the tunnels. (The POWs recalled the building as being old and filthy.) He said that it was *he* who had campaigned for the Americans to be moved from the dirty and dangerous work inside the tunnels to a more salubrious outdoor setting. In addition, he claimed that the POWs were better clothed than their guards, and that each of the POWs was given two blankets when they left Berga.

He also asserted that, on the "death march," he would often bicycle ahead and arrange for civilians to have soup and hot tea and other foods waiting for the POWs when they reached the villages (none of the POWs remembered this happening). Whenever a POW fell ill along the march, Merz contended, they were taken to the nearest hospital for professional medical treatment.[4]

Despite their protestations, on 15 October 1945, Ludwig Merz and Erwin Metz were found guilty on all charges and were sentenced to death by hanging. The following year, lawyers for the two condemned men submitted petitions for clemency.[5]

Writing about the trial, defense attorney Richard Ruppert excoriated the tribunal for its many errors, and especially for the refusal of the War Crimes Group to approve a request that eyewitnesses from among the survivors be brought from the United States to Germany to participate in the trial. It is deeply troubling that the court failed, for whatever reason, to give the survivors the chance to face their former tormentors and speak for themselves. Their absence severely weakened the prosecution's case; their testimony could have carried considerable weight to support the allegations against Merz and Metz. According to court documents, the commanding officer of the local detachment of the War Crimes Group at Dachau refused to allow defense and prosecution witnesses in the United States to travel to Germany, or to permit the counsels for the defense and prosecution to travel to the U.S. and obtain depositions from material witnesses, or to allow officers from the Judge Advocate General's Corps in the United States to obtain depositions from said witnesses.[6]

Ruppert noted, "Nothing except the presence of American witnesses, or complete depositions, can clarify the confusions and contradictions of the present meager basic evidence. . . . Speaking as a lawyer, the defense counsel here asserts that the failure of American witnesses to appear in person or by deposition was the sole reason for the length of the trial. Confronted by chapter after chapter in a volume of hair-raising accusations—none of which could be called testimony because none of it was tested by the cold water of an opposite point of view—defense counsel could never disprove any prosecution statement by the simple and short method of cross-examination. . . . If the Americans had been present, the trial would have been terse, complete, investigative, and final in its revelatory character. As it is, after weeks of trial, the reasons for the 60 American deaths [at Berga] are still confused and untangled [sic]."[7]

In January 1948, the War Crimes Review Board met to consider the petitions for clemency that had been submitted by Merz's and Metz's lawyers.

Besides his wife, Luise, a large number of Merz's subordinates came to his defense, writing letters to the court, attesting to his fine character, genial nature, and willingness to do everything within his power to help the POWs better their existence.[8]

Erwin Metz, too, claimed that he tried to be the prisoners' friend and did his utmost to be kind and generous to them. "I never once harbored a feeling of hatred towards the POWs," wrote Metz. "I considered them my friends and my saviours from tyranny and dictatorship. I owed them thanks, and showed my thanks by doing everything that could be done for them in order to better their fate for the brief weeks."

In defense of Metz, a guard, Paul Hockart, testified that Metz provided eating utensils and three blankets per man, and assured the court that the medical care at the camp was sufficient. A civilian doctor from Berga, Rudolf Miethe, testified the POWs either had health problems, such as diarrhea, before they came to

Berga or else came down with the ailment from drinking water from the polluted Elster River.

Metz also asserted that he gave higher-quality food to the POWs than to their guards—a patently false claim; he said that the prisoners received hot coffee in the morning; sausage five days a week; lunches consisting of stew with meat, vegetables, and potatoes; and hearty soup for dinner. (If this is true, then all of the survivors were suffering from collective amnesia, for no one recalled these types of substantial meals.)

Perhaps conveniently forgetting that there were no medical supplies in the camp, Metz made the astounding contention that, "If anyone is to be held responsible for this [the terrible state of health of the Americans], *the ten U.S. medics are to be held responsible. They bore the sole responsibility for the medical care.* [Metz's emphasis]

"When the new camp [Berga Two] was taken over," he contended, "I intended to ask for a German medical corps non-commissioned officer to take charge of the hospital [there was no hospital at Berga Two], but the U.S. medics asked me not to do that and said that they, together with the German doctor, would take complete charge of all medical care themselves. By looking at their identification papers, I could see that they 'had passed an examination.' They also remarked that the sick prisoners of war would obviously have more confidence in the medics who were their own fellow countrymen. I saw the merits of this and approved it."

Metz went on to accuse the medics of stealing food from the sick and enriching themselves at the expense of their fellow Americans: "The medics (U.S.) habitually took part of the general food supplies for themselves, took what the sick prisoners left, since they could not eat much any more, and likewise gave the sick prisoners only half of the special diet food in the gift [i.e., Red Cross] packages. I made a thorough investigation and interrogated individual sick prisoners as to what food they had received the last few days before this. Unfortunately, the accusations proved to be true. To me that was a monstrous deceit, a crime committed against the sick prisoners by their own medics and fellow-countrymen. I ordered that a strict check be kept that every bit of food be distributed and that the medics stand guard day and night in two-hour shifts. . . . The steps I took won me the hate of the medics because I had reprimanded them for their flagrant negligence of duty, for their lack of piety and, to put it bluntly, for their crime against the sick. I ask you: who must bear the responsibility? The answer is obvious: The U.S. medics. . . ."

To paint himself as the compassionate supervisor, Metz pointed out that he often complained to SS Leutnant Hack that the Americans should not be used for work in the tunnels, but his complaints were dismissed. Metz also said that the corpses of POWs who died of illness or were "shot while escaping" were piled near the barracks for no other reason than a lack of coffins.

In closing his appeal, Metz asserted that it was *he* who was the aggrieved party: "I, an innocent man, have been dying a living death for three years and my poor family (wife and three daughters) are not only forced to do without me as their breadwinner but are also forced, through no fault of their own, to suffer hardship and distress after having lost everything, even their native land. That is the thanks I get for having conducted myself humanely."[9]

Primarily because no Americans had been called as witnesses either for the prosecution or the defense, the War Crimes Review Board, in January 1948, recommended reducing Ludwig Merz's death sentence to five years in prison. The reviewers also stated that there was reasonable doubt as to Erwin Metz's culpability in the death of Morton Goldstein; Metz's sentence was reduced from death to twenty years.[10]

The leniency shown by the court met with howls of protest from the few people who even knew of the reduction of sentences. Edwin A. Gray, the father of a POW who died at Berga, wrote to New Jersey Senator H. Alexander Smith,

> I have been much concerned of late in reading numerous articles in the newspapers concerning the work of the Special Commission in recommending and apparently securing the commutation of sentences imposed upon many of the Nazi war criminals.
>
> Our son, who was a prisoner of war in Germany, died in April, 1945, the victim of one of these criminals. The man, Metz, was convicted upon the evidence of eye-witnesses and now we learn his sentence has been commuted and that he is to be freed.
>
> Neither Mrs. Gray nor myself have any desire to be vindictive. If Bob had died in combat, we would have accepted our loss as thousands of other parents have done. But, now, we carry with us always the thought that he was brutally murdered as a defenseless prisoner. Someone who apparently has no interest whatever in all those fine young men who gave their lives in this war, has decided that this sentence of the Trial Court was unduly harsh and, as they express it, that Metz was only an "agent" carrying out the orders of his superiors.

We have two younger sons who served later in both France and Germany. As a family, we believe that we have the right to protest as strongly as we can against the unfeeling injustice of both this action on the part of the Commission and its approval by the Army.

Of course, we understand that protests of this nature are of little avail and receive scant consideration. We believe, however, that those in authority who are sponsoring this action should know how we feel. We will greatly appreciate it, therefore, if you will be kind enough to see that this letter reaches whoever may be in charge of such matters.[11]

The person in charge of such matters on whose desk this, and many more angry letters, landed was none other than the illustrious General Lucius Dubignon Clay, the Military Governor of Germany, a distant relative of Henry Clay, and architect of the "Berlin Airlift" that kept the citizens of that war-ravaged city alive after the Russians had cut off all land transportation into and out of it. Clay also had the final word on which ex-Nazis would be punished for their crimes.* While he had great compassion for the besieged civilians of Berlin, he evidently had little to spare for the American victims of Nazism. Dr. Jacob Cantor, whose son Jerry had died from his infected scratches, had protested to the Army and received this response from General Clay:

> ... I can fully understand and appreciate the intensity of your feelings, as the father of one of the victims of the work camp at Berga. ... Undoubtedly, the responsible individuals deserve the severest kind of punishment.
>
> My function, as final reviewing authority, however, is to review the records of trial in these cases and to mete out punishment in accordance with the evidence which was presented in court. ... In this case, unfortunately, all of the persons responsible for the conditions at the camp had not been apprehended and were not before the court. As to MERZ, there was little evidence connecting him directly with any atrocities and there was considerable evidence to the effect that he did his utmost within his power to ameliorate conditions for

---

*It should be noted that Clay also commuted the sentence of Ilse Koch, the notorious wife of the commandant of the Buchenwald concentration camp; it is alleged that she decorated her home with lampshades made from the tattooed skin stripped from the bodies of prisoners.

the American prisoners. I considered five years' imprisonment for MERZ to be an adequate sentence.

The evidence showed that METZ was a sergeant in charge of the work details of the camp and was guilty of much brutality. The only evidence in the record, however, connecting him with the killing of an American [Morton Goldstein] involved an escape incident. There was direct conflict in the evidence as to whether the victim was actually trying to escape or whether he was summarily killed. Considering the evidence in the Record of Trial as a whole, I considered that the ends of justice were met by a sentence of life imprisonment. . . .[12]

It was not the last letter General Clay would write to outraged, grieving relatives.

Both Merz and Metz served time in Landsberg prison—the same prison in which Adolf Hitler was incarcerated after the abortive Munich *putsch* and where he wrote *Mein Kampf.* In 1951, Ludwig Merz was given credit for time already served and was released from prison. Erwin Metz's sentence was reduced to fifteen years; he was later freed after serving six years.

In 1955, Metz's U.S. Parole Officer, Paul J. Gernert, commented in his Supplement to Metz's application for "Good Conduct Release":

> Applicant was released on parole on November 13, 1954. . . . This parolee made a remarkable adjustment while on parole. He is the introvert type, willing, industrious, and warm-hearted, probably too soft for his own welfare. He, at first, found it difficult to realize all the changes that took place since his imprisonment, especially those in his own family, such as marriage of his daughters. Parolee's wife carried the burden of family providor [sic] and since his release on parole she completely broke down physically. Parolee, although in impaired health, has faithfully continued in his employment and is especially grateful for the opportunity to be released on parole. . . . Recommend that he be released on good conduct release.[13]

Like many of the POWs who survived, Dr. William Shapiro had no knowledge that a war-crimes trial had been held for Metz and Merz until he read Mitchell Bard's book *Forgotten Victims* in 1996. When informed by this author of the content of Metz's plea for clemency, Dr. Shapiro responded, "I was never contacted, except for answering a questionnaire by attorney Charles Vogel, an uncle of Bernard Vogel, who died in Berga. I understand that Charles Vogel tried many times to contact the prosecutors but they had treated him as an 'interfering' person.

"All of the following will be of no avail at present but, just to set the record straight, the testimony of Metz regarding the medics is patently false. First, we did not have identification papers which would refer to our 'passing an examination.' I had no 'so-called papers.' We were all stripped of our equipment, Red Cross arm bands (only Tony Acevedo was able to keep his), etc. We were trained in different locales in the USA, had different ratings, but most were just assigned when you got to the Replacement Depot in England or France. We had International Red Cross Cards upon which was our photo, army serial number, thumbprint, and signature. This card was issued to all medics prior to going overseas. As to the food, at no time did we receive the daily rations as Metz described them. Our rations consisted of ersatz coffee in the A.M., a dipper full of green grass, turnip heads, occasional rotted potato soup, and a slice of 25% sawdust-contained bread.

"As to the Red Cross packages, there was no 'special diet' in the packages that we received. I was part of the detail to go to the British POW camp and plead for the packages. Metz withheld the packages and did not distribute them for eight days, keeping many for himself.

"I know nothing about what happened to Merz, but according to what Mack O'Quinn [another researcher/historian] conveyed to me, Metz died in his bed in 1972. Mack had contacted Metz's daughter and got this information. As far as Lieutenant Hack is concerned, he was hung by the Russians upon his capture."[14]

Whether someone at the higher levels of American government made a conscious decision to allow the prosecution of Merz and Metz, and the subsequent reduction of their sentences, to fade away with little public fanfare or outrage is unknown. By the late 1940s, the Cold War between East and West was growing chillier and more dangerous by the day. The trials of the major Nazi figures at Nuremberg in the autumn of 1946 had angered many Germans and worried many Americans who thought it prudent to downplay the old wartime animosities for the sake of enlisting the newest U.S. ally, West Germany, in the confrontation with the Soviets. Thus, in the face of the belligerency of Stalin and his hard-line minions, the spirit of revenge that had existed against the Nazi criminals evaporated. "Let bygones be bygones, and turn West Germany into the first brick in the wall against the tide of Communism" seemed to be the prevailing attitude among many in the Truman administration.

As a consequence, the victims of Berga never got their day in court, never had the opportunity to confront their tormentors or tell their stories of what actually transpired. They were, in the end, sacrificed upon the altar of a new world order. While such an outcome may have ultimately aided the West in resisting Soviet expansionism, it did nothing to resolve the turmoil and sense of injustice that the survivors of Berga, and the families of those who perished, would carry with them for the rest of their days.

EPILOGUE

ONCE THEY RETURNED to America, the young ex-POWs—most of them still in their late teens or early twenties—did their best to put the awful past behind them and get on with their lives. Most did surprisingly well, given their wartime experiences. Peter Iosso observed that it was like they had been granted "a new life."[1] They got married; had children; established careers; and tried to bury the memories of the terrible sights and sounds and smells of war and their captivity.

Yet, no matter how hard they tried to forget, the nightmares continued. Cold weather that numbed their feet and hands became a painful reminder of days spent in a frozen foxhole, or in an unheated boxcar, or on a long march under guard. An itchy scalp reminded them of the lice that had once feasted upon them. The innocent backfire of a car became gunfire and caused them a momentary flinch. A whiff of rotting garbage brought back memories of corpses left outside their barracks. An unflushed toilet sent their minds racing back to the horribly unsanitary conditions of the boxcars and camps. The racket of a jackhammer reminded them of the drills hammering away at the slate wall in the tunnels of Berga. The bark of a dog snapped them back to

John ("Jack")
Crawford,
photographed
in 2004.
(Courtesy
Jack Crawford)

terror-filled moments when they were surrounded by armed guards and snarling German shepherds. The gory dreams of hundreds of heads blown apart along the highway of death caused them to bolt upright, sweating, heart pounding, in the middle of the night. When their spouses asked them what was wrong, invariably the answer was, "Nothing. Just a dream." A later generation of soldiers would have a name for it: Post-Traumatic Stress Disorder, PTSD.

Although many of the men returned to lead seemingly normal lives full of goodness and worth, they would be forever scarred by their experiences on the front lines, at Stalag IX-B, at Berga, and on the death march to Cham. For decades, most of them kept the terrible secrets of their incarceration and survival a closely guarded secret, off-limits to family members and reporters.

In many ways, the survivors of Berga would forever remain prisoners of the Nazis.

THE STALAG IX-B (BAD ORB) SURVIVORS

JACK CRAWFORD. Jack Crawford remained at Bad Orb until American troops liberated the camp on 2 April 1945. He was detailed to guard the German camp guards for about a week before being allowed to depart. Crawford came home and married his sweetheart, Theresa Heisse, in 1948; they had three sons and three daughters. He received a disability pension due to service-related health problems, mostly stomach. After the war, he was a sales representative for a paint company and retired to his hometown of Philadelphia.[2]

P. ROBERT FOWLER. P. Robert Fowler, a POW at Bad Orb and Berga, passed away in November 1998. His widow, Helen, provided the following information: "I didn't know Robert while he was in the military, as he was ten years older than me, but his mom always said he was never the same after he came back from the war; I can believe that. I have learned lots since his death about what he went through during his POW days— wish I had known it during our married life; I'm sure it would have made

P. Robert Fowler in 1983. (Courtesy Helen Fowler)

it easier to live with him. He hardly talked about his experiences, except about not having enough food. During the 125 days he was a POW, he did not have a bath, nor a change of clothes, and very little to eat. He lost about 70% of his body fat. He did not blame the German people. He would always say, 'They were as good to us as they could be.' My husband was a HERO. He died with COPD (a lung condition) that was caused from being exposed to God-knows-what and digging those underground factories, yet our government denied his claims for his lung condition. He was on oxygen the last two years of his life and was a very sick man, but he didn't complain. He always had a smile. He was, however, very disappointed that his government wouldn't approve his claim for his lung condition (he never smoked a cigarette his whole life). He fought for his claim for six long years. . . . He deserved better than this.

"The one thing that my husband could not understand was the apathy that young people had toward government. He believed that, as citizens of this country, we had the privilege and the responsibility to vote and let our voices be heard. . . . My husband always felt that voting was a very hard-earned privilege that he and everyone in the service fought for. In fact, the very last thing he did in this life was to vote."[3]

LEON HOROWITZ.   Leon Horowitz, whose pneumonia at Stalag IX-B prevented him from being sent to Berga, had a memorable story about an incident at Bad Orb after the 350 POWs had departed from Stalag IX-B on 9 February: "Additional American soldiers were brought to the camp, including more Jewish soldiers. In February, there's a Jewish holiday known as Passover. Among the new prisoners that had been brought to IX-B were a number of Jews among them. So we put the word out that we were going to have a Passover seder. There may have been ten or fifteen of us, and we sat around outdoors in a circle. We didn't have any prayer books, but a lot of us had had a lot of Hebrew schooling, and several of us knew many of the prayers by heart. At a seder, there's a lot of traditional food—unleavened bread, bitter herbs, matzoh, and so on. We didn't have any of that, so we made believe. The Germans up in the guard towers had no idea what we were doing."

Dr. Leon Horowitz
in 1998.
(Courtesy
Dr. Leon Horowitz)

After receiving a medical discharge in August 1945, he returned home and started classes at NYU in September. Upon graduation, he was accepted into medical school. In 1951, he married Florence Betty Phillips; they have been married ever since, and have five children and seven grandchildren. In 1955, the Horowitzes moved to Tulsa, Oklahoma, where he established a medical practice.

Thoughts of being captured in the winter and his subsequent incarceration in an unheated barracks stayed with Dr. Horowitz: "Many of us who had non-freezing cold injury today have symptoms such as not being able to tolerate cold; I can't hold a glass with ice in it because my fingers turn white and hurt like hell."

He retired in 1993 to Southlake, Texas, in order to be near three daughters and six grandchildren.[4]

ROBERT KLINE.   Robert Kline spent two months in an Iowa hospital following his return to the U.S. The lack of adequate dental care during his incarceration at Stalag IX-B resulted in the extraction of all his upper

Dr. Robert E. Kline,
photographed in 1994.
(Courtesy Robert Kline)

teeth. He was discharged from the service in October 1945 and attended Iowa State University, from which he graduated with a doctorate in Veterinary Medicine. He practiced in Melbourne, Iowa, for thirteen years, then he and his wife Lucille bought the Diamond K Ranch near Lyons, Colorado, retired from his practice, and became a feed-lot feed sales representative. The Klines have two daughters and two grandchildren.[5]

RICHARD LOCKHART.   Richard Lockhart has forever wondered why the Jewish soldiers at Bad Orb identified themselves, for it gave the Nazis the opportunity to "demonstrate once again the enormous capacity of some to impose the cruelest punishment on others, solely because of differences of race, religion, nationality, or culture. Those Jewish GIs in Stalag IX-B many have thought they would be exempt from the Nazi Holocaust. They were not, and their fate should never be forgotten."

After the war, Lockhart returned to Chicago and attended evening school at Northwestern University. In 1958, he started a governmental affairs management/lobbying firm and, as of 2004, at age eighty, still worked there. "I love what I do," he said. "Why should I retire?"[6]

CLIFFORD SAVAGE.   After spending several weeks at Stalag VII-A at Moosburg, Clifford Savage and the other POWs there were sent on a march similar to the one suffered by the Americans at Berga; his group was liberated on the road on 29 April 1945. After the war, he returned and became a self-employed paint and drywall contractor. He married Doris Renfrow on New Year's Eve, 1948. They have five children and seventeen grandchildren. He retired in 1982 to Olive Branch, Mississippi.[7]

JAMES V. SMITH.   James V. Smith returned to New York on 5 May 1945. Three days later, on V-E Day, Smith was in Fort Jackson, South Carolina, where he celebrated the end of the war in Europe.

On 3 December 1945, Smith was discharged and later married his long-time sweetheart, Mary Virginia Fuller. Before the war, he had worked at a local textile

Richard
Lockhart,
photographed in 2004.
(Courtesy Richard
Lockhart)

Recent photo of
Cliff Savage.
(Courtesy of
Cliff Savage

mill, Jordan Mills, for almost two years, right out of high school. After the war, Smith returned to the company and stayed there for thirty years. Eventually, he became secretary of the company, then treasurer, and finally vice president and a member of the board of directors. "Quite an advancement from where I had started," he said.

He and his wife had four children, and they had three grandchildren. He passed away in March 2004, shortly after being interviewed for this book.[8]

THE BERGA SURVIVORS

TONY ACEVEDO. He was married for thirty years to the woman he met on the train to Durango. After being discharged, he trained to become a chiropractor, but switched careers and became a design engineer, working in aerospace engineering at McDonald Douglas, North American, and Hughes Aircraft.

James V. Smith in
February
2004.
(Courtesy
Mary E. Smith)

The Acevedos had four children: a son who is today an analytical engineer; another who is a computer specialist for a European space firm; another who is an architectural engineer; and a daughter working for Raytheon. Tony and his wife divorced in 1985.

Maria Dolores, the woman he originally thought he would marry, then came back into his life. He said, "Maria was married to an Air Force man, but he died. After thirty-three years, I met her again; we have been together ever since. I can't marry her because she will lose her government benefits. But we have been very good friends; she needs my help more than I need her help. She has a very bad back."

Tony also spent time volunteering at the Veterans Administration hospital in Loma Linda, California, where he worked with former POWs. He also traveled the country talking with ex-POWs. In 2004, he was living in southern California.[9]

MORTON BROOKS. Morton Brooks was released from the hospital in December 1945 and received his discharge. A flood of veterans entered

Tony Acevedo in 1999
displays his medals.
(Courtesy
Tony Acevedo)

college at that time on the GI Bill* and Brooks was accepted by the University of Buffalo for the February term.

"I was very desirous of trying to make up the time that I had lost," he said. "I was able to repeat some of the courses that I had taken earlier, like Chemistry and Biology; I was able to finish up in about two and a half years. I wanted to be a psychologist, so went to Columbia for graduate work, and came out a psychologist.

"Fortunately, I met a girl named Selma, who later became my wife, and she was a marvelous therapist; she got me through a lot of difficult days."

The two met accidentally on the train from New York to Connecticut. "She was with her boyfriend; he was in the Army and he was home on furlough, and his unit was supposed to be sent to the Pacific. She and I got to talking and found out that we were going to the same place—an adult camp—in Connecticut for a week. We became sort of friends during the week that we were up

---

*The "G.I. Bill," or Serviceman's Readjustment Act, was legislation passed on 22 June 1944 and designed to provide federal assistance to veterans in the areas of health care, the purchase of homes and businesses, and, mostly importantly, higher education. For the next seven years,

Dr. Morton Brooks speaking to a high school class about the Holocaust and his experiences as a POW. (Courtesy Morton Brooks)

there, and we met again afterwards and found the chemistry between us. We got married and had two daughters and five grandsons."

After the war, he changed his surname from Brimberg to Brooks "because of the anti-Semitism I experienced from my fellow Americans. After what I went through during the war, this was very troubling to me."

Brooks never returned to Bad Orb or Berga after the war. "I haven't been able to get myself to do that. I wasn't even sure that I wanted to go back to Germany. I started a program of taking my grandsons on trips with me as they matured, and I took one on a cruise in 2002; one of the stops was Germany. I did go to see what Berlin looked like on a one-day tour, however."

Brooks had certain physical and emotional symptoms—such as Irritable Bowel Syndrome, spinal arthritis, and PTSD—that he attributed to his treatment as a POW, but he always tried to keep a positive outlook on life. "I've described my POW experience as a million-dollar experience I wouldn't want to repeat for two million. It gave me an understanding of behavior under extreme

the government subsidized college tuition, fees, and books for some eight million veterans; by 1951, the program had cost taxpayers approximately $14 billion but reaped incalculable benefits for veterans in particular and the nation as a whole. (www.higher-ed.org)

conditions and how brutal and sadistic people can be toward others. I don't feel as though only the Germans acted that way; some fellows in Japanese POW camps experienced the same thing. I guess it would be a contest to see who would be more brutal and sadistic. Germans were supposed to be an educated, sophisticated society. Even when we brought up the Geneva Convention to them—if you're not the military in power, then forget it."

He has closed his psychology practice and retired to Florida.[10]

GERALD DAUB.   After receiving his discharge at Fort Oglethorp, Georgia, in early December, Gerald Daub was back in school, studying architecture at the Pratt Institute in the second week of January 1946. After graduation, he enrolled in a summer art school for Americans near Paris, at the palace of Fontainebleau. On the ship from New York to France, he met an aspiring American painter, Joan Hughes. "We became friendly at the school, and we stayed that winter in Paris. She was at the painting academy called Academy Juliet and I was enrolled in the Beaux Arts in Paris and worked briefly for a very well-known architect, Le Corbusier. But the money that paid my salary ran out and I returned to America."

Daub became his father's partner and eventually took over the architectural firm. "I was finished with college and Joan was still a student in her second or third year at Syracuse. She graduated after six months or a year and we got married. Eventually, my father passed away and I ran the office by myself for about thirty years. I retired in 1998 and left the business to my son, David. I live in a place just south of Nyack."

His friend, Bob Rudnick, eventually came home by hospital ship. "He was hospitalized but pretty much recovered. We just resumed our lives in Brooklyn; he became a tax lawyer and an accountant, and we were the greatest of friends for the rest of our lives. At that time I lived in Tenafly, Bergen County, New Jersey, and he lived in Denbrook, about forty-five miles away. He had two girls and I had two boys. Our wives were very friendly. He owned a winter lodge in Mount Snow and we all skied together there. Joan and I owned a house in the Hamptons, so we vacationed together there in the summer. Both Bob and his wife have passed away, but we still see both of his daughters. The older girl was married last spring and I gave the bride away. It was a great honor for me."[11]

Gerald Daub, photographed in fall 2003, at a Holocaust symposium for high school students and teachers, Nashville, Tennessee. (Courtesy Gerald Daub)

NORMAN FELLMAN. After returning home, Norman Fellman was eager to go to college and couldn't stand to wait to be discharged. "I wanted to go to William and Mary, which had an extension in Norfolk, Virginia. They were accepting students in September and it was getting late and I was getting ready for discharge. I am trying to get out of the Army and they keep telling me, 'In a couple of days, in a couple of days.' One day I go down to where the discharge office is and there's nobody there—out to lunch, or whatever. I see this stack of discharge papers on the guy's desk, so I go through the stack and I find my name third from the bottom. I just removed it and put it second or third from the top, and the next day I was out. I just barely made it into school for the fall semester."

Fellman only allowed himself two years to get his schooling. "I wanted to get to work. I felt like I had a hell of a lot of catching up to do. I loved William and Mary; I went there for one year and then I went to the University of Virginia for a year. In those two years, I took all the business courses I could find.

Norman Fellman and
his wife, Bunny, pho-
tographed in 2003.
(Courtesy Norman
Fellman)

"While I was there, I met this nurse; I wound up marrying her. Her name was Ruth Faust, but she was called 'Bunny.' When she was in class, there were two or three Ruth's, so to keep them from confusing one another in their class, they gave her a nickname. She had a mannerism—she was very quick at everything she did and very precise, so they said she was quick like a bunny, and it became 'Bunny.'"

Fellman's father wanted him to go into the footwear business with him, so he got his son a job at Weinberg Shoe Manufacturing Company in Milwaukee to learn the ins and outs of the business. "They took me through an executive training program and I worked in each department of the factory. I came away with at least an appreciation of how footwear was made and the differences in quality. Then I joined my dad; he had tried to market some of his inventions that he made for the Navy. They insisted that he patent them so that none of his other inventions got taken away from him."

Fellman and his father worked together in retail for a number of years until his uncles bought the stores and the younger Fellman went into the wholesale footwear business. "I stayed in wholesale for five or six years, on the road, and then I opened my own store in Union, New Jersey. I had what was then, I think, a first—the only fine men's footwear shop on the highway. Not a discount store—it was a full-service shop. I was there for twenty years. It was very close to Newark, and we were near a very high-crime area. We were held up four or five times. The last time they held us up, there was weapons fire at the store—about four or five rounds. My wife asked me to close it or she was going to leave me; I debated it for about three seconds. I retired in 1986.

"When my dad was in his nineties, he was working on developing a combat boot for desert warfare. The Israeli army wanted to fly him to Israel and have him present the plans to them; Pop felt that he couldn't go that far because his doctors said he was close to the end. I still have a set of plans for those boots. He was quite a guy."

The Fellmans have three daughters and two grandchildren and live on a horse farm in Bedminster, New Jersey. Norman Fellman said, "It's been a good life. I got my pilot's license and flew an airplane for a while. Got a motorcycle, did that. Rode horses for years. I have done about everything I wanted to do."

He also began talking for the first time in decades about his POW experiences, having found that discussing his horrific memories has helped to dislodge the traumatic demons. "The more I talk about it, the easier it gets," he said.[12]

PETER IOSSO. After being discharged, Peter Iosso decided to go back to work in a factory—adjusting record-player turntables for General Instrument Corporation in Elizabeth, New Jersey, for a dollar an hour. Finding the work stultifying, Iosso, a high school dropout, realized that he wasn't going anywhere without an education. He entered an accelerated program for veterans that enabled him to complete his high school education and receive his diploma. While he excelled in all his courses, he was most proficient in French. He applied to Montclair State Teachers College, where he majored in French. He then received a scholarship to study in France at the University of Strasbourg.

"I had matured a little more while I was in France, then I came back to Montclair State. I was kind of a celebrity—you know, an exchange student returning to a local college. It was the fall of 1950 at Montclair when I met a pretty young woman in the cafeteria. Her name was Rhoda Thomson. We went out together. She was an English major and a French and Social Studies minor. We dated throughout 1951 and graduated in 1952 and got married."

A recent photo of
Peter Losso.
(Courtesy Peter Iosso)

Iosso received a teaching fellowship at the University of Wisconsin in Madison in the department of languages and his wife also found a teaching job in a nearby school. "I decided during that year that graduate work was not for me. I had trained to be a teacher of French and that's what I wanted to do."

After a brief stint teaching in Janesville, the Iossos returned to New Jersey, where he obtained a teaching position at Columbia High School in South Orange-Maplewood. He retired from teaching in 1985, and successfully battled prostate and kidney cancer. Sadly, Rhoda passed away in 2000.

Looking back on his seventy-eight years, Iosso reflected, "As an ex-POW, I have enjoyed a return to civilian life; schooling under the GI Bill; a long, fruitful marriage; a family—source of joy and satisfaction; a successful teaching career; retirement; and remission from cancer. However, despite all this goodness and serendipity, I am still haunted by the indelible images of that period of captivity, and I still have real pain and discomfort from the physical and psychological problems that were the direct result of that POW life."[13]

JOSEPH MARK.   Joseph Mark is another who has dealt with the physical and mental after-effects of being held as a prisoner of war. Physically, cold weather pains him. "I still have frozen feet," he said. "My feet bother me to this day."

He was not able to speak about his experiences for many years. Perhaps as a way to deal with his own trauma, he attended New York University and earned a doctorate in Clinical Psychology, spending fifty years as a psychologist. "I worked for the VA for about five or six years, and then I went into private practice, doing mainly psychotherapy."

He retired from his practice when he was eighty. The Marks have enjoyed living in New Jersey and wintering in Florida. He and his wife, Stella, have three sons and a daughter, and each one has two children.

Mark refused to let his POW experiences diminish his sense of humor and positive outlook on life: "One of the things that kept me going through all of that was my bitter hatred for Hitler and the things he did. I still have strong feelings against the Nazis and what they did to my buddies.

"The Germans and the Japanese are very unusual people. They can be involved in a military operation where they're killing people and then go home and play in a string quartet. It's very strange. Curiously enough, though, I don't have that hostility toward the Germans of today. I think of them as a different generation, different people, and I don't want to carry my anger with me all of my life—and I don't. In fact, I recently went out and bought myself a German Volkswagen Passat!"[14]

ERNEST MICHEL (no image shown).   The German-born Ernest Michel, a political prisoner who had survived five and a half years in various Nazi concentration, slave-labor, and extermination camps, made his way to America after learning that his family, except for his younger sister, who was safely in Palestine, had been wiped out by the Nazis. He said, "I came to this country in 1946 through the Harry Truman Displaced Persons Act, through one of the Jewish organizations. I learned English and eventually became an executive with the United Jewish Appeal, in New York, an organization I've been involved with ever since."[15]

Dr. Joseph Mark and his wife, Stella, shown enjoying retirement in a recent photo. (Courtesy Dr. Joseph Mark)

WILLIAM SHAPIRO. William Shapiro always felt his "good luck amulet" was the International Red Cross Card which proved that he was a non-combatant and, based upon the Geneva Convention of 1929, was to be accorded special treatment. "Well, I did not get all the special treatment but it clearly saved my life," he said. "Being a medic protected me from other roles, jobs, and risk factors which surely may have resulted in my being killed, being wounded, or dying as a prisoner. . . . The infantrymen in my platoon were always protective of me, and would cover me from enemy attack when it was within their control. There were countless anxious and life-threatening experiences, but my amulet must have helped.

"When I was taken prisoner, the panzer troopers who searched me must have had some understanding or feeling for a medic. They took all my other possessions, left me with four cigarettes, and I do not recall any harassment. After I was transferred to Arbeitskommando 621 in Berga, my card helped define my work detail, which was infinitely less arduous, with less risk for injury and brutality. As a medic, I experienced that miraculous interlude when I was fed, cleansed, and rested in Stalag IX-C."

After the war, Shapiro kept the Red Cross card in his wallet until he retired in November 1985. "Later that month, I was playing golf and my wallet was stolen from my locker—about forty-one years after the card was issued. I made many attempts to retrieve the wallet from the police, but the thief must have discarded it in some trash can. Physically, my good luck amulet is gone but it will always be remembered and, in my mind, it is always with me."

Shapiro courted his childhood sweetheart, Betty Ostrowsky, during the summer of 1945. "Sometime in July, I bought Betty a watch which, in that era, preceded the engagement ring for the recognized protocol of commitment. On August 8, 1945, the Japanese surrender led to a pandemonium of joy and celebrations. We and all our friends ran, shouted, and sang in the streets of Pelham Parkway. The girls were all dressed in their best party dresses. Crazily, we mounted and sat on the hoods of some cars that were slowly driving through the streets. We were happy. Our joy was an expression of our understanding that each of us could get on with our individual lives, free from the terror of going to the Pacific to end that war." Shapiro was discharged on October 20, 1945. "I have the telegram which I sent to my parents, and it states, 'Call me Mister.'"

He then attended New York University and was admitted to Boston University Medical School. He interned at Mount Sinai Hospital, New York City, where he did his residency in obstetrics and gynecology, and then started his own practice. He also rose up the academic ladder of the Mount Sinai Hospital and Medical School to become Senior Attending and Associate Professor of Ob/Gyn; he was there for thirty-five years.

"I stopped active practice because of my hearing loss secondary to my five months on the front lines; my concussion with all the loud explosions, etc., resulted in hearing loss over time. I then became a medical legal expert, defending OB/Gyns in negligence suits, and was consultant to two hospitals. After eight years, the statute of limitations—and my becoming tired of the work—helped me retire for good.

"After I returned to the States, Betty was the most important person to help me become reacclimated and 'rehumanized.' She was always supporting and encouraging. Happily, we have been married for fifty-seven years and have a great family. We have three sons who have all followed me in becoming

Dr. William Shapiro
in 2003. (Courtesy
Dr. William Shapiro)

physicians, but in different fields. They and their wives have given us seven grandchildren who we see frequently in Florida.

"Presently, we are physically well. I had a quadruple bypass in 2003 and I am now fully recovered. We live in an active tennis and golf community and have many friends, and social engagements as well as theatre, concerts, etc. We feel blessed and fortunate to experience this retirement.

"I am constantly amazed when I think of where we have come, what we have personally contributed to humankind in so many various ways. Of-times, I think of the millions of Jews and non-Jews killed by Hitler, Stalin, and other killers—not to forget the Muslim fanatics of today, who have destroyed the lives of young people who could have made inventions unknown and done so many things for the betterment of humankind. What I see and read about them makes me shudder for all our children. Again, we are repeating man's inhumanity to his fellow man."[16]

Remains of a barrack at Berga Two.
(Author photo 2004)

BERGA-AN-DER-ELSTER

Because Berga was in East Germany until the collapse of the Communist state in 1989, it is only recently that Westerners have begun to visit the region. The sprawling Buchenwald concentration camp near Weimar has drawn large numbers of visitors, but Berga is virtually unknown. High on a hill to the north of the town is a memorial to the victims of Buchenwald, but there are no signs, markers, or memorials to those who slaved in the tunnels along the Elster River, or died of disease, accidents, brutality, or outright murder.

The site of Berga One, the political prisoners' camp, is today an anonymous farm-equipment manufacturing facility, with no hint of the gallows, barracks, and other buildings that once existed.

The buildings still stand at Berga Two, the American camp up the hill on the south end of town. The site was turned into a youth camp (similar to Stalag IX-B) but was closed in 1994 and has remained abandoned since then. The tunnel entrances were sealed with concrete several years ago. But there are no signs, memorials, museums, or markers at any of the sites to inform current and future generations about the terrible things that happened there.

242

Sealed
entrance to one
of the tunnels.
(Author photo 2004)

Emil Kluge, the mayor
of Berga in 1945,
places a wreath to the
memory of
victims of Nazism.
(Courtesy National
Archives)

243

Two Berga citizens carry wreaths during memorial ceremonies in the town square. (Courtesy National Archives)

The townspeople of Berga, along with American GIs, attend a memorial ceremony in the town square for the camp's victims, May 1945.
(Courtesy National Archives)

POSTSCRIPT

In April 2004, Stephan Büttner, the young mayor of Berga, wrote for this book:

> April 2005 will be the 60th anniversary of the liquidation of the slave labor camp and POW camp called "Schwalbe V" in Berga. The approaching American troops and the approaching end of World War II gave rise to the German rulers' decision to evacuate slave laborers and POWs to send them on the death march. Many of them did not see their liberation.
>
> With great gratitude we remember the liberation by the Allies. One of the darkest chapters of German history was finished. The occupying powers accompanied the reconstruction and development of democracy in Germany. Today it is more important than ever before to join hands with all peace-loving people all over the world in a common effort to establish friendship and understanding against dictatorship and terrorism.[18]

APPENDIX

Unit Composition

In World War II, a U.S. Army infantry division was organized as follows:

	Officers	Warrant Officers	Enlisted Men	Total*
Division headquarters:	38	8	103	149
Headquarters and headquarters company:	6	0	113	119
Three rifle regiments (each):	139	5	2,974	9,354
Division Artillery:	130	9	2,021	2,160
Engineer Combat Battalion:	27	3	617	647
Medical Battalion:	34	2	429	465
Signal Company:	7	4	215	226
Ordnance Light Maintenance Co.:	9	1	137	147
Quartermaster Company:	10	0	183	193
Military Police Platoon:	3	0	70	73

Each infantry division had three rifle regiments; each regiment had three battalions of approximately 800 men each; each battalion had four companies of approximately 200 men each; each company had four platoons of approximately 40 men each; each platoon was composed of approximately 9–12 men.

---

* With attached chaplain, additional medical, and band, the total authorized strenth is 14,253. (Source: Stanton, p. 9)

NOTES

Prologue

1. 11th Armored Division, G–3 messages, 16–31 April 1945, Records Group 94, National Archives.
2. William L. Shirer, *The Rise and Fall of the Third Reich* (Greenwich, CT: Fawcett/Crest, 1960), pp. 1414–1418.

Chapter 1: Raw Recruits

1. Morton Brooks interview by author, Nov. 2, 2003.
2. Website: www.astpww2.org.
3. Brooks interview by author, Nov. 2, 2003.
4. Gerald Daub interview by author, Nov. 16, 2003.
5. Shelby Stanton, *World War II Order of Battle* (New York: Galahad Books, 1984), pp. 176–177.
6. Anthony Acevedo interview by author, Nov. 20, 2003.
7. Stanton, pp. 139–140; and website: www.army.mil.

8.   Acevedo interview by author, Nov. 20, 2003.

9.   Stanton, p. 140.

10.   Norman Fellman interview by author, July 20, 2003.

11.   Joseph Mark interview by author, Nov. 20, 2003.

12.   William Shapiro correspondence with author, March–April 2004.

13.   Stanton, pp. 104–106.

14.   Peter Iosso interview by author, Aug. 15, 2003.

Chapter 2: Trial by Fire

1.   Website: www.st.vith.be.

2.   Hugh M. Cole, *U.S. Army in World War II—The European Theater of
       Operations—The Ardennes: Battle of the Bulge* (Washington, DC: U.S. Army
       Center of Military History, 1994), pp. 39–42.

3.   Ibid., pp. 51–56.

4.   Bell I. Wiley; William R. Keast; and Robert R. Palmer, *U.S. Army in World
       War II—The Army Ground Forces: The Procurement and Training of Ground
       Combat Troops* (Washington, DC: Historical Division, Department of the
       Army, 1948), pp. 470–473.

5.   Robert P. Kissel, "Death of a Division." Website: www.military.com. (Date
       unknown)

6.   Cole, pp. 139–141.

7.   Charles D. McMullen, website: www.axpow.org.

8.   Danny S. Parker, *Battle of the Bulge: Hitler's Ardennes Offensive, 1944–1945*
       (Philadelphia: Combined Books, 1991), pp. 39–40; and Charles B.
       MacDonald, *A Time for Trumpets: The Untold Story of the Battle of the Bulge*
       (New York: Quill/William Morrow, 1985), p. 40.

9.   *New York Times,* Dec. 15, 1944.

10.   Doris Kearns Goodwin, *No Ordinary Time: Franklin and Eleanor Roosevelt:
       The Home Front in World War II* (New York: Simon & Schuster/Touchstone,
       1994), pp. 549–553 and 570–571.

11.   Cole, p. 71.

12.   Helmut Heiber and David M. Glantz, eds., *Hitler and His Generals: Military
       Conferences 1942–1945* (New York: Enigma Books, 2003), pp. 533–541.

13.   Shirer, pp. 1415–1418.

14.   Paul Carell, *Hitler Moves East, 1941–1943* (New York: Bantam, 1966), p. 9.

15.   Dwight D. Eisenhower, *Crusade in Europe* (Garden City, NY: Doubleday, 1948), p. 342; and Cole p. 71; and Parker, pp. 67, 75, 81, 116–117, 169–171.

16.   Cole, pp. 72–73.

Chapter 3: The Surprise

1.   Cole, pp. 139–141 and 151–152.

2.   Shapiro memoir.

3.   Cole, p. 59.

4.   Omar N. Bradley, *A Soldier's Story* (New York: Rand McNally, 1951), p. 459.

5.   Iosso interview by author, Aug. 15, 2003; and memoir.

6.   Robert Kline interview by author, Nov. 10, 2003.

7.   Clifford Savage interview by author, Nov. 13, 2003.

8.   *New York Times,* Dec. 18, 1944.

9.   Cole, pp. 156–159.

10.   Iosso interview by author, Aug. 15, 2003; and correspondence, 2003.

11.   Mark interview by author, Nov. 2, 2003.

12.   James V. Smith interview by author, Feb. 9, 2004.

13.   Cole, pp. 654–655.

14.   Savage interview by author, Nov. 13, 2003.

15.   Smith interview by author, Feb. 9, 2004.

16.   Cole, pp. 143 and 162.

17.   Ibid., pp. 156–158.

Chapter 4: Captive

1.   Eisenhower, p. 342.

2.   "The Battle of St. Vith, Belgium—17–23 December 1944. An Historical Example of Armor in the Defense." U.S. Army Armor School (Reprinted by Merriam Press, Bennington, VT, 2003), p. 21.

3.   Cole, pp. 157–158.

4.   Shapiro memoir.

5.   Cole, pp. 161 and 171–172; and Charles Whiting, *Death of a Division* (New York: Stein and Day, 1981), pp. 75 and 91.

6.   "Battle of St. Vith." U.S. Army Armor School, p. 21.

7.   Kline interview by author, Nov. 10, 2003.

8. Whiting, p. 96.
9. Kline interview by author, Nov. 10, 2003.
10. Whiting, pp. 91–97.
11. Ibid., pp. 89–99.
12. "Battle of St. Vith," U.S. Army Armor School, p. 21.
13. Smith interview by author, Feb. 9, 2004.
14. Mark interview by author, Nov. 2, 2003.
15. Crawford interview by author, Nov. 25, 2003.
16. House memoir.
17. Cole, p. 170.
18. Eisenhower, p. 342.
19. Harry C. Butcher, *My Three Years with Eisenhower* (New York: Simon and Schuster, 1946), p. 724.
20. Ibid., p. 730.

Chapter 5: Bad Times at Bad Orb

1. *New York Times,* Dec. 18, 1944.
2. *Time,* Jan. 1, 1945.
3. David A. Foy, *For You the War Is Over: American Prisoners of War in Nazi Germany* (New York: Stein and Day, 1984), pp. 12–13.
4. Ibid., pp. 86–117.
5. Ibid., pp. 12–14.
6. Mark interview by author, Nov. 2, 2003.
7. Shapiro memoir.
8. Savage interview by author, Nov. 13, 2003.
9. Fowler memoir.
10. Ibid.
11. McMullen, website: www.axpow.org.
12. Lockhart interview by author, Dec. 19, 2003.
13. Mark interview by author, Nov. 2, 2003.
14. Shapiro memoir.
15. Lockhart interview by author, Dec. 19, 2003.
16. Crawford interview by author, Nov. 25, 2003.
17. Smith interview by author, Feb. 9, 2004.

18. "American Prisoners of War in Germany (Ground Force Privates Captured in the 'Bulge')." Prepared by Military Intelligence Service, War Department, 1 November 1945; National Archives.

19. MacDonald, *A Time for Trumpets*, p. 46.

20. House memoir.

21. Foy, p. 114.

22. House memoir.

23. Marion K. Blackburn, sworn statement, 23 July 1945, "Army JAG War Crimes," RG 153, Box 34, Folder 2, National Archives.

24. Thompson memoir.

25. House memoir.

26. Sign at main gate of camp.

27. Lockhart interview by author, Dec. 19, 2003.

28. Crawford interview by author, Nov. 25, 2003.

29. Fowler memoir.

30. Smith interview by author, Feb. 9, 2004.

31. House memoir.

32. Owen R. Chaffee, sworn statement, 12 Sept., 1945, "Army JAG War Crimes," RG 153, Box 34, Folder 2, National Archives.

33. House memoir.

34. Smith interview by author, Feb. 9, 2004.

35. Mitchell G. Bard, *Forgotten Victims: The Abandonment of Americans in Hitler's Camps* (Boulder, CO: Westview Press, 1994), pp. 5 and 72.

36. Leon Horowitz interview by author, Nov. 26, 2003.

37. Mark interview by author, Nov. 2, 2003.

38. Dan J. Ferrand, sworn statement, Sept. 12, 1945, "Army JAG War Crimes," RG 153, Box 34, Book 2, Folder 2, National Archives.

39. Smith interview by author, Feb. 9, 2004.

40. Crawford interview by author, Nov. 25, 2003.

41. Bard, p. 72.

42. Smith interview by author, Feb. 9, 2004.

43. Ibid.

44. "Rudolf Höss, Excerpts from the Autobiography of," in *Survivors, Victims, and Perpetrators: Essays on the Nazi Holocaust,* Joel E. Dimsdale, ed. (Washington, DC: Hemisphere, 1980), p. 296.

45. Foy, p. 114.

46. Sam Higgins, *Survival: Diary of an American Prisoner of War in World War II* (Central Point, OR: Hellgate Press, 1999), p. 85.

47. John Sabini and Maury Silver, "Destroying the Innocent with a Clear Conscience: A Sociopsychology of the Holocaust," in Dimsdale, ed., *Survivors, Victims, and Perpetrators* (Washington, DC: Hemisphere, 1980), pp. 346–347.

48. Ibid., p. 348.

49. Bernard L. Squires, sworn statement, July 5, 1945, "Army JAG War Crimes," RG 153, Book 7, Folder 2, National Archives.

50. Albert A. Kadler letter, 28 April 1945, "Army JAG War Crimes," RG 153, 100–486, Box 34, Book 1, National Archives.

51. Edward R. Cassidy, sworn statement, July 25, 1945, "Army JAG War Crimes," RG 153, Book 7, Folder 2, National Archives.

52. Joseph C. Matthews, sworn statement, July 17, 1945, "Army JAG War Crimes," RG 153, 100–425, Box 245, Book 6, Folder 1, National Archives.

53. Cassidy, sworn statement, July 25, 1945, "Army JAG War Crimes," RG 153, Book 7, Folder 2, National Archives.

54. Lockhart interview by author, Dec. 19, 2003.

55. Vernon S. Jenkins, sworn statement (date unknown) 1945, copy provided to author by Richard Lockhart.

56. Lockhart interview by author, Dec. 19, 2003.

57. Cole, pp. 668–676.

Chapter 6: Caught in a North Wind

1. Jeffrey J. Clarke and Robert R. Smith, *U.S. Army in World War II: The European Theater of Operations. Riviera to the Rhine* (Washington, DC: Center of Military History, 1994), p. 392.

2. Daub interview by author, November 16, 2003.

3. Clarke and Smith, pp. 464–470.

4. Brooks interview by author, Nov. 2, 2003; and Stanton, p. 128.

5. Clarke and Smith, pp. 492–505.

6. Daub interview by author, Nov. 16, 2003.

7. Horowitz interview by author, Nov. 26, 2003.

8. Brooks interview by author, Nov. 2, 2003.

9. Unit Citation, provided to author by Morton Brooks.
10. Brooks interview by author, Nov. 2, 2003.
11. Donald C. Pence, "The Battle of Philippsbourg, Jan. 1–20, 1945." Website: www.trailblazersww2.org.
12. Acevedo interview by author, Nov. 20, 2003.
13. Fellman interview by author, July 20, 2003.
14. Acevedo interview by author, Nov. 20, 2003.
15. Fellman interview by author, July 20, 2003.
16. Daub interview by author, Nov. 16, 2003.
17. Clarke and Smith, p. 527.
18. Daub interview by author, Nov. 16, 2003.
19. Brooks interview by author, Nov. 2, 2003.
20. Martin Hagel, sworn statement, June 8, 1945, "Army JAG War Crimes," RG 153, Box 34, Book 2, Folder 2, National Archives.
21. Smith interview by author, Feb. 9, 2003.
22. Crawford interview by author, Nov. 25, 2003.
23. Fellman interview by author, July 20, 2003.
24. Lockhart interview by author, Dec. 19, 2003.
25. Smith interview by author, Feb. 9, 2003.
26. William Thompson, unpublished memoir. Provided to author by William Thompson.
27. Fred G. Koenig, sworn statement, July 20 1945, "Army JAG War Crimes," RG 153, 100–425, Book 6, Folder 1, National Archives.
28. Smith interview by author, Feb. 9, 2003.

Chapter 7: The Last Train to Berga

1. Horowitz interview by author, Nov. 26, 2003.
2. Lockhart interview by author, Dec. 19, 2003.
3. Fellman interview by author, July 20, 2003.
4. House memoir.
5. Daub interview by author, Nov. 16, 2003.
6. Horowitz interview by author, Nov. 26, 2003.
7. Daub interview by author, Nov. 16, 2003.
8. Fellman interview by author, July 20, 2003.
9. Horowitz interview by author, Nov. 26, 2003.

10. Daub interview by author, Nov. 16, 2003.
11. Howard P. Gossett, sworn statement, July 20 1945, "Army JAG War Crimes," RG 153, 100–425, Box 34, Book 7, Folder 1, National Archives.
12. Daub interview by author, Nov. 16, 2003.
13. Smith interview by author, Feb. 9, 2003.
14. Stella Mark interview by author, Nov. 2, 2003.
15. Acevedo interview by author, Nov. 20, 2003.
16. Fellman interview by author, July 20, 2003.
17. Iosso memoir.
18. Acevedo interview by author, Nov. 20, 2003.
19. Horowitz interview by author, Nov. 26, 2003.
20. Daub interview by author, Nov. 16, 2003.
21. Bard, p. 75.
22. Brooks interview by author, Nov. 2, 2003.
23. *Historical Atlas of the Holocaust,* United States Holocaust Memorial Museum (New York: Simon & Schuster Macmillan, 1996), pp. 147–148; and pamphlet, "Buchenwald Memorial" (Weimar, Germany: Buch- und Kunstdruckerei Kessler, 2003).
24. Information in "Army JAG War Crimes," RG 153, 100–425, Box 49, Book 4, National Archives.

Chapter 8: Berga

1. Fellman interview by author, July 20, 2003.
2. Daub interview by author, Nov. 16, 2003.
3. Iosso interview by author, Aug. 15, 2003.
4. Brooks interview by author, Nov. 2, 2003.
5. Shapiro memoir.
6. Fellman interview by author, July 20, 2003.
7. Brooks interview by author, Nov. 2, 2003.
8. Paul A. Van Horne, sworn statement, June 19, 1947, "Army JAG War Crimes—Clemency," RG 153, 100–486, Vol. 1, Part 2, Folder 2, National Archives; and "Action of the Modification Board," Vol. 1, "Army JAG War Crimes," RG 153, 100–486, Box 49, National Archives.
9. Shapiro memoir.
10. Iosso memoir.

11. Daub interview by author, Nov. 16, 2003.
12. Iosso interview by author, Aug. 15, 2003.
13. Daub interview by author, Nov. 16, 2003.
14. Shapiro memoir; and Bard, p. 78; and "Action of the Modification Board," Vol. 1, "Army JAG War Crimes," RG 153, 100–486, Box 49, National Archives.
15. "Action of the Modification Board," Vol. 1, "Army JAG War Crimes," RG 153, 100–486, Box 49, National Archives.
16. Shapiro memoir.
17. Stanley B. Cohen, sworn statement, June 1, 1945. "Army JAG War Crimes," RG 153, 100–425, National Archives.
18. Shapiro memoir.
19. Joseph P. Kos, sworn statement (date unknown), "Army JAG War Crimes," RG 153, 100–425, Box 33, Book 5, National Archives.
20. Shapiro memoir.
21. Ernest Michel interview by author, June 1, 2004.
22. Brooks interview by author, Nov. 2, 2003.
23. Fellman interview by author, July 20, 2003.
24. Daub interview by author, Nov. 16, 2003.
25. Brooks interview by author, Nov. 2, 2003.
26. Fellman interview by author, July 20, 2003.
27. Shapiro memoir.
28. Fellman interview by author, July 20, 2003.
29. Acevedo interview by author, Nov. 20, 2003.
30. Iosso memoir.
31. Acevedo interview by author, Nov. 20, 2003.
32. Milton S. Harold, sworn statement, Oct. 8, 1945. "Army JAG War Crimes," RG 153, 100–425, Book 6, Folder 2, National Archives; and Charles Vogel, letter to War Crimes Branch, June 18, 1948, "Army JAG War Crimes," RG 153, 100–486, Box 49, Book 4, National Archives.
33. Shapiro memoir.
34. Ibid.
35. Ibid.
36. Brooks interview by author, Nov. 2, 2003.
37. Norman Martin, sworn statement, Nov. 13, 1945, "Army JAG War Crimes,"

RG 153, 100–148, Box 48, Book 1, Folder 2, National Archives.

38. Iosso memoir.

39. Shapiro memoir; and "Action of the Modification Board," Vol. 1, "Army JAG War Crimes," RG 153, 100–486, Box 49, National Archives.

40. Brooks interview by author, Nov. 2, 2003.

41. Fellman interview by author, July 20, 2003.

42. Daub interview by author, Nov. 16, 2003.

43. Brooks interview by author, Nov. 2, 2003.

44. Stanley B. Cohen, sworn statement, June 1, 1945, "Army JAG War Crimes," RG 153, 100–425, National Archives.

45. Shapiro memoir.

46. Acevedo interview by author, Nov. 20, 2003.

Chapter 9: The End of Hope

1. Daub interview by author, Nov. 16, 2003.

2. Fellman interview by author, July 20, 2003.

3. Ibid.

4. Daub interview by author, Nov. 16, 2003.

5. Fellman interview by author, July 20, 2003.

6. Shapiro memoir.

7. Mark interview by author, Nov. 2, 2003.

8. Fellman interview by author, July 20, 2003.

9. Norman Martin, sworn statement, Nov. 13, 1945, "Army JAG War Crimes," RG 153, 100–148, Box 48, Book 1, Folder 2, National Archives.

10. Mark memoir.

11. Daub interview by author, Nov. 16, 2003.

12. Brooks interview by author, Nov. 2, 2003.

13. Acevedo interview by author, Nov. 20, 2003.

14. Ibid.

15. Fellman interview by author, July 20, 2003.

16. Brooks interview by author, Nov. 2, 2003.

17. John Nichol and Tony Rennell, *The Last Escape: The Untold Story of Allied Prisoners of War in Europe 1944–45* (New York: Viking, 2002), pp. 193–194.

18. Acevedo interview by author, Nov. 11, 2003.

19.   Shapiro memoir.

20.   Iosso memoir.

21.   Shapiro memoir.

22.   Mark memoir.

23.   Shapiro memoir.

24.   Ibid.

Chapter 10: *Totenmarsch*

1.   Thompson memoir.

2.   Smith interview by author, Feb. 9, 2004.

3.   Crawford interview by author, Nov. 25, 2003.

4.   *Historical Atlas of the Holocaust,* pp. 204–209.

5.   Erwin Metz, petition for clemency, Feb. 1, 1948, attached to: War Crimes Board of Review No. 1, United States vs. Erwin Metz, et al., Case No. 12–1836, Feb. 20 1948, "Army JAG War Crimes," RG 153, Box 49, National Archives.

6.   Daub interview by author, Nov. 16, 2003.

7.   Bard, pp. 97 and 123.

8.   Brooks interview by author, Nov. 2, 2003.

9.   Shapiro memoir.

10.   Fellman interview by author, July 20, 2003.

11.   Norman Martin, sworn statement, Nov. 13, 1945, "Army JAG War Crimes," RG 153, 100–148, Box 48, Book 1, Folder 2, National Archives.

12.   Mark interview by author, Nov. 2, 2003.

13.   Iosso memoir.

14.   Shapiro memoir.

15.   Michel interview by author, June 1, 2004.

16.   Iosso memoir.

17.   "Army JAG War Crimes," RG 153, 100–425, Box 49, Dossier File 1944–1949, National Archives.

18.   Bard, p. 100.

19.   Roy Moser, sworn statement, "Army JAG War Crimes," RG 153, 12–2163, Box 412, National Archives.

20.   George von Roeder, *Short History of the 357th Infantry Regiment.* Weiden,

Germany: Ferdinand Nickl Buchdruckerei, 1945, p. 69.

21. "Army JAG War Crimes," RG 153, 100–425, Box 49, Dossier File 1944–1949, National Archives.

22. Iosso memoir.

23. Michel interview by author, June 1, 2004.

24. Bard, p. 98.

25. Milton S. Harold, sworn statement, Oct. 8, 1945, "Army JAG War Crimes," RG 153, 100–425, Book 6, Folder 2, National Archives.

26. Daub interview by author, Nov. 16, 2003.

27. Shapiro memoir.

28. Mark interview by author, Nov. 2, 2003.

29. Acevedo interview by author, Nov. 20, 2003.

30. Iosso memoir.

31. Roeder, p. 69.

32. Brooks interview by author, Nov. 2, 2003.

33. Mark interview by author, Nov. 2, 2003.

34. Ibid.

35. Brooks interview by author, Nov. 2, 2003.

Chapter 11: Liberation

1. 11th Armored Division, G–3 messages, 16–31 April 1945, National Archives Records Group 94.

2. Ibid.

3. Major James Q. Simmons, Jr., M.D., Acting Division Surgeon, 11th Armored Division. "Medical Annex" of 611–0.3, A/A Reports and Supporting Documents, 1 April–8 May 1945, National Archives.

4. Wayne A. Aldinger, "A Combat Infantryman's Story, 1943–1946." Memoir in U.S. Army Military History Institute.

5. G–3 Journal, Combat Command A, 11th Armored Division, 1011 hours, 23 April 1945, 611–3.2, National Archives.

6. G–3 Journal, Combat Command A, 11th Armored Division, 1526 hours, 23 April 1945, 611–3.2, National Archives.

7. Daub interview by author, Nov. 16, 2003.

8. Mark interview by author, Nov. 2, 2003.

9. Shapiro memoir.
10. Daub interview by author, Nov. 16, 2003.
11. Mark interview by author, Nov. 2, 2003.
12. "Unknown 'Forced March' Vet to Be Honored," *Jewish Journal,* Nov. 7, 2003.
13. Shapiro memoir.
14. Brooks interview by author, Nov. 2, 2003.
15. Daub interview by author, Nov. 16, 2003.
16. Shapiro memoir.
17. Daub interview by author, Nov. 16, 2003.
18. Shapiro memoir.
19. Mark interview by author, Nov. 2, 2003.
20. Fellman interview by author, July 20, 2003, and document provided to author by Fellman.
21. Brooks interview by author, Nov. 2, 2003.
22. Fellman interview by author, July 20, 2003.
23. Iosso memoir.
24. Mark interview by author, Nov. 2, 2003.
25. Acevedo interview by author, Nov. 20, 2003.
26. Michel interview by author, June 1, 2004.
27. Brooks interview by author, Nov. 2, 2003.
28. Shapiro memoir.
29. Daub interview by author, Nov. 16, 2003.
30. Fellman interview by author, July 20, 2003.
31. Iosso interview by author, Aug. 15, 2003.
32. Mark interview by author, Nov. 2, 2003.
33. Acevedo interview by author, Nov. 20, 2003.

Chapter 12: Aftermath

1. "Army JAG War Crimes," RG 153, 100–486, Box 245, Book 6, 12–390, Case File 1944–1949; also, "Clemency," Volume 1, Part 2, Folders 1 and 2, 100–486; also Box 49, Book 4; also "Action of the Modification Board, Vol. 1, National Archives.
2. Charles Vogel letter, March 25, 1946. "Army JAG War Crimes," RG 153, 100–486, National Archives.

3. "Action of the Modification Board," "Army JAG War Crimes," RG 153, 100–486, Box 49, Vol. 1, National Archives.

4. Erwin Metz, petition for clemency, 1 February 1948, "Army JAG War Crimes," RG 153, 100–486, Box 49, National Archives.

5. "Clemency," "Army JAG War Crimes," RG 153, 100–486, Box 49, Vol. 1, Part 2, Folders 1 and 2, National Archives.

6. Richard Ruppert, petition for re-hearing, "Army JAG War Crimes," RG 153, 100–486, Box 49, Vol. 1, Part 1, Folder 2, National Archives.

7. Ibid.

8. "Clemency," "Army JAG War Crimes," RG 153, 100–486, Box 49, Vol. 1, Part 2, Folder 2, National Archives.

9. Erwin Metz, petition for clemency, Feb. 1, 1948, "Army JAG War Crimes," RG 153, 100–486, Box 49, National Archives.

10. "Report of War Crimes Board of Review, No. 1," "Army JAG War Crimes," RG 153, 100–486, Box 49, Vol. 1, "Clemency," Part 1, National Archives.

11. Edwin Gray letter, Oct. 7, 1948, "Clemency," "Army JAG War Crimes," RG 153, 100–486, Box 49, Volume 1, Part 2, Folder 2, National Archives.

12. Lucius Clay letter to Dr. Jacob A. Cantor, Sept. 4, 1948, "Clemency," "Army JAG War Crimes," RG 153, 100–486, Box 49, Vol. 1, Part 2, Folder 2, National Archives.

13. Paul J. Gernert, "Supplement to Application of Parolee Erwin Metz for Good Conduct Release." Undated (probably July or August 1955). "Army JAG War Crimes," RG 153, 100–486, Case File 1944–1949, National Archives.

14. Shapiro interview by author, April 15, 2004.

Epilogue

1. Iosso interview by author, May 3, 2004.

2. Crawford interview by author, Nov. 25, 2003.

3. Helen Fowler correspondence with author.

4. Horowitz interview by author, Nov. 26, 2003.

5. Kline interview by author, Nov. 10, 2003.

6. Lockhart interview by author, Dec. 19, 2003.

7. Savage interview by author, Nov. 13, 2003.

8. Smith interview by author, Feb. 9, 2004.

9. Acevedo interview by author, Nov. 20, 2003.

10. Brooks interview by author, Nov. 2, 2003.

11. Daub interview by author, Nov. 16, 2003.

12. Fellman interview by author, July 20, 2003.

13. Iosso interview by author, Aug. 15, 2003.

14. Mark interview by author, Nov. 2, 2003.

15. Michel interview by author, June 1, 2004.

16: Shapiro memoir and interview by author, April 15, 2004.

Postscript

1. Büttner letter to author, 2003.

SELECTED
BIBLIOGRAPHY

Oral Histories

Anthony "Tony" Acevedo (Company B, 275th Regiment, 70th Infantry Division),
    interviewed by author, October 15, 2003.

Morton Brooks (C Company, 242 Regiment, 42nd Infantry Division), interviewed by
    author, November 2, 2003.

John J. "Jack" Crawford (590th Field Artillery Battalion, 106th Infantry Division),
    interviewed by author, November 25, 2003.

Gerald Daub (F Company, 397th Regiment, 100th Infantry Division), interviewed by
    author, November 16, 2003.

Norman Fellman (Company B, 275th Regiment, 70th Infantry Division), interviewed
    by author, July 20, 2003.

Leon Horowitz (Company F, 397th Regiment, 100th Infantry Division), interviewed by
    author, November 26, 2003.

Peter Iosso (Company E, 422nd Regiment, 106th Infantry Division), interviewed by
    author, November 21, 2003.
Robert E. Kline (Company M, 423rd Regiment, 106th Infantry Division), interviewed
    by author, December 3, 2003.
Richard T. Lockhart (Anti-Tank Company, 423rd Regiment, 106th Infantry Division),
    interviewed by author, December 19, 2003.
Joseph Mark (Headquarters Company, 3rd Battalion, 106th Infantry Division),
    interviewed by author, November 2, 2003.
Stella Mark, interviewed by author, November 2, 2003.
Ernest W. Michel, interviewed by author, June 1, 2004.
Clifford Savage (Company M, 393rd Regiment, 99th Infantry Division), interviewed by
    author, November 13, 2003.
James V. Smith (Company H, 423rd Regiment, 106th Infantry Division), interviewed
    by author, February 9, 2004.

Unpublished or Privately Published Memoirs

Aldinger, Wayne A. "A Combat Infantryman's Story." 1943–1946. Memoir in U.S. Army
    Military History Institute.
Fowler, P. R. (Robert) (28th Infantry Division). Unpublished memoir provided to
    author by Helen (Mrs. Robert) Fowler.
House, Peter, Sr. "Life in Stalag IX-B: Story of an American Held in a German POW
    Camp." Unpublished memoir, provided to author by Peter House, Jr.
Iosso, Peter. Unpublished memoir, provided to author by Peter Iosso.
Mark, Joseph. Unpublished memoir, provided to author by Dr. Joseph Mark.
Shapiro, William J. (Company D, 110th Infantry Regiment, 28th Infantry Division).
    "An Awakening: A Personal Recollection and Appraisal of My Prisoner-of-War
    Experience." Unpublished memoir, provided to author by William Shapiro.
Thompson, William. Unpublished memoir, provided to author by William Thompson.

Official Sources

"Action of the Modification Board." National Archives Records Group 153, 100–486,
    "Army JAG War Crimes," Vol. 1, National Archives and Records Administration,
    College Park, MD.
"American Prisoners of War in Germany—Stalag IX-B. (Ground Force Privates
    Captured in the "Bulge.")" Prepared by Military Intelligence Service, War

Department, 1 November 1945; National Archives.

"Battle of St. Vith, Belgium—17–23 December 1944: An Historical Example of Armor in the Defense." U. S. Army Armor School. Reprinted by Merriam Press, Bennington, VT, 2003.

Blackburn, Marion K. Sworn statement, 23 July 1945. National Archives Records Group 153, 100–486, "Army JAG War Crimes," Book 6, 12–390, Box 245, Folder 2, Case File 1944–1949.

Cassidy, Edward R. Sworn statement, 25 July 1945. National Archives Records Group 153, 100–425, "Army JAG War Crimes," Box 34, Book 7, Folder 2, Dossier File 1944–1949.

Chaffee, Owen R. Sworn statement, 12 September 1945. National Archives Records Group 153, 100-486, "Army JAG War Crimes," Book 7, Folder 2, Case File 1944–1949.

Cohen, Stanley B. Sworn statement, 1 June 1945. "Army JAG War Crimes," National Archives Records Group 153, 100-425, Dossier File 1944–1949.

Distinguished Unit Citation for First Battalion, 242nd Infantry Regiment, 42nd Infantry Division.

11th Armored Division, G–3 messages, 16–31 April 1945, National Archives Records Group 94.

Ferrand, Dan J. Sworn statement, 12 September 1945, "Army JAG War Crimes," National Archives Records Group 153, Box 34, Book 2, Folder 2, Case File 1944–1949.

Gernert, Paul J. "Supplement to Application of Parolee Erwin Metz for Good Conduct Release." Undated (probably July or August 1955). National Archives Records Group 153, 100–486, "Army JAG War Crimes," Case File 1944–1949.

Gossett, Howard P. Sworn statement. "Army JAG War Crimes," National Archives Records Group 153, 100–425, Book 7, 12–390, Box 245, Folder 1, Dossier File 1944–1949.

Harold, Milton S. Sworn statement, 8 October 1945. "Army JAG War Crimes," National Archives Records Group 153, 100-425, Book 6, Folder 2.

Jenkins, Vernon S. Sgt. Sworn statement regarding mistreatment of POWs at Stalag IX-B, date unknown. National Archives.

Kadler, Albert A. Letter, dated 28 April 1945, from Swiss Legation describing a visit to Stalag IX-B on 23 March 1945. National Archives Records Group 153, 100-486, "Army JAG War Crimes," Box 34, Book 1.

Koenig, Fred G. Sworn statement, 20 July 1945. National Archives Records Group 153, 100–425, "Army JAG War Crimes," Book 6, Box 245, Folder 1, Dossier File

1944–1949.

Kos, Joseph P. Sworn statement (date unknown), "Army JAG War Crimes," RG 153, 100-425, Box 33, Book 5, National Archives.

Martin, Norman. Sworn statement, 13 November 1945. National Archives Records Group 153, 100–425, "Army JAG War Crimes," Dossier File 1944–1949.

Matthews, Joseph C. Sworn statement, 17 July 1945. National Archives Records Group 153, 100–486, "Army JAG War Crimes," Box 245, Book 6, 12-390, Folder 2, Case File 1944–1949.

Metz, Erwin. Petition for clemency, 1 February 1948, attached to: War Crimes Board of Review No. 1, United States vs. Erwin Metz, et al., Case No. 12-1836, 20 February 1948, National Archives.

Moser, Roy. Sworn statement, "Army JAG War Crimes," National Archives Records Group 153, 12-2163, Box 412.

National Archives and Records Administration: Records Group 153, 100–486, "Army JAG War Crimes," Box 245, Book 6, 12-390, Case File 1944–1949; also, "Clemency," Volume 1, Part 2, Folders 1 and 2, 100–486; also Box 49, Book 4; also "Action of the Modification Board, Volume 1, 100-486.

Simmons, James Q., Jr., Acting Division Surgeon, 11th Armored Division, "Medical Annex" to 611-0.3, "After-Action Reports and Supporting Documents," 1 April–8 May 1945, National Archives.

United States Third Army After-Action Report (two volumes), 1945 (place published unknown).

Van Horne, Paul A. Sworn statement, 19 June 1947, "Army JAG War Crimes— Clemency," National Archives Records Group 153, 100-486, Vol. 1, Part 2, Folder 2.

Wiley, Bell I.; Keast, William R.; and Palmer, Robert R. *U.S. Army in World War II—The Army Ground Forces: The Procurement and Training of Ground Combat Troops.* Washington, DC, Historical Division, Department of the Army, 1948.

Books

Army Almanac, The: A Book of Facts Concerning the Army of the United States. Washington, DC: U.S. Government Printing Office, 1950.

Bard, Mitchell G. *Forgotten Victims: The Abandonment of Americans in Hitler's Camps.* Boulder, CO: Westview Press, 1994.

Béon, Yves. *Planet Dora: A Memoir of the Holocaust and the Birth of the Space Age.* Boulder, CO: Westview Press, 1997.

Bonn, Keith E. *When the Odds Were Even: The Vosges Mountain Campaign—October 1944–January 1945.* Novato, CA: Presidio, 1994.

Bradley, Omar N. *A Soldier's Story.* New York: Rand McNally, 1951.

Butcher, Harry C. *My Three Years with Eisenhower.* New York: Simon and Schuster, 1946.

Carell, Paul. *Hitler Moves East, 1941–1943.* New York: Bantam, 1966.

Clarke, Jeffrey J., and Smith, Robert R. *U.S. Army in World War II: The European Theater of Operations. Riviera to the Rhine.* Washington, DC: Center of Military History, 1994.

Colby, John. *War from the Ground Up: The 90th Division in World War II.* Austin, TX: Nortex Press, 1991.

Cole, Hugh M. *U.S. Army in World War II: The European Theater of Operations. The Ardennes: Battle of the Bulge.* Washington, DC: Center of Military History, 1994.

Eisenhower, Dwight D. *Crusade in Europe.* Garden City, NY: Doubleday, 1948.

Foy, David A. *For You the War Is Over: American Prisoners of War in Nazi Germany.* New York: Stein and Day, 1984.

Heiber, Helmut, and Glantz, David M., eds. *Hitler and His Generals: Military Conferences 1942–1945.* New York: Enigma Books, 2003.

Higgins, Sam. *Survival: Diary of an American Prisoner of War in World War II.* Central Point, OR: Hellgate Press, 1999.

Hilberg, Raul. *The Destruction of the European Jews.* New York: Holmes & Meier, 1985.

Historical Atlas of the Holocaust: United States Holocaust Memorial Museum. New York, Simon & Schuster Macmillan, 1996.

History of the 90th Division in World War II, A; 6 June 1944 to 9 May 1945. 1946 (place published unknown).

MacDonald, Charles, B. *U.S. Army in World War II: The European Theater. The Siegfried Line Campaign.* Washington, DC: GPO, 1951.

———. *A Time for Trumpets: The Untold Story of the Battle of the Bulge.* New York: Quill/William Morrow, 1985.

McKale, Donald M. *Hitler's Shadow War: The Holocaust and World War II.* New York: Cooper Square Press, 2002.

Nichol, John, and Rennell, Tony. *The Last Escape: The Untold Story of Allied Prisoners of War in Europe 1944–45.* New York: Viking, 2002.

Parker, Danny S. *Battle of the Bulge: Hitler's Ardennes Offensive, 1944–1945.* Philadelphia: Combined Books, 1991.

Roeder, George von. *Short History of the 357th Infantry Regiment*. Weiden, Germany: Ferdinand Nickl Buchdruckerei, 1945.

Sabini, John P., and Silver, Maury. "Destroying the Innocent with a Clear Conscience: A Sociopsychology of the Holocaust," in *Survivors, Victims, and Perpetrators: Essays on the Nazi Holocaust*. Dimsdale, Joel E., ed. New York: Hemisphere, 1980.

Seventh United States Army in France and Germany, 1944–1945, The. Vol. II. Heidelberg, Germany: Aloys Gräf, 1946.

Shirer, William L. *The Rise and Fall of the Third Reich*. New York: Crest/Fawcett, 1964.

Stanton, Shelby L. *World War II Order of Battle*. New York: Galahad Books, 1984.

Steward, Hal D. *Thunderbolt*. Washington, DC: 11th Armored Division Association, 1948.

Whiting, Charles. *Death of a Division*. New York: Stein and Day, 1981.

Articles

Band, Gary. "Unknown 'Forced March' Vet to Be Honored." *Jewish Journal*, 7 November 2003.

Cunningham, Ed. "Battle of the Bulge." *Yank* magazine, 2 March 1945.

Ramsey, Winton G., ed. "The Battle of the Bulge." *After the Battle* magazine, No. 4, 1974.

Miscellaneous

"Buchenwald Memorial." Pamphlet published by the Buchenwald Memorial Foundation, Weimar-Buchenwald.

Clay, Gen. Lucius D. Letter to Dr. Jacob A. Cantor, September 4, 1948; National Archives Records Group 153, 100–486, "Army JAG War Crimes."

Gray, Edwin A. Letter to Senator H. Alexander Smith, dated 7 October 1948; in National Archives Records Group 153, 100–486, "Army JAG War Crimes."

Guggenheim, Charles. *Berga: Soldiers of a Different War*. Television documentary. Public Broadcasting System, 2003.

Pence, Donald C. "The Battle of Philippsbourg, Jan. 1–20, 1945."

Vogel, Charles. Letters from Charles Vogel, Vogel and Vogel, Counsellors at Law, New York City, to War Crimes Branch, dated 25 March 1946, and 18 June 1948; in "Army JAG War Crimes," RG 153, 100-486, National Archives.

Websites

www.astpww2.org. "Army Specialized Training Program."
www.axpow.org. "Ex-POW Biographies."
www.higher-ed.org. "G.I. Bill—Act of June 22, 1944."
www.lonesentry.org. "Photos of Stalag IX-B."
www.military.com. "Death of a Division," by Kissel, Robert P.
www.trailblazersww2.org.

Index

Index